THE COMPLETE GUIDE TO JOINING THE
PEACE CORPS:

WHAT YOU NEED TO KNOW EXPLAINED SIMPLY

BY SHARLEE DIMENICHI

With Foreword By Shannon Heintz
Returned Peace Corps Volunteer
Kenya 2005-2007

THE COMPLETE GUIDE TO JOINING THE PEACE CORPS:
WHAT YOU NEED TO KNOW EXPLAINED SIMPLY

Library of Congress Cataloging-in-Publication Data

DiMenichi, Sharlee, 1974-
 The complete guide to joining the Peace Corps : what you need to know explained simply / by Sharlee DiMenichi.
   p. cm.
 Includes bibliographical references and index.
 ISBN-13: 978-1-60138-284-9 (alk. paper)
 ISBN-10: 1-60138-284-7 (alk. paper)
 1. Peace Corps (U.S.)--Handbooks, manuals, etc. 2. Peace Corps (U.S.)--Vocational guidance--Handbooks, manuals, etc. 3. Cross-cultural orientation--United States--Handbooks, manuals, etc. 4. Volunteerism--United States--Handbooks, manuals, etc. I. Title.
 HC60.5.D56 2010
 361.6023'73--dc22
                                  2008037929

PROJECT MANAGER: Melissa Peterson • mpeterson@atlantic-pub.com
PEER REVIEWER: Marilee Griffin • EDITOR: Sheila Reed
INTERIOR LAYOUT: Harrison Kuo • BACK COVER DESIGN: Holly Marie Gibbs
FRONT COVER & INTERIOR DESIGN: Meg Buchner • megadesn@mchsi.com

Printed on Recycled Paper

Printed in the United States

We recently lost our beloved pet "Bear," who was not only our best and dearest friend but also the "Vice President of Sunshine" here at Atlantic Publishing. He did not receive a salary but worked tirelessly 24 hours a day to please his parents. Bear was a rescue dog that turned around and showered myself, my wife, Sherri, his grandparents Jean, Bob, and Nancy and every person and animal he met (maybe not rabbits) with friendship and love. He made a lot of people smile every day.

We wanted you to know that a portion of the profits of this book will be donated to The Humane Society of the United States. *—Douglas & Sherri Brown*

The human-animal bond is as old as human history. We cherish our animal companions for their unconditional affection and acceptance. We feel a thrill when we glimpse wild creatures in their natural habitat or in our own backyard.

Unfortunately, the human-animal bond has at times been weakened. Humans have exploited some animal species to the point of extinction.

The Humane Society of the United States makes a difference in the lives of animals here at home and worldwide. The HSUS is dedicated to creating a world where our relationship with animals is guided by compassion. We seek a truly humane society in which animals are respected for their intrinsic value, and where the human-animal bond is strong.

Want to help animals? We have plenty of suggestions. Adopt a pet from a local shelter, join The Humane Society and be a part of our work to help companion animals and wildlife. You will be funding our educational, legislative, investigative and outreach projects in the U.S. and across the globe.

Or perhaps you'd like to make a memorial donation in honor of a pet, friend or relative? You can through our Kindred Spirits program. And if you'd like to contribute in a more structured way, our Planned Giving Office has suggestions about estate planning, annuities, and even gifts of stock that avoid capital gains taxes.

Maybe you have land that you would like to preserve as a lasting habitat for wildlife. Our Wildlife Land Trust can help you. Perhaps the land you want to share is a backyard—that's enough. Our Urban Wildlife Sanctuary Program will show you how to create a habitat for your wild neighbors.

So you see, it's easy to help animals. And The HSUS is here to help.

2100 L Street NW • Washington, DC 20037
202-452-1100 • www.hsus.org

Dedication

For Stefan

With thanks to Nancee and Kenneth DiMenichi, Chandra Vitelli Bleice, Traci Sacks, Sam Donnelly, Eric Hanus, George Polk, and Susan Cushman

Table of Contents

Chapter 6: Alternatives to the Peace Corps   71

Chapter 7: Protecting Yourself from Crime   77

Chapter 8: Medical Concerns   81

Chapter 9: Packing and Training   85

Chapter 10: Living In-country   89

Foreword

The decision to join the Peace Corps is a personal one; everyone has a catalyst for wanting to serve. For me, it was a Coca-Cola bottle on a 6th-grade science teacher's desk — where had it come from? The answer was Sri Lanka, where my teacher served as a Peace Corps volunteer (PCV), and after seeing pictures and hearing stories of his childhood in Africa, I was sold. I *had* to be a Peace Corps volunteer. For me, being a PCV was a life goal, but making it through the process was fraught with questions. In *The Complete Guide to Joining the Peace Corps*, Sharlee DiMenichi helps to demystify the process with reflections from returned volunteers and information about the government bureaucracy that is the Peace Corps.

Why join the Peace Corps? Where will you go? How will you live? What will you do? The questions are many — some can be answered now, and some will only be answered once your journey begins. In this book, DiMenichi helps to answer some of the basic questions regarding Peace Corps service, but there is one crucial thing to remember when reading memoirs, stories, and guides to the Peace Corps: No one's service is the same. Your experiences, your stories, your successes, and your failures will be your own — just as my stories are my own.

I have been reading tales of Peace Corps life for over a decade. My mind was full of what to expect, how life would be, and what volunteering Peace Corps-style was really about. When I was not dropped in the bush upon my arrival, I was disappointed. What was this two-month "cultural training"? What happened to "Here's your hut. See you in two years"? Not in today's Peace Corps. Today, you have the luxury of a two-month crash course in language and culture. Going to my site, I was not sure what to expect, but I was expecting to have to gather my own water for drinking, bathing, and cooking — and there was no way I would have electricity (or *stima,* as they call it in Kenya). When I found out that I would have running water and electricity, I thought I was being robbed of the "real" Peace Corps experience. I was a Peace Corps Princess; this is not what I wanted. Little did I know that aside from the "luxury" of running water — which, by the way, was only drinkable after filtering and boiling — my challenges would be many.

The key to the Peace Corps is remembering that everyone comes from somewhere else and that everyone's challenges at site are valid. Living in a large town does not make service easier or cushier. In fact, it can make it very hard to connect with your new home. In Nyahururu, Kenya, many vans of tourists on safari pass down the main road and through town every day. To many in this town of 15,000, I was simply another *muzungu* traveler making my way through their town. It can become very tiresome to have to explain, "Yes, I live down the road. No, I do not own the building, neighborhood, or street — I rent just like the Kenyans." It can become very frustrating to have to bargain for a fair price at the market. With all the tourist traffic, it becomes very easy to take advantage of a *muzungu* wanting a mango. At the same time, it is nice to be able to be anonymous, like we are in America. Not being in a village means that people in your neighborhood — not in the whole town — know your business. The constant verbal battle at the soko, or local market, is not only good for your language skills, but it also helps you build special relationships with a few trusted mamas who never cheat you — they befriend you, help you, and make you feel at home.

As the ad campaign asks, "Life is calling; how far will you go?" Ask yourself, "How far will I go?" I hope the answer is, "I will go anywhere." Your journey begins with applying and sticking it out through a long process and, hopefully, as you set foot in a new land. As you go through the process of applying, it is important to remember that in actuality, you are applying for a job. "Volunteer" may be part of your future title, but the government invests thousands of dollars in each volunteer, and the selection process is arduous and can be intimidating. That is why it is important to know why you are applying.

Having that conviction, whatever your reasoning, will give the wherewithal to stick with the process.

My experiences in the Peace Corps have not fundamentally changed who I am. I have always wanted to work with people to better their lives. My time in the Peace Corps has helped me to understand that many times people have the answers to their problems — they just need help making the solution a reality. The Peace Corps has helped me listen; it has helped a hopeless wanderer and traveler find a path in life. Your "job" in the Peace Corps, as in any social service work, is to put yourself out of a job, to help people grow in their own capacity, and ensure your community has ownership of any program you work on. Work *with* people, not for people. Work *with* a community, not for a community. Work *with* an organization, not for an organization. Peace Corps skills are life skills.

Due to my Peace Corps experience — and a good friend who believed in my capacity — I am working in a field I love, for an agency I believe in. Teaching public health, peer education, and family planning in America is full of new challenges for me. Working for Planned Parenthood allows me to empower people to make their own informed choices about their reproductive health. My time in the Peace Corps has opened many doors at home. It has allowed me the confidence, and instilled in me the capacity for empathy and empowerment, to do outreach in communities that are fundamentally different from my own. I have a perspective on the world and a first-hand understanding of complex issues due to my time in the Peace Corps. No amount of class work will equate to two years of field work in HIV prevention and care and family planning.

Applying can be daunting — just do it. You never know what will happen if you do not apply. Traveling to your country of service can be daunting — it is nerve-wracking for everyone else getting on that plane, too. You never know what you are capable of until you are pushed. Waking up and realizing you are a Peace Corps volunteer in a foreign county — there to help a community fulfill some of its own needs — is amazing, empowering, frustrating, and overwhelming — and, ultimately, it will be an experience that changes your life. I know this book will help answer some of the basic questions about Peace Corps service. The other questions will have to be answered day-by-day in your country of service.

Good Luck. Hear stories. Read memoirs. See pictures. But know your journey will be yours alone. Your Peace Corps experience is something you will own completely. It will be hard; it will be rewarding; it will be daunting; it will change your life.

Shannon Heintz
Raleigh, North Carolina
Returned Peace Corps Volunteer
Kenya 2005-2007

Shannon Heintz is a graduate of the Evergreen State College. She served as a public health volunteer in Peace Corps Kenya from 2005-'07. Currently, she is the community health educator for Planned Parenthood Health Systems in Raleigh, North Carolina. She hopes to return to Africa one day to help women and men grow their capacity to receive family planning services.

Introduction:
What is the Peace Corps?

A President's Idealistic Legacy

On the eve of the Camelot era, presidential candidate John F. Kennedy shared — with an assembly of college students from the University of Michigan — his vision of an international service project that would become the Peace Corps. The students responded with overwhelming enthusiasm, and on March 1, 1961, President Kennedy created the Peace Corps by executive order. From its beginning, the Peace Corps has sent U.S. citizens overseas for two-year stints to learn about residents of developing countries, to support development projects, and to encourage international friendships. According to their Web site (**www. peacecorps.gov**), the Peace Corps' mission has three simple goals:

1. Helping the people of interested countries in meeting their need for trained men and women.

2. Helping promote a better understanding of Americans on the part of the peoples served.

3. Helping promote a better understanding of other peoples on the part of Americans.

The Peace Corps is an independent U.S. government agency, providing requested assistance to countries around the world through the work of volunteers. Since its inception, nearly 200,000 Americans have served in 139 host countries.

A Thumbnail Sketch of Peace Corps History

Even though its essential purposes have stayed the same, the Peace Corps has changed over its nearly five decades. The Corps began with programs in Ghana and what is now Tanzania. In its inaugural year, the Corps sent 750 volunteers to 13 countries in Latin America, Africa, South Asia, Asia, and the Caribbean. Early volunteers worked in education, medicine, health care, and community development. The number of volunteers peaked at more than 15,000 in 1966; ebbed to 5,380 in 1982; and now stands at approximately 7,700.

In its first two decades, the Peace Corps evolved from being an agency in the State Department to joining forces with other national service programs to form the government agency ACTION, which was described as "the Federal Domestic Volunteer Agency." The Peace Corps added business projects in the 1980s, the decade during which it became an independent federal agency. In the 1990s, the Peace Corps expanded into China and countries of the former Soviet Union, and teams of returned Peace Corps volunteers (RPCVs) began offering disaster relief in developing countries. During the new millennium, the Peace Corps expanded its work to include HIV/AIDS education and care. In some countries, Peace Corps programs focus on establishing Internet access to remote locations, making communication between volunteers and their loved ones easier than in the past.

For a full account of the Peace Corps' history, visit **www.peacecorps.gov/ index.cfm?shell=learn.whatispc.history.decades**.

Management and Support

The Peace Corps has a team of directors who provide leadership and support to the volunteers. The following sections detail the positions and describe their roles in the Peace Corps.

Head of the Corps

Aaron S. Williams, RPCV, became director of the Peace Corps in August 2009 after having served in the Dominican Republic from 1967 to 1970. Williams is the fourth director to have previously served as a volunteer in the Peace

Corps. President Barack Obama nominated Williams, who was a member of the White House transition team. Williams also spent time at the U.S. Agency for International Development (USAID) where he was a career minister in the Senior Foreign Service (SFS). Other accomplishments include receiving the USAID Distinguished Career Service Award and the Presidential Award for Distinguished Service. Williams sits on the Council on Foreign Relations (CFR) and has worked to deliver international aid to the Middle East, Africa, Latin America, and Asia. Williams is fluent in Spanish and is a graduate of Chicago State University with an MBA from the University of Wisconsin. Williams met his wife, Rosa, during his service as a volunteer in the Dominican Republic.

Within the organizational ranks of the Peace Corps, the director advocates for the Peace Corps to Congress, which sets the service organization's annual budget. The director works with host-country governments and the Secretary of State to advance the Peace Corps' agenda.

Regional directors

A regional director (RD) is responsible for establishing new Peace Corps work sites. An RD must also develop a rapport with the host-country government, determine the volunteer expertise needed at each post, and prepare for the arrival of each team of Peace Corps volunteers (PCVs).

There are currently three RDs with the Peace Corps: Lynn Foden, acting regional director, Africa; David Burgess, acting regional director, Europe, Mediterranean, and Asia; and Roger Conrad, acting regional director, Inter-America and the Pacific.

Country director

The role of each country director (CD) is to promote the well-being of volunteers by developing safety policies and making sure staff members are trained to adjust to their new culture. Country directors are also responsible for a budget of up to $4 million per CD and host country. CDs work with assistance groups in host countries to establish and plan Peace Corps projects.

Associate Peace Corps director

The associate peace corps director (APCD) is responsible for selecting and arranging housing for PCVs. The APCD also visits work sites regularly and advises the staff as needed. APCDs provide technical advice and guidance to the country director; supervise staff in all areas of administrative management; and are responsible for budget formulation and execution, human resources, procurement, property, computer systems maintenance, and general services to the post. They are also responsible for the fiscal integrity of the country program.

The U.S. government

The Peace Corps is an independent agency within the executive branch of the U.S. government. The President of the United States appoints the Peace Corps director and deputy director, and these appointments must be confirmed by the U.S. Senate. The Senate Committee on Foreign Relations and House Committee on Foreign Affairs are charged with general oversight of the activities and programs of the Peace Corps. The Peace Corps' annual budget is determined each year by the congressional budget and appropriations process. Funding for the Peace Corps is included in the State, Foreign Operations, and Related Programs Appropriations bill. Generally, the Peace Corps budget is about 1 percent of the foreign operations budget. The budget for fiscal year 2009 was $340 million and is $400 million for 2010.

The Present Day Peace Corps

In 2011, Peace Corps will celebrate its 50th anniversary. To commemorate the anniversary, the Peace Corps has created an expandable, searchable digital collection of key materials, historical documents, and images. Current and former volunteers can add their stories and images to the collection. You can browse the Digital Library by visiting **http://archive.peacecorps.gov**.

Celebratory events begin in March 2011 with the Kennedy Service Awards and continue with activities, tributes, and volunteer projects in host countries throughout the world and celebrations at U.S. colleges and universities that have helped shape the Peace Corps and the Peace Corps' legacy in the future. In September 2011, Washington, D.C., will host celebratory events, including a 50th anniversary celebration and volunteer reunion on the National Mall, diplomatic reception at the Library of Congress, and congressional reception on Capitol Hill and concludes with a wreath-laying ceremony at the grave of President Kennedy.

The fanfare will follow efforts to expand the Peace Corps through increased funding and recruitment. Recently, 20 countries requested PCVs, but there was not enough funding to send new volunteers. In April 2009, President Obama signed the Edward M. Kennedy Serve America Act, which supports expanding the Corps, officially recognizes September 11th as a National Day of Service and Remembrance, and encourages all Americans to recommit to service in their communities throughout the year. The president hopes to double the number of volunteers by 2011.

President Obama's enthusiasm for the Peace Corps echoes that of its founder. In President Kennedy's final State of the Union address on January 14, 1963, he lauded the Peace Corps as a unique means of sharing American goodwill. "Nothing carries the spirit of American idealism and expresses our hopes better and more effectively to the four corners of the earth than the Peace Corps," President Kennedy said.

Today, volunteers serve in 76 host countries. Sixty percent of volunteers are female, and 93 percent of volunteers are single. Minorities make up 16 percent of the volunteer base, and the average age of volunteers is 28, with 7 percent of volunteers being over the age of 50. Eighty-nine percent of volunteers have at least an undergraduate college degree. Volunteers work with local governments, communities, schools, and entrepreneurs to address changing and complex needs in education, health and HIV/AIDS, business, information technology, agriculture, youth development, and the environment.

Recent Peace Corps' news includes the return of volunteers to Rwanda in April 2009 after a 15-year absence, the return of volunteers to Sierra Leone in June 2010 after a 15-year absence, and the creation of the Peace Corps/ Indonesia program in December 2009, with volunteers arriving in mid-2010.

CHAPTER 1

The Benefits of Joining the Peace Corps

"The toughest job you'll ever love" is the Peace Corps' familiar slogan. It is also the reason thousands of volunteers leave everyday conveniences to embark on two-year adventures in developing countries. While monetary compensation is only a modest stipend, what the 7,700 volunteers gain in having the opportunity to improve the quality of life of men, women, and children in host countries is a reward that is personally gratifying. PCVs also leave their two years of service with a confidence born of succeeding in spite of scarce material resources.

Letting Experience Re-grind Your Lens

One characteristic incumbent upon all PCVs is their ability to adapt to new situations regardless of where or in what capacity they serve. Many PCVs find that daily life in their countries of service takes on the qualities of an adventure. Adjusting to foreign, and perhaps forbidding, surroundings makes ordinary routines anything but a daily grind.

Commuting to work in the United States often means crowded subways and jammed highways; commuting to a Peace Corps work site in Nepal means hiking three hours with some of the world's most stunning mountains as a backdrop, according to RPCV Darren Miller, who served from 1991 to 1993.

Doing the laundry in the United States involves the solitary drudgery of schlepping your clothes up and down the basement stairs; doing the laundry by hand outdoors in Micronesia could involve carloads of people stopping to stare at the spectacle of a man washing clothes, according to RPCV Mark Kohn, who served from 1979 to 1981.

Going to the doctor in the United States usually requires a short drive to the office; going to the doctor in Micronesia required a three-day boat ride during which Kohn got to witness a baby's birth.

In the United States, taking a bus usually means smelling diesel fuel while trying to block out the sound of other passengers yapping on cell phones because your MP3 player has died. In Nepal, taking a bus can mean feeling the coach negotiate hairpin-turns while sitting on the roof with the luggage because there is not enough room between seats for long American legs, according to Miller.

Through encountering and adapting to foreign circumstances, PCVs grow in self-sufficiency, resourcefulness, and creativity. The chance to do something unprecedented in one's life and develop character through adventure is among the non-monetary rewards of service.

Personal growth is not the only intangible benefit of joining the Peace Corps. Volunteers also have the opportunity to alleviate some of the suffering caused by global disparities in wealth, improve the lives of residents of developing nations, and learn a new language and culture. Volunteers frequently find their understanding of how people live with economic hardship deepened by their experience in the Peace Corps.

One Haitian man had to discreetly urinate into a cup that he emptied out the window of the public bus he rode to get treatment for an illness that prevented him from being able to use the bathroom at normal intervals, according to RPCV Richard Ireland, who served from 1998 to 2001. Most Haitians cannot afford to own cars.

The children in RPCV Donna Statler's Belizean host family offered their guest the only beans in the house, although they expected to have only tea that day. She politely declined to eat after she realized doing so would mean depriving the children of food.

Most volunteers leave the Peace Corps with an expanded understanding of the culture of their country of service. Through two years of becoming acquainted with an unfamiliar country, volunteers grow to look with new eyes at American habits they once took for granted. Kohn found his view of time changed while serving in the Peace Corps. Living in the present became more possible for Kohn, who served in Micronesia and adopted a sense of time closely attuned with that of residents of his host country. Fishing was an essential source of food and livelihood when Kohn served in Micronesia, so residents had to forgo any other commitments if they had a bountiful catch at hand. "If you have an appointment with someone on Tuesday, and the fish were running and they don't show up until Friday, you can't be mad at them," Kohn said.

Volunteers often must adapt not only to a different concept of time, but also to a different concept of personal space. Gone is the anonymity with which one can walk down a public street in the United States. Groups of children shouting "Foreigner!" frequently followed Richard Lipez, who taught secondary school in Ethiopia from 1962-1964.

CASE STUDY: A JOURNEY BEYOND YOUR COMFORT ZONE

Heather Windom
Macedonia
Education

"It took about a year from application to assignment for my Peace Corps adventure to begin. I had heard that only one out of 10 applicants were chosen, so I was thrilled I was given the chance to go. Letters of reference, essays, and phone interviews accompanied my application — all designed to give the Peace Corps as much information about me as possible.

I was assigned to Macedonia, the former-Yugoslavia country located just above Greece. Before my departure, I received a detailed informational book-let, logistics, and a cultural welcome CD with music and language phrases.

My group landed in Skopje, Macedonia, after two flights and a day of traveling. A large bus took us to a town two hours east of Skopje called Kochani. We arrived at a hotel that would be our home for the first week. During that week, we learned the Cyrillic alphabet, met the U.S. Ambassador and the Peace Corps country director, and got to know one another. At the end of the week, each of our host families came to pick us up.

My host family, Vaska and Aleksandar, was charming and set me at ease immediately. Vaska is a kindergarten teacher and Aleksandar a doctor. Their two children, Maria, 12, and Zoran, 20, quickly became my friends and guides around their town, called Vinica.

For the next three months, I spent time learning the language, learning to cook Macedonian cuisine, and immersing myself in the culture. The time with my host family was wonderful and beyond what I had hoped for.

After three months, I was sent to Rostushe a remote village on the western side of Macedonia, quite a distance from where my host family lived. The Peace Corps pays for each volunteer to have a language tutor if they choose. I found an amazing tutor and friend in the village and, for my first six months there, we worked together for many hours each week. After endless hours of homework, I became about 85 percent fluent in Macedonian. Learning the language was the biggest hurdle, and it was also the key to my success.

For the next two years, I lived the life of a villager high in the Macedonian mountains that bordered Albania. I taught students from 5th to 8th grade about ecology and English. I set up an English club for high school and college students interested in continuing their studies, and I created an English library and media center to promote continued education for children and adults. I helped conduct summer camps for Roma children who learned everything from swimming to lessons about the environment.

I fell in love with the people. I learned about Muslim and Orthodox Christian religions, went to weddings, funerals, and dances, and lived in a 200-year-old stone house that was the perfect sanctuary for me. I made wonderful friends and learned everything I could about the culture, traditions, and history of Yugoslavia. I had the time of my life.

It was in my best interest to have stuck it out through the challenges and occasional doubts. I am a better person for having joined the Peace Corps. I recommend it to anyone who has enough flexibility and open-mindedness to commit themselves to an endeavor beyond their comfort zone. It will be a journey of the heart and soul, one that connects the volunteer to the rest of the world in ways only achieved by true participatory and egoless actions.

Building Your Résumé

Although volunteers receive just a small stipend, which the Peace Corps sets according to the cost of living in each host nation, joining the Corps can be a wise career move.

College graduates who join the Corps gain experience in their field and often serve in positions of greater responsibility than entry-level jobs. Peace Corps experience makes a job candidate a standout among applicants fresh out of school. But work experience is only part of what an employer sees when reviewing the résumé of a RPCV.

The character-building aspects of service in the Peace Corps are so widely known that employers typically make positive assumptions about the independence, leadership ability, and work ethic of a returning volunteer. Another advantage to being an RPCV is access to the huge network of professionals who live across the country and work in a variety of professions.

The Peace Corps Office of Returned Volunteer Services (RVS) provides career and education assistance to RPCVs. RVS offers the Hotline bulletin, an online bulletin of employment and educational opportunities for RPCVs, that is published twice a month and career publications and events. You can find the current issue of Hotline and at **www.peacecorps.gov/index. cfm?shell=resources.returned.hotline.**

A Better Shot at a Federal Job

For one year after returning, volunteers receive non-competitive eligibility when applying for federal jobs. Returning volunteers need only meet the minimum qualifications of the job descriptions. Those with non-competitive eligibility are considered federal employees and are eligible for positions typically filled by promoting from within. Those with federal jobs that require Peace Corps service will begin at a higher level of pay, plus the two years of service counts toward the accrual of retirement benefits and vacation time.

CASE STUDY: LESSONS LEARNED

Kristin Webster
Romania

The first few months were delightful. I was excited about being accepted into the Peace Corps, and everything was interesting because it was new. With Peace Corps staff and other volunteers around, I did not feel the isolation that often happens on site. I was glad to have an affectionate host family.

It is hard to quantify everything I learned. I learned things like traditional cooking and dancing, and even took up knitting with some of the local senior citizens. But I also learned how to be a quicker problem solver, to live independently, to budget effectively, and to be a better and more creative cook, among other things. Of course, 27 months of immersion in Romania also provided me with a solid education in legends, history, folk beliefs, and a great appreciation for a culture I had previously known nearly nothing about.

I have only returned about three months ago, and I am still struggling with adjusting. I often feel like it is hard for me to relate to people I meet because so few people seem to know what the Peace Corps is, and they know even less about Romania. It gets frustrating that for the past two years of my life, Romania was the center of my world, and yet it is so far in the periphery for the average American. And as far as Peace Corps countries go, Romania does not seem remotely exotic. I understand why the third goal of Peace Corps is to share the countries we serve in with people back home.

An Edge for Getting into Graduate School

Those seeking advanced degrees will also find the Peace Corps advantageous. Having served in the Peace Corps strengthens the graduate school applications of volunteers by demonstrating they can handle the rigors of a challenging situation. Financial assistance for RPCVs is also available at some colleges and universities.

About 60 universities offer Master's International (MI) degrees, which involves a year of intensive study and two years of Peace Corps service. To enter a MI degree program, prospective students must submit an application to the Peace Corps and graduate school at the same time. The application must be completed at least six months before the semester in which study is planned. Returned volunteers who enroll in MI programs typically excel, according to RPCV John Coyne, who worked as an associate Peace Corps director. "In a sense it makes them more interesting for the professor," said Coyne, who served in Ethiopia from 1962 to 1964.

The Peace Corps Web site at **www.peacecorps.gov** has more information on the Master's International program. *See Chapter 14 for more information on the Master's International degree.*

PEACE CORPS FAST FACTS

- *The length of service is 27 months, which includes an average of three months of in-country training and 24 months of volunteer service.*

- *Applications are accepted on a rolling basis. Over the past year, the Peace Corps has received over 15,000 applications, an 18 percent increase over the previous year.*

- *The application process averages nine to 12 months. The minimum age for Peace Corps service is 18; there is no upper age limit. Volunteers must be U.S. citizens.*

- *Competitive applicants demonstrate commitment to community service, leadership experience, and a willingness to learn a new language. One in three applicants serves abroad.*

- *Volunteers receive a living allowance that covers food, housing, and incidentals, enabling them to live in a manner similar to people in their local communities.*

- *Volunteer safety and security is the Peace Corps' highest priority. The agency devotes significant resources to provide volunteers with the training, support, and information they need to stay healthy and safe.*

Help with Student Loan Debt

Even though the Peace Corps promises character-building experiences and an opportunity to serve others, the fact remains — the job does not pay the bills. Still, joining the Peace Corps could mean that certain bills, like federal student loans, can be deferred for up to three years. Interest does not accrue during deferment on Perkins Loans — federal government-provided loans for low-income stuents — and subsidized direct loans. Stafford Loans, — a form of federal financial aid — consolidated loans, and unsubsidized direct loans will accrue interest, while payments are deferred. PCVs can cancel 15 percent of their unpaid Perkins Loan debt for each of their first two years of service. For the third and fourth year of service, PCVs can cancel 20 percent of their unpaid Perkins Loans.

Those volunteers who have subsidized Stafford Loans can have the federal government pay the interest during the period of deferment.

Free Health Care

The Peace Corps employs medical officers in each country to provide free care to volunteers. Fully staffed physician offices are available in every country of service. The distance from PCVs' work sites to the clinics can be quite lengthy, so in some host nations, doctors make house calls. Peace Corps medical insurance covers all costs associated with medical care. Volunteers also receive a health kit and intensive training in self-treatment. Should volunteers require evacuation to countries with more advanced medical facilities than their host countries can offer, the Peace Corps will pay for transportation.

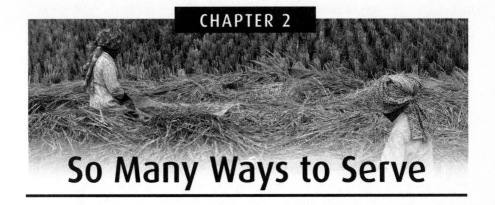

CHAPTER 2

So Many Ways to Serve

P eace Corps volunteers serve at the invitation of host-country governments and work on projects that have been identified as areas of need by country officials, professionals, and residents. Some PCV projects can be as intricate as establishing computer labs with Internet access, to as simple as the building containers for clean drinking water. Volunteers also address problems such as environmental degradation, AIDS-related issues, and a lack of access to education.

Project support and supervision for volunteers can vary from county to country. In some cases, PCVs must motivate themselves because they are breaking new ground or have scarce resources. In other cases, volunteers can get excessive oversight from professionals and lay individuals.

No matter the location or the assignment, these three Peace Corp goals are tantamount in every project: assist with development, improve the United States' image abroad, and increase Americans' knowledge of the world.

If these goals are the catalyst that make you consider living abroad for two years, the next step is to match your educational background and experience with the right assignment. The Peace Corps will try to place volunteers in areas where they apply, but it cannot guarantee a location or assignment. The following sections will provide an overview of the different project areas available to PCVs.

Education Requirements to Join the Peace Corps

Applicants are not required to have a college degree to join the Peace Corps, although 89 percent of volunteers do have at least an undergraduate college degree. Opportunities are available for those with a combination of job experience and education, though some opportunities require a four-year degree. Opportunities for applicants with an associate's degree are also available. Each individual position and sector has specific education requirements, which are detailed in the following sections and on the Peace Corps' Web site. Specific Web sites where education requirements can be found are listed where applicable in the following section. When submitting an application for service, the Peace Corps will decide if you have the required educational and/or work experience to serve with the organization.

Education

Education is the most popular Peace Corps service area. Thirty-five percent of volunteers work in the education sector. Successful applicants should have a combination of college study and teaching experience. Most education positions begin in May/June, and all education positions require at least a bachelor's degree and a minimum GPA of 2.5. For more on requirements for specialized fields in the education sector and their requirements, visit **www. peacecorps.gov/index.cfm?shell=learn.whatvol.edu_youth**. The following are sub-fields within the education service area.

Elementary education

Volunteers who qualify to teach primary education must have a bachelor's degree in elementary or early-childhood education. A teaching certificate is not required, and applicants can qualify with a bachelor's degree in other fields, or by drawing on their experience working with young children, or curriculum development. Other teaching experience should include work as a substitute, or as a teacher in early childhood programs or elementary schools.

Volunteers who work in elementary education will assist teachers with professional development, instructional methods, and occasional class instructions. Volunteers in elementary education specialize in a particular segment of the sector such as child psychology, English instruction, teaching a language other than English, science, environmental studies, AIDS prevention, or remedial classes.

Secondary education

Volunteers who qualify to train secondary English teachers must have at least a bachelor's degree in education, English, English as a second language (ESL), or a foreign language. A master's degree in ESL instruction, applied linguistics, or foreign language can improve an applicant's chance of acceptance. Applicants need not be certified to teach, but experience as a student teacher, teacher's assistant, or substitute is a plus.

University instructors

Volunteers who qualify to teach English at the college level must have at least a master's degree in English with a concentration in writing, literature, rhetoric, or speech.

Volunteers with a master's degree in linguistics, a language other than English, or other fields in the humanities — or who have taught English as a second language — improve their chances of acceptance. Other teaching experience should include work as a teacher's assistant, substitute, or tutor. Experience working on student publications or as an adult literacy tutor is a plus.

Volunteers who work at the university level will collaborate with other teachers and teach classes in all aspects of languages.

Special education

Volunteers who qualify to work in special education must have a bachelor's degree in education and certificates qualifying them to teach students with special needs. Applicants who have experience working with people with physical, emotional, learning, or developmental disabilities, or those who have experience with people with visual and auditory impairments, may qualify. Experience working on the staff of a group home, or having been a volunteer with the Special Olympics, is a plus.

Volunteers who work in special education provide resources for instructors of students with disabilities and advise them on classroom management.

Mathematics

Volunteers must have a bachelor's degree in mathematics, computer science, or engineering. Volunteers who minored in mathematics and those certified to teach mathematics at the secondary level, but who have degrees in unrelated fields, may also qualify.

Science

Volunteers who seek a science-teaching assignment must have a bachelor's degree in general science, biology, chemistry, physics, or engineering. Volunteers with a degree in secondary education with a concentration in science may qualify. Those who have degrees in any field with certification in secondary science may also qualify. Applicants should have experience tutoring small groups, or have volunteer experience with youth programs.

English

Volunteers who wish to teach secondary English must have a bachelor's degree in any field and experience teaching or tutoring ESL or English. Volunteers should also have experience with youth-oriented community organizations, or have worked in daycare centers.

Volunteers who teach English at the secondary level must conduct conversational classes, teach ESL, instruct students in English as it relates to other subjects, and develop curriculum material with other teachers.

Youth Development

PCVs who work in youth development are responsible for establishing community projects to help children, teens, and young adults who are likely to drop out of school, become unemployed, or contract HIV. Five percent of volunteers work in the youth-development sector.

Volunteers who qualify for youth outreach should have at least three months' experience working in youth services; six months' experience working full-time with youth (preferably in a city); or have experience as physical educators. Volunteers with training in conflict resolution, experience in AIDS education, fundraising, or helping young people with disabilities is a plus.

To learn more about this sector and its requirements, visit **www.peacecorps. gov/index.cfm?shell=learn.whatvol.youth**.

Community Development

Community development volunteers support Peace Corps endeavors by running public information campaigns and determining residents' needs. Successful applicants should have a bachelor's degree in any discipline, but a degree in psychology with a concentration in counseling, community development, or social work is a plus. PCVs must have recent experience in counseling, organizing, or leadership. Experience in adult education or assessing community needs is a plus.

To learn more about this sector and its requirements, visit **www.peacecorps. gov/index.cfm?shell=learn.whatvol.youth.comdev**.

Environmental Education

PCVs who work in environmental education promote recycling and conservation of trees and wildlife. Volunteers help host-country nationals conserve the natural resources they use to make a living. Volunteers who work in environmental education will teach youth groups and students in elementary through high school and set up environmental organizations and sanitation programs in cities. Fourteen percent of volunteers work in the environmental sector.

Successful applicants must have a strong science background and a bachelor's degree in ecology, environmental science, or natural-resource conservation. Volunteers with related work or volunteer experience can compensate for a degree in a non-environmental field. PCVs should have work experience in organizing conservation projects, grant writing, teaching, and camp counseling.

To learn more about the specialized fields PCVs contribute to in the environmental sector and their requirements, visit **www.peacecorps.gov/ index.cfm?shell=learn.whatvol.env**.

Conservation and Park Management

Volunteers who work in conservation and park management train rangers, assist with wildlife counts, and promote sustainable harvesting of resources.

Successful applicants must have a bachelor's degree in management of wildlife, natural resources, recreation, or park administration. PCVs should have worked at parks, zoos, or museums; other work experience includes taking flora and fauna inventories, grant writing, or participation in tree-planting efforts.

Environmental Engineering

PCVs who work in environmental engineering concentrate on water utilities and trash collection.

Applicants must have at least a bachelor's degree in environmental or civil engineering. Volunteers without a college degree may qualify if they are certified to handle hazardous materials or to operate water treatment plants.

PCVs who are in outstanding physical condition, have knowledge of bookkeeping, and have a background in construction or public health are considered strong candidates.

Business

Business volunteers address problems such as joblessness, burgeoning populations, and poorly trained employees. Some PCVs serve in an advisory capacity to facilitate economic growth by guiding a variety of businesses, municipal governments, schools, and community organizations. Volunteers share expertise in fiscal planning, business design, product development, and marketing. Fifteen percent of volunteers work in the business sector.

Applicants with a variety of educational backgrounds qualify. Successful applicants must have a bachelor's degree in business or related fields. Experience in accounting, running small businesses, cooperatives, or credit unions could compensate for bachelor's degrees in non-business fields.

Volunteers without a degree should have at least four years' experience managing a business; those who have owned or managed a small business are considered strong candidates. Successful applicants will demonstrate an aptitude for handling many tasks simultaneously. Popular backgrounds for applicants include human resources, marketing research, fundraising, and agriculture.

To learn more about the specialized fields PCVs contribute to in the business sector and their requirements, visit **www.peacecorps.gov/index. cfm?shell=learn.whatvol.busdev_01**.

The following are subfields within the Peace Corps' business service area.

Business development

Volunteers who work in business development teach in technical schools, high schools, universities, community organizations, and institutes. PCVs also design curriculum materials, help increase the financial power of women and minorities, and assist with government plans for economic growth.

Successful applicants must have a MBA or master's degree in public administration, management, accounting, banking, or finance with two years of related work experience. Applicants with a bachelor's degree and five years of related work experience may qualify.

Successful applicants for positions in business development have at least two years of related experience and experience as the owner and operator of their own business. Volunteers will be conversant with diverse management philosophies, have relevant computer skills, and have experience developing budgets.

Those applicants who work in development of non-governmental organizations (NGOs) draft fiscal plans, strategic plans, and mission statements. PCVs are also responsible for recruiting and training volunteers for NGOs.

Civil planning

Some business volunteers will devote their time to planning at the municipal and regional levels. These PCVs are responsible for impact assessment, infrastructure and budget planning, and serving as liaisons between government organizations and communities.

Successful applicants must have at least a bachelor's degree in planning, public administration, or public policy. Applicants with a bachelor's degree in architecture or related fields and at least a year of work in planning may qualify. Other volunteers with a bachelor's degree in unrelated fields, five years of related work experience, and three years of employment in planning may also qualify. Some applicants will have experience working with service groups or planning commissions.

Agriculture

Agricultural volunteers help farmers provide balanced diets and establish food security within communities. They also help farm families become financially self-sufficient and learn how to conserve natural resources. PCVs also assist farmers with business procedures such as analyzing profitability of crops and forming agribusiness associations. Five percent of volunteers work in the agriculture sector.

To lean more about the specialized fields PCVs contribute to in the agriculture sector and their requirements, visit **www.peacecorps.gov/index. cfm?shell=learn.whatvol.agr**.

The following are sub-fields that you can go into within the Peace Corps' agriculture service area.

Agriforestry

Volunteers who work in agriforestry are not required to have a college degree, but they must have one year of related experience. Successful applicants will have worked at least three months in gardening, landscaping, planting trees, managing livestock, or raising fish, and they should have a familiarity with environmental issues; tutoring experience is also helpful.

PCVs who work in applied agriculture promote organic growing, farm management, and agricultural methods. Volunteers encourage composting and organic methods to repel vermin.

Successful applied-agriculture applicants must have a bachelor's degree in agricultural science. Those without a degree must have three years' experience farming full-time. Some applicants will have worked on organic farms, operated farm equipment, and knowledge of crop storage.

Agribusiness

Agribusiness and farm management volunteers work with small farmers, co-ops, and non-governmental organizations to teach business planning, marketing, fiscal analysis, and networking.

Successful applicants must have a bachelor's degree in agribusiness or farm management, or a degree in business with one year of farming experience. Applicants without a degree must have at least three years of work experience in agribusiness. An extensive knowledge of gardening, business, research, and networking is a plus.

Animal husbandry

PCVs who work in animal husbandry — the agricultural practice of breeding and raising livestock — help farmers provide balanced diets for their families, increase their income, encourage livestock inoculations, establish gardens and beekeeping operations, and instruct farmers in marketing and land allocation.

Applicants must have a bachelor's degree in animal husbandry, zoology, livestock science, or biology. Applicants can have a bachelor's degree in unrelated fields and a minimum of 18 months of work experience with farm animals.

Applicants without a degree but who have a minimum of three years' experience working with livestock may qualify. Volunteers with a background in veterinary medicine, a familiarity with gardening, and experience managing businesses may also qualify.

Health

Volunteers in the health field focus on the health of mothers and children, diet and cleanliness education, disease-prevention information, improving sanitation, and increasing the availability of potable water. Twenty-two percent of volunteers work in the health and HIV/AIDS sector.

Successful applicants must have a bachelor's degree in a health-related field or in any field combined with relevant professional or volunteer work. Volunteers who are registered nurses and those who have other health care certificates may qualify.

To learn more about the specialized fields PCVs contribute to in the health sector and their requirements, visit **www.peacecorps.gov/index.cfm?shell=learn. whatvol.health**.

The following are sub-fields within the Peace Corps' health-service area.

Public health

Some volunteers devote their time to community health education. They recruit teachers to inform residents about the health of mothers and children, diet, and sanitation. Volunteers also coordinate activities to raise funds for health supplies and instruct peer counselors about STD prevention.

Successful applicants must have bachelor's degrees in any field and a background in public health. Applicants can be registered nurses or volunteers or workers in AIDS education, family-planning guidance, emergency response, or direct patient care.

Some volunteers dedicate their efforts to public health education. They work with residents to increase awareness of healthy practices and disease and illness prevention. Volunteers will instruct host-country nationals in elementary and secondary schools, conduct community health surveys, develop educational initiatives, and collect epidemiological data.

Successful applicants must have at least a bachelor's degree in a health-related field. Applicants will have completed health-related volunteer work or studied pre-medicine. Applicants with experience as nutritionists, dietitians, registered nurses, midwives, or physician assistants may qualify, as well as applicants who have studied survey methods and disease-tracking procedures.

Water quality and sanitation

Health volunteers who concentrate on water quality and sanitation help increase the public's awareness of good hygiene practices, build better quality water tanks, and construct latrines.

PCVs can have a bachelor's degree in any field, but applicants with bachelor's degrees must have a minimum of three months of relevant experience. Volunteers without degrees must have worked in some aspect of construction or plumbing for at least a year. Volunteers should have performed community education related to health or the environment. Applicants should be able to physically endure the requirements of the job.

HIV/AIDS Outreach

All PCVs in Eastern Europe, Africa, Central Asia, and the Caribbean are trained in HIV/AIDS outreach. Health volunteers might work in orphanages dedicated to children who are HIV-positive, develop AIDS prevention programs, or counsel those affected by the disease.

Even volunteers in programs unrelated to the HIV/AIDS crisis will have an opportunity to help host-country nationals.

To lean more about the specialized fields PCVs contribute to in the HIV/AIDS outreach sector and the Peace Corps' efforts to combat these diseases in host countries, visit **www.peacecorps.gov/index.cfm?shell=learn.whatvol.hivaids**. Requirements to work in this field are also available on this Web site.

Volunteers who specialize in education will teach AIDS care and prevention, instruct peer counselors, and establish support groups for orphans and those who are HIV-positive.

Volunteers who work in business development help establish and generate funding for HIV clinics and AIDS education programs.

Information Technology

Volunteers who work in information technology increase economically disadvantaged communities' access to computers and the Internet. PCVs specializing in information technology offer education and technical support to schools, national and local governments, non-governmental organizations, and businesses. PCVs establish databases and computer networks for government offices and businesses; help business owners and farmers use computers to find new markets; and help connect schools to the Internet.

Successful applicants must have a bachelor's degree in computer science or information systems, or a bachelor's degree in communications or any other field — provided they have at least 15 credit hours in computer science and two years of related work experience. Applicants should have at least five years' work experience as a computer programmer, systems analyst, or in a related position. Volunteers with an associate's degree in a relevant field or two years in a related discipline may qualify.

Successful applicants must understand fundamental computer functions and demonstrate an aptitude for organizing and leading others; experience in Web-based sales is a plus. Some applicants will have experience teaching others to make multimedia presentations, writing curricular materials, and developing Web sites.

To learn more about information technology and the requirements, visit: ***www. peacecorps.gov/index.cfm?shell=learn.whatvol.busdev_01.itwork.***

Food Security

Volunteers do not distribute food, but they do support host-country nationals with their own nutritional needs. PCVs who work in agriculture, environment, and health/nutrition are most directly involved in promoting food security. Projects include teaching residents how to garden and farm without destroying the soil, acting as a liaison between farmers and markets, and helping growers build business associations, apply for loans, and buy seeds.

Peace Corps projects have always indirectly helped communities achieve food security. To help address the worldwide food crisis, the Peace Corps has made food security a special priority since 2008.

Learn more about the efforts of the Peace Corps to promote food security by visiting: www.peacecorps.gov/index.cfm?shell=learn.whatvol.foodsecurity.

A Snapshot of Peace Corps Regions

Projects in each region aim to support the Peace Corps goals of fostering international ties, supporting development within host countries, and enabling volunteers to learn from their counterparts in their countries of service.

The focus of Peace Corps projects varies from region to region. PCVs in areas with a high incidence of HIV infection participate in AIDS prevention outreach regardless of their field of expertise. In regions with precarious food supplies, all volunteers address food security issues.

For specific information on the regions in which the Peace Corps operates, visit their interactive map at www.peacecorps.gov/index.cfm?shell=learn.wherepc.

Africa

With 26 countries of service, the African climate ranges from tropical to arid. Official languages include Zulu, French, Arabic, English, and many indigenous tongues. Many countries of service are former colonies that have become republics; some have figurehead monarchies. Volunteers assist with AIDS prevention and treatment, business development, water and sanitation, and education.

Caribbean

In all eight Caribbean countries of service, PCVs help residents prepare for and recover from natural disasters. Most residents are Christian, but a minority of residents are Rastafarian. Inhabitants speak English, French patois, Spanish, and English patois.

Eastern Europe and Central Asia

Linguistic diversity is a hallmark of this 12-country region. Inhabitants of Eastern Europe and Central Asia speak Russian and Greek, as well as Gagauz and Lezgi. Residents are Muslims, Christians, and followers of the Yezidi religion. Each country of service in the region has a project in education. The climate ranges from temperate to Mediterranean, from dry to semi-arid. Geographic features include mountains, beaches, steppes, deserts, and plains. The region includes former Soviet states and a former Yugoslav state. Earthquakes, droughts, and tsunamis are among the natural hazards.

Asia

All five countries of service in Asia have Peace Corps projects in education. Languages spoken include Mandarin, Spanish, Khmer, French, Russian, Turkic, Khalkha Mongol, English, Filipino, Tagalog, and Thai. Inhabitants are Buddhist, Muslim, Christian, Shamanist, and atheist. The climate ranges from tropical to desert to continental to subtropical. Monsoons occur regularly in some areas. Countries are governed by the National Assembly, members of the Communist party, and monarchs.

Central America and Mexico

Most of the eight countries in Central America and Mexico have Peace Corps projects that focus on environmental conservation. The climate ranges from tropical to subtropical to temperate to cool. Languages spoken include English, Spanish, Creole, Garifuna, German, Quiche, Kelchi, Nahuatl, and Miskito. Most residents follow Christianity or adhere to indigenous faiths. Terrain includes swamps, plains, mountains, and volcanoes. Countries of service are democracies and republics.

Middle East

Jordan is the only country of service in the Middle East. Peace Corps projects focus on education and youth development. Jordan is a constitutional monarchy, and residents speak Arabic and English. They follow Christianity, Islam, and the Druze religion.

Pacific Islands

Linguistic diversity is a notable characteristic of the seven countries of service in the Pacific Islands. Inhabitants speak Japanese, Anguar, Palauan, English, Tobi, Sonsoralese, Filipino, Trukese, Pohnpeian, Yapese, Kosrean, Ulithian, Woleian, Nukuoro, Kapingamarangi, and Tongan. Religions include Christianity, Islam,

Hinduism, Baha'i, and Modekngei. Political systems include constitutional governments and parliamentary democracies. The climate is tropical; typhoons and cyclones occur. Features of the terrain include mountains, plains, desert, plateaus, and volcanoes. PCVs work on projects in development of youth and communities, natural-resource conservation, education, information technology, business, environment, agriculture, and community health.

South America

The Peace Corps offers quite a few projects in the seven countries of service in South America. Inhabitants speak English, Creole, Dutch, Carib, Ndjuka, Saramaccan, Sranan, Tongo, Spanish, Guarani, and Quechua. PCVs work on agriculture, natural-resource management, environmental education, youth development, water and sanitation, business, environmental conservation, health, community development, beekeeping, municipal development, elementary education, sanitation, agriforestry, hygiene education, sanitation, water quality, and economic development.

```
CASE STUDY: LEARNING FROM
YOUR COUNTRY OF SERVICE
```

```
David Wright
Water and Sanitation, Ecuador,
1985-1987
Rural Education and Development,
Belize, 1987-1990
```

One of the images that remains with David Wright is that of 17 men jumping up and down on a water tank that he built in Ecuador. As a volunteer on water and sanitation projects, Wright helped introduce a kind of water tank construction that used less cement than builders typically used for similar structures. Engineers from Ecuador did not believe Wright's tank would hold up as well. "These Ecuadorian engineers were very skeptical. They said, 'We don't think your tank is very strong, so we're going to get up on top of it and jump up and down,'" Wright recalled.

There are now at least 2,000 similarly constructed tanks in Ecuador.

Wright left his business as a passive solar-heating consultant to join the Peace Corps at age 40. Inspired by a television commercial in which a RPCV described using her cooking and baking skills as a home economics educator, Wright applied to serve as a construction worker.

Wright advises prospective volunteers to closely examine their motives for applying to the Corps. He had a successful Peace Corps experience because he realized his pre-service goals of learning a new language, understanding another culture, and becoming familiar with the economic hardships that people in the developing world face.

Having grown up in the United States, Wright was unprepared for the slow pace of life and work in Ecuador. The first day Wright walked to work in the small Andean town where he served, he had difficulty adjusting to the slow pace of the townspeople. "I wound up walking in the street and passing everyone," Wright said.

Residents would often ask where he was going in such a hurry. Talking with colleagues required a similar adjustment. In the United States, work-related conversations often focus on the tasks at hand. But in Ecuador, talking business before asking about a colleague's family is considered rude. Employees also generally worked at a slower pace than in the United States and dealt with problems in a less confrontational manner. "I had to adjust myself to the idea that I wasn't necessarily wasting time or not doing my job," Wright said.

The intercultural openness Wright developed in the Peace Corps has served him well throughout his career. After finishing two terms, Wright took positions supervising and training volunteers. He eventually moved to Southeast Asia to work with the International Rescue Committee and now works in Indonesia as an environmental health adviser with CHF International.

The opportunity to understand how to work and live in another culture makes the Peace Corps especially valuable for people seeking an international career. To get the most out of Peace Corps service, volunteers should remain open to learning from those in their countries of service. "I think it's very important that you do not assume you have all the answers going in," Wright said.

CHAPTER 3

Volunteers of Many Stripes

resh-faced college graduates with newly minted degrees are the classic
image of PCVs. It is true that many people still join the Corps right out
of college, but the ranks of PC volunteers have diversified, to reflect the way
society has changed after nearly five decades.

To capitalize on the value of diversity, the Peace Corps recruits volunteers from
various backgrounds at different stages of their personal and professional lives.
A college degree is optional, and retirees are welcome — although 89 percent
of volunteers have at least an undergraduate degree, and only 7 percent of
volunteers are over the age of 50. The Peace Corps has opportunities available
for individuals without college degrees who have professional skills, work
experience, and a commitment to service. For those who have wanted to join
the Peace Corps but thought the opportunity had passed — think again.

To learn more about the different opportunities available to potential volunteers
regardless of your college or work experience, visit **www.peacecorps.gov/
index.cfm?shell=learn.whovol.**

Volunteers with Work Experience

In the Peace Corps, your work experience counts. The Corps encourages
applications from people whose jobs have taught them skills in building,
farming, tree maintenance, hazardous-materials management, water
treatment, and other related fields.

Volunteers for water-treatment projects need a year of experience in
woodworking, construction, plumbing, or stone work. Volunteers in forestry

and agriculture need a year of experience at a nursery or fish farm. To be assigned to a project in agribusiness, it is necessary to have spent three years managing a farm or related enterprise. To serve as an environmental or water engineer, applicants must be certified to treat water or sewage, or to handle hazardous materials. *For details on Peace Corps programs that are open to volunteers with work experience, please refer to Chapter 2.*

Volunteers with Associate's Degrees

The Peace Corps does not require volunteers to have a four-year degree. A two-year college degree (in some cases, combined with work experience) can qualify an applicant for service — though, again, the majority of PCVs do hold bachelor's degrees. PCVs with associate's degrees usually work in positions such as business advisers, computer scientists, and NGO developers.

Applicants with an associate's degree in trade education can teach technical classes; an LPN can assist with AIDS prevention and education; those with agricultural science or animal husbandry can volunteer for projects in their disciplines; and any two-year degree qualifies a volunteer for an assignment in youth development.

To view the eligibility requirements for applicants with an associate's degree, visit **www.peacecorps.gov/index.cfm?shell=learn.whovol.collegestu.associate.**

Volunteers of Various Races

One of the Peace Corps' reasons for existing is to give residents of host countries a chance to get to know Americans. The Peace Corps is committed to having a racially diverse pool of candidates, many of whom may speak several languages. The chart at right details the Peace Corps' most recent data at the time of writing for volunteers of color:

Racial minorities account for 16 percent of all PCVs. The percentage of African-Americans in the

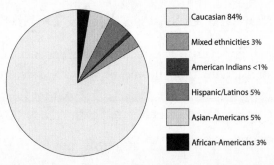

Caucasian 84%

Mixed ethnicities 3%

American Indians <1%

Hispanic/Latinos 5%

Asian-Americans 5%

African-Americans 3%

Peace Corp has nearly doubled since 1998, as has the percentage of Latinos. In 1998, 4 percent of PCVs were Asian, 4 percent were a mixed race, and less than 1 percent were American Indians.

To see specific information for applicants of color, visit **www.peacecorps.gov/ index.cfm?shell=learn.whovol.peopleofcolor**.

LGBT Volunteers

The Peace Corps welcomes lesbian, gay, bisexual, and transgender (LGBT) volunteers. The Corps provides in-country support, and connects them with other volunteers of the same sexual orientation. LGBT volunteers often find residents of their host communities less than tolerant of people whose gender identities differ from that of traditional males and females. Host-country nationals also often disapprove of romantic relationships between members of the same gender. A prospective PCV must decide how to respond to the attitudes and mores of life in a host country where their sexual orientation is an issue.

Spouses Serving Together

Married couples are welcome in the Peace Corps, but they usually must wait a longer period of time beyond the typical nine to 12 months for their assignments because they must be placed together. Seven percent of volunteers serving in the Peace Corps are married. The applicants must be married for at least one year before applying for service. Couples with minor children must document how their children will be cared for and financially supported in their absence.

Mature Volunteers

Volunteers who have spent decades working in their disciplines have a wealth of knowledge to share with their host-country counterparts, and many residents welcome the experience and expertise of the mature volunteer. Again, there is no upper age limit for volunteer serving in the Peace Corps, and 7 percent of volunteers are over the age of 50.

To view specific information for older applicants, visit **www.peacecorps.gov/ index.cfm?shell=learn.whovol.older**.

Concerns for older volunteers

Language education

Volunteers who have not been inside a classroom in decades might worry that they cannot learn a foreign language, but they will likely find the immersion-style language education that the Peace Corps provides quite effective. Tutors are also available for those who need extra assistance after training.

Severely ill or injured grandchildren

Grandchildren are among the relatives covered under the Peace Corps' emergency-leave policy. The Corps will pay for round-trip transportation if a volunteer needs to return to the United States to see a seriously ill grandchild.

Health check

Volunteers over the traditional age might have concerns about the medical examination. But the health review for older volunteers is no more rigorous than it is for younger ones. The Peace Corps provides medical care and evacuation services, if needed.

Retirement income

Peace Corps applicants who receive social security could find their payments decreased because of their Peace Corps stipend. To find out how the Peace Corp stipend could affect social security income (whether for retirement or disability), contact the Social Security Administration.

To determine the impact Peace Corps income will have on disbursements from your pension, 401(k), or other private retirement plans, contact your employer's human resources department

Federal employees will receive their full retirement annuities and Peace Corps pay at the same time.

NOTABLE RPCVs

- *Sen. Christopher Dodd (D — Conn.), served in the Dominican Republic from 1966 to 1968*

- *Mildred Taylor, Newberry Award-winner and author of Roll of Thunder, Hear My Cry, served in Ethiopia from 1965 to 1967*

- *Joe Acaba, mission specialist and educator at NASA, served in the Dominican Republic from 1994 to 1996*

- *Joyce Neu, founding executive director of the Joan B. Kroc Institute of Peace and Justice, served in Senegal from 1972 to 1974*

- *Bob Shacochis, American Book Award recipient and author of Easy in the Islands, served in the Eastern Caribbean from 1975 to 1976*

- *Jim Doyle, former governor of Wisconsin, served in Tunisia from 1967 to 1969*

- *Richard Wiley, winner of the PEN/Faulkner Award and author of Ahmed's Revenge and Soldiers in Hiding, served in Korea from 1967 to 1969*

- *Samuel Gillespie III, senior vice president of Exxon Mobil Corp., served in Kenya from 1967 to 1969*

CASE STUDY: VOLUNTEERING AT AN OLDER AGE

Donna Statler
Belize
Education
1989-1991

Donna Statler did not have a lifelong desire to join the Peace Corps. In fact, the urge to join took Statler by surprise and was part of a transformation that included getting a divorce and returning to school. Statler's metamorphosis began in her early 30s and continued right until she left for Belize at age 38.

Serving as an ambassador for ordinary Americans was one of Statler's most rewarding aspects of working in Belize.

Many host-country nationals picture the United States as Hollywood's glamour or Manhattan's excitement, but Statler's agrarian background helped her show the residents of Belize that they might have more in common with people in the United States than imagined.

Statler, who regularly visits Belize, has helped Belizeans study in the United States and has a scholarship named after her at the high school in her former community of service. Statler is happy to have established international ties with the residents and to have made a good impression on behalf of the United States. "They look at Americans in a positive light," Statler said.

During her time in Belize, Statler witnessed her own self-discovery and personal growth. Forming international ties and connecting with members of her community of service were not the only rewards of serving in the Peace Corps; Statler also underwent a significant amount of personal growth. Learning she could rely on herself and thrive in a foreign country was one of the most meaningful aspects of service. "The most rewarding [aspect] to me was just that I could make it," Statler said.

Endurance has been a hallmark of Statler's life, and she used her experience as one of 12 children growing up on a farm to demonstrate she could adapt to life in Belize and teach members of an agricultural community. When applying to the Peace Corps, applicants should emphasize relevant life experience, such as agricultural work or travel. A bachelor's degree with a minor in special education strengthened Statler's application.

Flexibility and the confidence to work without extensive supervision were key qualities that helped Statler succeed as a PCV. As a teacher trainer, Statler taught instructors how to make school subjects more meaningful to students who work on family farms. She also painted classrooms and built desks. Once when a teacher was unexpectedly absent, Statler found herself in front of dozens of 4- and 5-year-olds with no books, no electricity, and no lesson plans. Conducting a class in a foreign country without many of the resources that teachers in the states take for granted confirmed Statler's confidence in her ability to adapt and solve problems.

Statler's service in the Peace Corps made her a stronger and more impressive candidate in job interviews. The experiences Statler had in the Peace Corps gave her the confidence to apply for jobs that previously she might have felt underqualified to try, including one working with convicted sex offenders. "Before Peace Corps, I wouldn't have said '*I know I can do a great job*,'" Statler said.

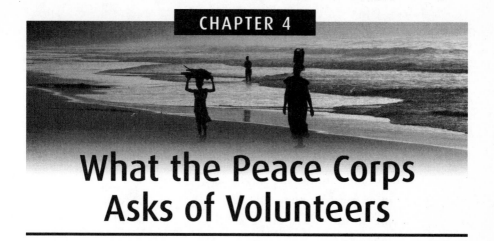

CHAPTER 4

What the Peace Corps Asks of Volunteers

P art of carefully considering whether to commit to two years of service is understanding what the Peace Corps expects of volunteers. Successful volunteers will possess certain beliefs, attitudes, and life experiences. Below is an overview of the requirements for a successful stint in the Peace Corps.

A Willingness to Leave Home for 27 Months of Service

Each applicant must carefully consider what effect a two-year absence will have on their professional and personal life.

Volunteers could be asked to work on a project that uses their current skills, but in a very different job capacity. There could be so many obstacles outside your control that it would be next to impossible to complete the original service. Sacrificing the stability of your current career could be unsettling and a major cause for regret.

For those involved in a relationship other than a marriage, the time apart could take a sad toll. Non-married couples stand a lower chance of being accepted into the Peace Corps because volunteers are often torn between the demands of the Peace Corps and the demands of attempting to maintain a relationship from half a world away. Due to the rudimentary postal services in many Peace Corps countries and the possible inability to communicate via the Internet or telephone, many volunteers cannot maintain regular contact with partners in the United States. It could be strenuous to remain in a relationship with a partner in the United States when contact could be rare.

Volunteers would do well to determine whether family obligations would allow them to live abroad for two years. The Peace Corps requires volunteers to document arrangements they have made to financially support their dependents in their absence. In addition to financial responsibilities, volunteers must also consider if they can make adequate provisions for the care of any sick or elderly relatives for whom they are responsible. Likewise, volunteers must be prepared to miss many of the milestones that grandchildren, nieces, and nephews will achieve in their absence.

Leaving friends, members of religious communities, and civic organizations tends to be less heart-wrenching, but consider the impact your departure will have on such relationships and whether you are willing to live with the change.

A Strong Desire to Improve the Lives of Others

PCVs should be motivated to learn as much as they can about their host countries and the people who live there. It is important for volunteers to improve their skills during their years of service so that they can add to the quality of life for those they serve. Volunteers should approach their work as an opportunity to exchange skills and collaborate with colleagues, instead of simply imparting what they know.

A Willingness to Establish and Maintain Trusting Relationships with Members of Your Host Community

Your work on projects, as well as your safety, will rely heavily on such relationships. To develop a social network within your host community, PCVs must adapt to its customs and values. Such adjustment requires volunteers to listen and observe without passing judgment. Volunteers will also need to put aside some of their assumptions about matters such as the status of women, corporal punishment, eating habits, and promptness. Undergoing such pervasive and profound changes requires solid emotional health and considerable flexibility.

To keep community relationships intact, volunteers must accept accountability for their actions during work and non-work hours. Communities of service are often small and close-knit, so any conduct by a volunteer tends to spread quickly.

Excellent conduct is imperative because volunteers are representing America and Americans.

Adherence to Peace Corps Rules and Laws of the Host Country; Caution in Matters of Health and Safety

With medical care being remote or rudimentary in most countries of service, the proverb "An ounce of prevention is worth more than a pound of cure" should be observed. Peace Corps rules exist to prevent death, injury, or illness to volunteers, and violation of these rules could result in a volunteer's being fired and sent back to the United States. Accidents have caused most volunteer deaths and, because of this, volunteers must wear helmets when riding motorcycles. Similarly, volunteers must take the medicines provided to prevent diseases, and or sickness. With the exception of alcohol, recreational drugs are prohibited. Volunteers also may not enter war zones. *See Chapters 7 and 8 for more information on health and safety matters.*

Peace Corps trainees learn about the laws of their countries of service during training, but applicants should contact embassies ahead of time. *See those listed in Appendix B for an overview of laws in countries they are considering.*

A Willingness to Go on Any Assignment

PCVs use their stipend to pay for food, housing, and modest entertainment. The standard of living will likely be much lower than volunteers are used to in the states. In many countries of service, walking or cycling are the primary means of transportation. Residents of many host countries use outdoor bathrooms and wood for fuel. Prospective volunteers should not only consider the personal and cultural richness they will gain by working in their host communities, but also the material comforts they could lose for two years.

A Commitment to Accurately and Respectfully Portray Residents of Your Host Country Upon Your Return to the United States

One of the Peace Corps' goals is to educate Americans about residents of developing countries. It is important that returned volunteers present a fair and balanced report on their host country and the people they served. Volunteers have a responsibility to present cultural and historical context about their host countries that will help people in the U.S. overcome some of the stereotypes that might exist. Through the National Peace Corps Association, returned volunteers can dispel prejudices and misconceptions by discussing their experiences with schoolchildren and civic groups.

CASE STUDY: SETTING
REALISTIC EXPECTATIONS

Mark Kohn
Agriculture Generalist
Federated States of Micronesia,
Island of Kosrae
1979-1981

Realistic expectations are key to a fulfilling experience in the Peace Corps. Volunteers should respect the knowledge that people in their countries of service have and not join expecting to change the world. PCVs should also keep in mind that they might not "see the world," as such, but will be helping to improve the lives of small groups of people and getting to know a corner of the world that they might not otherwise have traveled. This makes a stint in the Peace Corps an exceptionally valuable experience. "I got to experience and see things I only dreamed about. I actually — in small, hard-to-fathom ways — made a difference in another culture," Kohn said.

Just as realistic expectations are essential to succeeding as a volunteer, so is being flexible. Applicants should be willing to go anywhere and do any job. Remaining flexible regarding locations and assignments helped Kohn secure an invitation to join the Peace Corps in spite of competing with applicants who had more-advanced degrees.

Kohn had an associate's degree and had worked as a mailman and an assistant manager of a book shop. A stint working with senior citizens as a VISTA volunteer, a lifelong interest in overseas service, and the desire to heal from a broken heart prompted Kohn to apply to the Peace Corps.

Spending two years in a location that had no telephone service at the time, and where the wait between available airline flights was measured in weeks, made the loneliness daunting at times. Kohn began his service with two other PCVs, but they left the island early. The residents were extremely attentive, going out of their way to keep Kohn company, even if they did not know him, but language and cultural barriers still caused him to feel isolated on occasion. Over time, Kohn began to immerse himself in the language, and he learned the skills needed for his work and personal life. Kohn left the Peace Corps more focused, self-sufficient, and ready to start the next chapter of his emotional and professional life.

Kohn credits the Peace Corps with giving him the resourcefulness and self-confidence to succeed in his career as a social worker with the Wisconsin Department of Corrections. RPCVs should use examples from their service to convince prospective employers that they are committed and flexible. "When being interviewed for post-Peace Corps jobs, be sure to stress the aspect of all the hardships you experienced and all the moments you had to think on your feet. Employers like to know their staff can handle whatever comes their way," Kohn said.

CASE STUDY: THE INTANGIBLE REWARDS OF SERVICE

Richard Lipez
Education
Ethiopia, 1962-1964

Post-Eisenhower idealism inspired Richard Lipez to drop out of graduate school and join the Peace Corps. "I was, first of all, caught up in the whole Kennedy-era romance of widening the United States' view of the world," said Lipez, who has a bachelor's degree in English.

Lipez left a small town in Pennsylvania to see a world in which Americans felt more welcome than they do today. Ethiopia, where he taught secondary school, was full of post-colonial optimism — which had yet to give way to revolutionary rage.

In part due to the social climate, Lipez adjusted smoothly to life and work in Africa. Loneliness was not an issue for Lipez because there were approximately 50 other volunteers in the capital (where he taught during his first year of service), and roughly eight other PCVs in the small town where he spent his second year. Ethiopians treated Lipez and his fellow volunteers with kind interest, staring at them in public and exclaiming at the sight of foreigners when they walked by. "It wasn't really that hard to be an object of sort of friendly curiosity," Lipez said.

What frustration Lipez did experience came mostly from coping with bureaucratic obstacles that stood in the way of his teaching. Pupils in the small town school had too few books, so when Lipez and his fellow volunteers found a warehouse full of schoolbooks, they thought the problem had been solved. Their glee subsided when the supervisor of the warehouse refused to let them take any books for fear the students would soil or lose them. The Department of Education would charge the supervisor personally for the cost of any books that went missing or were returned in less-than-perfect condition. Lipez and his colleagues eventually got official approval to use the books, but not without a trip to the capital and negotiating to ensure that the cost of lost books would not come out of the supervisor's pocket.

The kind of adaptability, patience, and problem-solving Lipez used to get the books released are qualities prospective volunteers should note in their applications. Other traits to emphasize include a deep interest in other cultures and an active imagination.

Openness to cross-cultural friendships and a keen imagination served Lipez well in the Peace Corps — and beyond. Lipez counts literary inspiration among the benefits of service. He is the author of a series of mystery novels in which a RPCV is a recurring character. A long-standing bond with members of his host community is another cherished outcome of service. Lipez and his partner recently visited Ethiopia for a reunion with his former students, who held a series of feasts in their honor.

Volunteers leave their host countries with many such intangible rewards for their service. "For ourselves, it was just the most profoundly educating and wonderful experience," Lipez said.

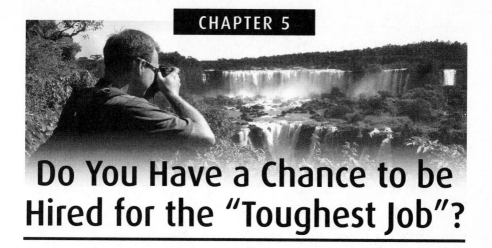

CHAPTER 5

Do You Have a Chance to be Hired for the "Toughest Job"?

I f the promise of adventure, immersion in a new culture, and enhanced career prospects has piqued your interest, you might be wondering whether you have what it takes to join the Peace Corps.

The Peace Corps welcomes diverse applicants. Volunteers vary in age, gender, and ethnicity. One of the Peace Corps' goals is to increase host-country nationals' understanding of the people of the United States. Hiring volunteers who reflect the diversity of the people in the United States helps inhabitants of countries of service transcend the stereotypical views of Americans. Although volunteers' backgrounds vary, they must meet certain requirements to serve.

Basic Requirements

- PCVs must be at least 18 years old; there is no maximum age limit.

- All successful applicants must be U.S. citizens. Federal tax dollars fund the Peace Corps, and it is one of the benefits citizens receive in return for their contributions. Including foreign nationals among the volunteer force would undermine the Peace Corps' goal of encouraging inter-cultural exchange between Americans and citizens of developing countries.

- Volunteers may not bring dependent children. Couples who have been married at least 12 months before the date they would be scheduled to leave the United States are eligible.

Couples who want to serve together have a slimmer chance of being accepted because the Peace Corps must find projects in the same host country that are suited to the skills of both partners. Less than 10 percent of PCVs are married. Married couples can strengthen their chances of getting into the Peace Corps if they are flexible in their geographic preferences. If both partners are basically proficient in Spanish or French — languages for which there is a high demand — they will have a significantly higher probability of being accepted. Married applicants who wish to join without their spouses must document their partner's consent.

- To enter the Corps, applicants must undergo an extensive physical exam to prove they are fit to serve.

Managed illnesses, including psychiatric illnesses, generally do not preclude acceptance. There are some health problems for which the Peace Corps cannot provide the accommodations required under the Americans with Disabilities Act (ADA), so applicants with those issues will not be accepted. For certain illnesses, applicants must undergo a waiting period to ensure their conditions will not radically change. A list of illnesses that require a waiting period or that are cause for nonacceptance can be found on the Peace Corps Web site at **www.peacecorps.gov/index.cfm?shell=learn.howvol.faq**.

- PCVs must commit to two years of service in addition to three months of training.

To see if you possess the basic requirements to be accepted by the Peace Corps, take their eligibility quiz at **www.peacecorps.gov/index.cfm?shell=learn.howvol.qualify**.

What Makes Some Applicants Shine?

The strongest applicants will draw on their work, life, and volunteer experience to provide evidence of personal qualities that make them suited to Peace Corps service. RPCVs and former Peace Corps staff suggest an applicant have these traits:

- Professionalism
- Leadership and community service experience
- Foreign language fluency
- Candor
- Openness to intercultural exchange
- Flexibility in geographic preferences
- Flexibility in types of projects on which one is willing to work
- Patience
- Self-motivation
- Optimism
- Physical energy
- Emotional stability

Taking the Language Proficiency Exam

Applicants are required to take a proficiency exam. The exam measures an applicant's ability to communicate rather than the knowledge he or she has gained over the years. The exam gives prospective volunteers an opportunity to make a strong case for their acceptance into the Peace Corps.

Now that you have decided that you might be qualified, read on to learn what to expect as you complete your application.

CASE STUDY: HOW TO BE AN ATTRACTIVE APPLICANT

John Coyne
Education
Ethiopia
1962-1964

Inspired by the idealism of the Kennedy era, John Coyne signed up for the Peace Corps while it was still in its infancy. After two years of teaching English in Addis Ababa, Ethiopia, Coyne spent another two years working as an associate Peace Corps director. Coyne's experience as a volunteer and staff member left him with some words of wisdom for prospective volunteers, current PCVs, and those who have returned.

Applicants who are willing to work in any program with a current opening have a better chance at being accepted. Potential volunteers who are willing to serve in any region are also more likely to find themselves holding an invitation packet. Many applicants are college students, but those with five years of work experience in welding, carpentry, and small business ownership also have strong chances of acceptance.

Successful applicants must go beyond convincing the recruiting staff that their skills and interests match open positions. Prospective volunteers should establish credibility by being completely candid. "The first is to be totally honest because they're going to do a check on you," Coyne said.

Peace Corps staff members evaluate applications individually, but they will rarely accept prospective volunteers with certain life circumstances or medical conditions. Significant medical obstacles include cancer, severe asthma, and major depression. Applicants who have current trouble with the law, who owe large amounts of money, or have children to support usually will not be accepted.

Succeeding as an applicant requires somewhat different qualities than succeeding as a volunteer. The most successful volunteers are those who have an ironic sense of humor, openness to other cultures, and flexibility. "You cannot be rigid, or you'll find out very fast that the American way is not the only way," Coyne said.

After working in what was once a completely foreign culture, PCVs often r-envision their professional lives. Post-Peace Corps work takes different forms for volunteers, but often, people who entered service with a particular passion find that the scope of their interest has become global. So, people who thought they were eventually destined for law school leave the Peace Corps wanting to practice international law. Other volunteers who started service with an interest in business discover they now want to work for an international company.

After returning, Coyne, who has a master's degree in English, edited books on returned volunteers' experiences. Coyne co-founded *RPCV Writers and Readers*, a newsletter of former volunteers. The newsletter evolved into the Web site **www.peacecorpswriters.org**, which publishes short writings by former volunteers, reviews of books by RPCVs, interviews with authors, and other items of interest to applicants.

> Returned volunteers find re-adjusting to life in the United States much more stressful than getting used to life in their countries of service. In their countries of service, volunteers trained with other people who were having a similar experience, but upon returning, some find themselves isolated from friends and family. RPCVs can ease their transition by developing a routine, such as going to work or school, joining an organization of RPCVs, traveling with other volunteers, and writing about their service experience. Some volunteers might find it helpful to continue traveling after their Peace Corps service. Regardless of how they choose to cope with leaving the Peace Corps, volunteers should recognize that it is normal to find readapting stressful. "Readjustment is probably the most difficult part of the whole Peace Corps experience," Coyne said.

The Application Process in a Nutshell

On average, the application process can take six to 12 months to complete, but it can take longer in some cases due to reference checks, medical evaluation, determining applicant suitability for assignments, and the availability of assignments. After being accepted by the Peace Corps, most people depart for their country assignment within two to three months.

What you need to get the ball rolling

The first step in becoming a PCV is to submit the application. You can submit an application online by visiting **www.peacecorps.gov/applyonline**. A paper application can also be submitted. Contact 800-424-8580 or visit a regional recruitment office to receive a paper application and speak with a Peace Corps recruiter if you have questions about the application. To find a recruitment office near you, visit **www.peacecorps.gov/index.cfm?shell=meet.regrec**. To find out more information, you can also attend an information event near you. For a listing of currently scheduled events, visit **www.peacecorps.gov/index. cfm?shell=meet.events**. The Peace Corps can also be found on Facebook, Twitter, and YouTube.

The online application does not need to be completed in a single session. You will create a PIN number and password for your application so you can work on it at your own pace. Most people complete the application within two weeks. During this stage of the process, you will need to submit the following items:

- **A health status review form**
  The health status review form covers your physical, dental, and psychological health.

- **College transcripts, official or unofficial**
  This is required unless you have ten years of applicable professional experience.

- **The six-page application form**
  The application includes two essays, three references, employment history, résumé, community and volunteer experience, and education background.

- **Three references**
  One of the reference letters must come from a current or former supervisor; a current or former volunteer supervisor should provide the second; and a friend who has known the applicant for two years or more should write the third letter of recommendation. Relatives, spouses, or romantic partners may not provide references.

- **List of financial obligations**
  This should include outstanding student loan, mortgage, or other financial obligations.

The application is similar to a job application, but is much more in-depth. In addition to listing your work experience and educational history, applicants will have to disclose any previous attempts to join the Peace Corps, and there is an extensive section where applicants must list and describe relevant and practical experience gained through hobbies and volunteer work. You will be able to monitor the progress of your application throughout the application process by visiting **www.peacecorps.gov/mytoolkit/login/login.cfm?**.

The essays

Applicants must write two 250- to 500-word essays. In one essay, applicants will be asked to discuss their inspiration for wanting to join the Peace Corps, and they must explain how their motivation links to their history and goals. The second essays asks applicants to tell a story about a time they had to adjust to a new environment, what they learned from adjusting, and the personal qualities or aptitudes that enabled them to make the transition.

SAMPLE ESSAY

By Julia Abigale Johansen, Education, Ukraine 2007-2009

Tonight was one of the best nights of my life, and it was exactly the reason I went into teaching ESL. I was invited to dinner by one of my former students. I went expecting a sit-down dinner, with maybe four or five people, perhaps six, and instead was treated to an awesome Saudi Arabian dining experience. We had tons of amazing food and engaging conversations. Because we were outside of the classroom, it gave us an opportunity to relate as people in an informal setting. It was a chance for them to show off parts of their culture they are proudest of to one of their teachers. I got to see a slice of Saudi culture that I would not have otherwise.

I have a true sense of wanderlust. No way would I ever be content staying in the same city, the same state, or even the same country while the world was out there to explore. I know in my heart that just being a tourist would never give me the satisfaction of really being a part of a culture. I am not content with the experience equivalent of a fast food restaurant; I want to savor my experiences.

When I first heard about the Peace Corps years ago, I knew it was exactly what I was looking for. The exchange of culture and ideas is what really breaks down prejudices. Until I started teaching ESL, I was not aware of how many prejudices I had, and I am so grateful every day to break down my own stereotypes and the students' as well. I want to know people outside of what the media tells me, not as a tourist, but as an honored guest. People like me and organizations like the Peace Corps help dispel myths perpetrated by media and tourists. The Peace Corps would give me the chance to experience a people in a way that I would not normally get to and would provide a profound life experience — there is something important that happens during a volunteer experience, doing something out of love rather than out of need for money.

I have wanted to teach ESL for about as long as I have wanted to join the Peace Corps, and the reason why I have not tried to do either until now is that I wanted to do them right. They are so important to me that I wanted to make sure I had all the qualifications, all the degrees, all the preparation out of the way.

> *At this point I have finished my master's degree and am completely qualified to teach anywhere in the world, and I am pausing in embarking on my career for the chance to join the Peace Corps because I want to start my career by doing something important and significant, and not based on how much money I can make. Sure, money is important, but right now, for me the experience is more important, and I would be honored and excited to be accepted into the Peace Corps.*

The interview

Do your research and dress professionally. The one meeting with the interviewer will significantly influence the outcome of your application. Prepare to discuss your inspiration for joining the Peace Corps and your teaching experience. Even if you do not know the language of your preferred country of service, discussing the challenges you have overcome while learning any foreign language will help. Applicants are not required to have passed a foreign language proficiency exam or to hold a degree in the language of their preferred host country, but having such qualifications to mention during the interview would improve your chances.

Be prepared for questions outside of the norm for a basic job interview. What are your methods for handling stress? How would those methods work outside the realm of your usual support system? Or what are your thoughts on having to change your appearance or habits to adapt to the culture of a host country? Applicants must be prepared to discuss cultural differences and any commitments that would make it difficult to finish their service.

Peace Corps recruiters conduct interviews by phone or face-to-face. Recruiters try to have a relaxed conversation that can range from less than an hour to two hours long.

The nomination

After the interview and your completed application have been received, a recruiter will review your application and determine whether you are qualified to join the Peace Corps. If you are, you will be nominated to work in a general sector and location, and given an expected departure date. However, this nomination is only a recommendation by the recruiter that you move forward in the application process.

The health review

The Peace Corps publishes a long list of health problems that usually cannot be accommodated in countries of service, as well as those that require waiting periods. Some issues that cannot be accommodated are potentially fatal allergies, metastasized cancer, recurring heart problems, HIV, muscular dystrophy, psychosis, schizophrenia, chronic major depression, and recurrent hepatitis. Other conditions require applicants to be symptom-free or stable for certain periods before joining the Peace Corps. Situations requiring waiting periods include abnormal Pap smears, cancer, braces to straighten teeth, herniated disks, and cystic acne. Visit **www.peacecorps.gov/medical** for information on conditions that the Peace Corps is typically unable to accommodate, or ask a recruiter for a list.

The legal review

Applicants must prove creditors will be satisfied in their absence by documenting their plans to pay their debts, or to legally defer any student loans. Prospective volunteers must state whether they have used illegal drugs or have consumed alcohol while underage; describe any criminal record(s), disclose any lawsuits in which they are involved; and, if they have a dishonorable discharge from the military, they must explain why. If an applicant is married and a spouse does not plan to join the Peace Corps, the applicant must attach a spouse's notarized statement that he or she has knowledge of the application. Divorced applicants must list the names of their former spouses and provide copies of divorce papers.

After the legal review, applicants are evaluated by a placement officer to determine how their skills compare to the skills of other applicants. The officer may contact you with follow-up questions. Applicants whose skills are in demand will then be matched to openings. The officer will take into account when you are available to leave and the availability of accommodations needed, should you have any special medical requirements.

The invitation

If you are qualified, the placement officer will extend an invitation to join the Peace Corps. You will be provided with a specific country of service and given a job description. You will receive a welcome packet, your date of departure, job assignment, and more. Invitations are typically sent out two to three months — but at least six weeks — before the volunteer will leave for service.

The Peace Corps' travel office will issue you an electronic ticket for travel to orientation session. You will meet other trainees before leaving for your host country for in-country training.

Choosing a Field for Service

Some of the service fields might sound more intriguing than others. To compare your background with the educational and professional requirements of the assignments that interest you, make an exhaustive list of your experience.

For each job or hobby, jot down all the personal qualities and professional skills necessary for the job, and list the skills or knowledge learned from the job or hobby. When reviewing your experience, think about how you remained committed to your goals against overwhelming physical and emotional odds. About 30 percent of PCVs leave before they finish their two-year commitment. To leave early, PCVs need only contact the staff of their nearest Peace Corps office and ask to go home. PCVs who leave to attend to family emergencies in the United States can return to service. Remaining in the Peace Corps for two years will require intense determination, so it is important for an applicant to know whether he or she has the mental fortitude to perseverance.

You might be qualified to serve in several areas of the Peace Corps. Answer the following questions about each position or hobby to help you decide which assignments you should apply for:

- What tasks gave me the greatest sense of accomplishment?

- What are some of my most compelling memories of working/ volunteering at this position or participating in this hobby?

- Which aspects of this job or volunteer position would I do in my free time if I did not have to concern myself with earning money?

- Which parts of this job, volunteer position, or hobby were most challenging?

- What did I learn from meeting the challenges?

- What character strengths did I develop by addressing the challenges?

- What disappointed me about this job, volunteer position, or hobby?

- How much did the disappointment impact my overall experience?

- How did I personally fall short in this job, volunteer position, or hobby?

- Have I remedied the shortcomings?

- If I cannot remedy the shortcomings, how would I work around them in the future?

Use the descriptions in Chapter 2 to determine which assignments would most likely offer rewards that were important in previous work, volunteer, or hobby experience. Choosing an assignment that matches some of your previous experience not only allows you to build a convincing case that you are up to the job, but it also gives you a glimpse of what challenges to expect and how you would react to them.

Where in the World You Could Go

Peace Corps staff tries to place applicants in their preferred location, but they cannot guarantee placement. During the application process, a prospective volunteer can refuse to go to any location they dislike, but once an assignment has been granted, it is unlikely it will be changed. An applicant can increase their chances of acceptance by being willing to go anywhere.

With eight regions to choose from, PCVs have options that range from frigid to tropical, rural to urban, and ancient to modern. Some awake to the crowing of roosters, while others rise to morning prayer calls echoing from domed rooftops. Corps members' workplaces can range from hand-tilled gardens to cutting-edge computer labs.

Determining What You Want

Put simply, determining where you would like to serve means taking stock of your preferences and learning about the areas in which you might work to learn which areas are good matches for your personality, interests, and experiences.

Before reading about the countries in which PCVs work, take some time to reflect on the type of place in which you would fit. Use a notebook for your thoughts so you can review them during your decision-making process.

Learning from Previous Travels

Make a list of all the places you have traveled for recreation or business. Be sure to include long journeys or vacations, day trips, or weekend camping trips. This list will provide an overview that can help your assessment. After the list is complete, set a timer for five minutes and write down everything you can remember about the experience. You might have to leave some of the questions blank, but try to provide enough information to give yourself a good overview.

- What did I expect before I went to this place?
- In what ways did the place live up to my expectations?
- In what ways did the place differ from my expectations?
- What problems did I encounter?
- How did I cope with the problems?
- What did I find exhilarating?
- What did I find tiring?
- How intensely was I homesick?
- How long did the homesickness last?
- What triggered homesickness?
- To whom did I turn for help?
- How often did I see other people I knew?
- Would I have preferred to see more or less of the other people I knew?
- Did I find myself wanting to stay longer or to leave early?
- Could I see myself living in such a place?
- If I had had to stay for several months, would I have preferred a place that was more urban, or less urban than this one was?
- How often did I contact people at home?

- If I had to do the trip over, would I want to have more contact with people at home?

- What are some of my most cherished memories of this place?

- How similar to my home was this place, and how did I react to the differences?

Your responses to these questions will give you some idea of your ideal country of service. Of course, the ideal country does not exist, but having a sense of what your perfect spot would be like can help you choose a location that comes as close as possible.

Call in Some Advisers

To further define your ideal county of service, applicants should ask those closest to them to describe the perfect community they could live in for two years, assuming they could live in one of the countries the Peace Corps serves. Ask your relatives and friends to go into as much detail as possible and to explain their reasoning. Notice what characteristics the communities have in common, and consider using them as qualities to look for when determining your preferred country of service.

Rating Your Requirements

Peace Corps volunteers work in eight regions of the world, so there is a lot of variety in potential countries of service and work assignments. Below is a list of factors to consider when deciding where to serve:

- Climate
- Degree of development
- Access to telephones
- Prevalence of AIDS
- Types of other diseases common in the country
- System of government
- Types of assignments available
- Religions practiced
- Languages spoken
- Terrain

Rate the importance of each consideration on a scale of one to 10, and note any factors that could be deal breakers. For instance, if you have a medical condition that is exacerbated by humidity, a hot climate could make some regions off-limits.

How to Apply

Prospective volunteers can apply at the Peace Corps Web site: **www.peacecorps. gov**. Applicants will go through an eligibility quiz with questions about their work experience, college major, linguistic ability, age, and citizenship status. After the account has been established, applicants will receive a personal identification number (PIN) that allows them to save their application and access it later. For those who prefer a paper application, they can request one by calling the Peace Corps at 800-424-8580.

Application Time

"Ready...set...wait..." might be a good motto for those applying to serve in the Peace Corps. It can take up to a year to get a response to your application. Filling out the application can take from one day to several weeks, depending on the extent of your work history, medical information, and volunteer experience. To complete the application, you will need documents regarding your loans, a list of volunteer positions you have held, your résumé, schools you have attended, graduation dates, a list of degrees earned, and the names and contact information of three references.

When Will You Set Off on Your Journey?

Departure dates vary, but your recruiter will provide a general idea of when you can expect to leave. Volunteers often depart several months after they accept their invitation.

CASE STUDY: TIPS FROM AN ACCEPTED VOLUNTEER

Lindsay Jenson
Accepted volunteer in an agricultural
extension program in Latin America
Actual departure date: TBD

A desire to learn from people who live in developing countries, a long-standing commitment to service, and a taste for adventure were motivating factors for Lindsay Jenson.

Jenson studied in Mexico and France. She served as an interpreter for workers on her church's school building project in Nicaragua, so she knows firsthand the value of understanding people of other cultures. Through Peace Corps service, Jenson looks forward to encountering a less consumerist view of life.

Jenson's previous volunteer service and study abroad made her application more competitive, as did her minor in Spanish and her volunteer work within the United States. Jenson has a bachelor's degree in public relations and works as a volunteer coordinator for Habitat for Humanity through AmeriCorps/VISTA. She recommends that prospective volunteers do as much volunteer work as they can before applying, even if they serve in the United States. Jenson applied in 2007 then joined AmeriCorps/VISTA to strengthen her chances of acceptance.

Prospective applicants should spend a lot of time gathering information to help them determine whether they are suited to serving in the Peace Corps and to help them prepare their applications. "Research, research, research. Talk with RPCVs; read the blogs of current volunteers; or go to the library and read books about the Peace Corps and RPCV stories. Applicants can ask their recruiter every question they can think of. The recruiter can also provide contact information of RPCVs in your area," said Jenson.

Reading the accounts of returned volunteers has heightened Jenson's eagerness to begin serving. "I'm excited about the experience and what I'm going to learn about the community and myself," Jenson said.

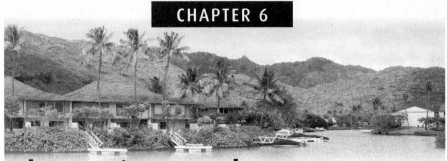

CHAPTER 6

Alternatives to the Peace Corps

Why the Peace Corps Might Pass You By

There are quite a few situations that could make a prospective volunteer ineligible. Some possibilities include if work experience does not match current projects; the amount of unpaid debt is too high; the interviewer sensed relationships problems; there is a lack of language proficiency; there are restricted geographic preferences; applicant has dependent children with no alternative means of support; there are medical conditions for which the Peace Corps cannot provide accommodations; or the applicant has narrow project interests.

For a variety of reasons, the Peace Corps accepts only approximately one applicant in every three. If your application is not approved, there are still many international service opportunities. Some last a week, some a year or longer. The cost of travel to and from the country of service often falls to volunteers, and some programs charge fees to participate. Scholarships are sometimes available; many religious or civic organizations could finance for your travel. There are numerous service projects available, and there is bound to be something that suits your interests, talents, budget, and time frame. The overview here will get you started.

Evaluating an Alternative Program

"No matter which voluntary service organization you are considering, it is important to ask questions that allow you to evaluate its motives, methods, and effectiveness. You want to be sure that the organization you devote your time and energy to is in line with your goals and values before you commit to working with them," wrote Paul Backhurst in the 11th edition of *Alternatives to the Peace Corps.*

Backhurst recommends researching organizations with which you are considering traveling to find out their political or religious affiliations, their relationships with residents of host countries, and the type of training needed. Also find out where the organization's money comes from and whether there is any available to defray the costs of your service. Costs for which you should budget include airfare, in-country travel expenses, food, housing, and vaccinations. College fellowships and private grants are some other possible sources of money for your trip.

Short Stints

Serving abroad for one to several weeks allows a volunteer to contribute to projects with a variety of missions. Host-country residents are often willing to help with lessons on culture and language. Short-term volunteers often serve in the summer, perhaps between graduation and beginning a job. However, many programs accept volunteers on a rotating basis throughout the year. Assignments could include restoration of culturally significant buildings, digging at an archaeological site, educating residents about AIDS prevention, working on organic farms, constructing houses, or teaching English. Volunteers can return home with the satisfaction of knowing they worked on a project intended to better the lives of their new friends.

Spring Break Programs

For those ready to end the party-vacation cycle, there is the alternative spring break. Such vacations offer sightseeing, volunteer opportunities, language lessons, and introductions to other cultures. Volunteers on alternative spring breaks build playgrounds, preserve turtles, construct houses, or conserve rainforests.

The United Way offers alternative spring break programs through which participants can volunteer to help victims of Hurricane Katrina continue to rebuild their lives or assist with community development in cities and towns across the country. For more information, see **www.liveunited.org/asb**.

Break Away coordinates alternative spring breaks during which volunteers can work with projects focusing on homelessness and education. For more information, see **www.alternativebreaks.org**.

Cross-Cultural Solutions runs one-week spring break programs abroad that combine volunteer work with cultural experiences and language lessons. For more information, visit **www.crossculturalsolutions.org**.

Becoming an Exchange Student

College students should check out their school's international office, sometimes called the office of international opportunities, to start researching opportunities to study abroad. Be sure to ask about language requirements, prerequisite courses, credits earned, and price of tuition. Costs differ among programs. In some cases, students do not pay more for tuition and living expenses than they would in the United States.

For those who have graduated from college, it is not too late to study abroad. Check out short-term programs to learn martial arts, a new language, journalism, painting, cooking, archaeology, or film appreciation.

The Rotary Club offers Ambassadorial Scholarships to students pursuing bachelor's degrees and graduate degrees, as well as to professionals who wish to take professional development courses. The scholarships support overseas study in hopes of fostering international relationships. For information about Ambassadorial Scholarships, log on to **www.rotary.org**.

Transitions Abroad is an information resource for people who want to study, volunteer or work abroad. The Transitions Abroad Web site at **www.transitionsabroad.com** lists study abroad programs ranging from journalism classes in Prague to martial arts training in Thailand, to language immersion programs in France, to archaeological digs in Jordan.

Hosting an exchange student

Welcoming a student from abroad is a way to expand your cultural knowledge, hone your language skills, and make a new friend. A host family would provide meals, a bed (preferably in the student's own room), a place to study, and transportation. The family and the student would typically undergo criminal background checks and compatibility screenings. Short-term and year-long stays are possible.

Hosts are adults, but need not be married or have children. The Center for Cultural Interchange at **www.cci-exchange.com/usprograms/host.aspx** offers information on hosting exchange students.

People to People Ambassador Programs

People to People Ambassador Programs (**www.peopletopeople.com**) offers short-term travel programs for students, athletes, educators, and professionals. Ambassadors travel abroad for two to three weeks in groups of approximately 35 as a way to foster local and global networking. They participate in cultural exchange and humanitarian activities, and tour culturally significant sites. For professionals, the organizations offer the opportunity to spend about a week in another country visiting workplaces and talking with others in their field. Trips also include sightseeing and home visits.

CASE STUDY: LOOKING ELSEWHERE FOR VOLUNTEER OPPORTUNITIES

Zachary Shtogren
Environmental Education
Dominican Republic, 2005
Journalist
Catalonia Today
Teacher
Benjamin Franklin International
School, Barcelona

Learning from a wrong turn could best summarize the value of Zachary Shtogren's time in the Peace Corps.

Inspired by a professional interest in international development, as well as generosity and desire for adventure, Shtogren served as an environmental educator in the Dominican Republic in 2005. Even though Shtogren found the language and cultural-training classes rigorous and competent, the technical training did not go beyond what he had learned in introductory college courses.

The emphasis on interpersonal aspects of Peace Corps work continued past pre-service training. Volunteers typically focus on establishing intercultural ties, rather than accomplishing concrete development goals. Those looking to begin a career in international development should consider other avenues.

The impact volunteers have on their host communities varies widely, regardless of professional qualifications. Shtogren, who has a degree in environmental studies and worked as an environmental educator before joining the Peace Corps, grew disenchanted with the Peace Corps and began to question the program's overall efficacy, especially its drop-out or "early termination" rate.

"Any real-world overseas development organization losing this many of its staff a year would be taking a very hard look at its effectiveness," said Shtogren, who now works as a journalist and teacher.

Although Shtogren did not find the Peace Corps useful for the purpose of finding work in international development, he noted that it can strengthen the résumés of those looking for government jobs or any positions in the public sector.

Potential applicants should assess their characters before beginning the application process. "The most successful volunteers are those who are patient, emotionally resourceful self-starters," Shtogren said. So many different positions are available that applicants with varied backgrounds have a strong chance of acceptance. Prospective volunteers can strengthen their applications by presenting themselves as optimistic and energetic.

Those applying should fully understand the nature of the organization. Shtogren said that the most rewarding part of his service was "realizing the Peace Corps is fundamentally a goodwill tour for young people and a hiring platform for the Department of State. When I realized this, I was ready to leave."

CHAPTER 7

Protecting Yourself from Crime

Theft, burglary, sexual assault, carjacking, mugging, and murder are among the crimes that occur in Peace Corps countries of service. As foreigners, who are wealthy by comparison to most host-country residents, Peace Corps volunteers stand out as targets for theft and burglary. Navigating unfamiliar geographic and cultural territory makes volunteers vulnerable to violent crimes. The Peace Corps Office of Safety and Security is responsible for helping PCVs stay safe. The office offers comprehensive safety training, determines whether volunteers' living quarters are secure, and designs emergency response methods.

PCVs are forbidden to enter zones the Corps considers too dangerous, often due to civil war. Volunteers must also notify the Peace Corps before they leave their host country to travel.

Safety and security rules vary by host country. In some countries of service, PCVs may not ride motorcycles without helmets. In others, volunteers are forbidden to travel at night by taxi. In some countries, PCVs must avoid going to the beach alone. During pre-service training, volunteers learn the safety rules of their respective host countries.

To view information released by the Peace Corps and their latest volunteer safety report, visit their site on safety and security at **www.peacecorps.gov/index.cfm?shell=learn.safety.safeandsec**.

Crime Statistics

According to the Annual Report of Volunteer Safety, released in January 2010, provides safety data for 2008, which is the most recent data collected by the Peace Corps. In 2008, PCVs endured 22 rapes/attempted rapes, 18 major sexual assaults, and 88 other sexual assaults. The Peace Corps defines rape as the unwelcome penetration of the victim's vagina or anus with the perpetrator's mouth or penis. A major sexual assault is one in which the attacker uses a weapon or injures the victim. If the victim fights off the attacker, a major sexual assault has occurred, according to the Peace Corps' definition.

Volunteers reported two kidnappings in 2008. PCVs experienced 37 aggravated assaults, 12 major physical assaults, and 43 other physical assaults that year. The Peace Corps defines aggravated assaults as attacks in which assailants use weapons, or cause such injuries as fractured bones or missing teeth. Major physical assaults are attacks that land victims in the hospital for fewer than two days, prompt doctors to order X-rays that do not show broken bones, or require surgery. If the victim fought off the attacker, a major physical assault has occurred, according to the Peace Corps' definition.

Volunteers reported 182 robberies, 317 burglaries, 757 thefts, and five acts of vandalism in 2008. Two PCVs died while serving in 2008. There was one accidental death and one death due to illness. There were no murders in 2008. Accidents are the primary cause of PCV deaths. Since the Peace Corps began, approximately 252 volunteers have died while serving. Murder has claimed the lives of 21 volunteers during the Peace Corps' existence.

For a more detailed overview of these statistics, visit the Peace Corps Web site at **www.peacecorps.gov/index.cfm?shell=learn.safety** and view the *Volunteer Safety Report.*

It Pays to Know Your Neighbors

Becoming part of your host community is crucial in reducing your risk of crime. The more your neighbors get to know your habits, the more they can check on you if you do not arrive home at your usual time. Commuting to work with your neighbors may also help discourage taunts and harassment.

Improving your odds

Although no security strategy is foolproof, you can adopt habits that reduce your risk of becoming a crime victim.

- **Know the territory.** Familiarity with your country of service is one of your best defenses. While crime can happen anywhere, some neighborhoods and roads are safer than others. Similarly, going out during hours when you are likely to be alone increases your risk of attack and theft. Eighty-two percent of sexual assaults against PCVs occurred when the victim was alone. In more than half of non-sexual assaults, victims were by themselves. See *Appendix B for a list of high-crime areas.* The Peace Corps cautions volunteers to avoid high-risk parts of each country of service.

- **Put down the bottle.** For your own safety, curb your alcoholic consumption. In 40 percent of assaults against PCVs, the victims or assailants had been drinking.

- **Recognize your host country's coupling customs.** Women in the United States live under the protection of laws that recognize that wearing revealing clothes does not necessarily constitute consent to hear sexual comments from strangers, and that pursuing sex with one man does not inherently reflect willingness to engage in sexual relations with anyone else. But women in many host countries express openness to sexual advances by dressing in particular ways and using certain body language. Wearing clothing that host-country nationals consider revealing or looking at strangers in what locals perceive as an overly familiar way could lead some to believe that sex or sexual advances are welcome. Community residents will be more likely to recognize an impending crime and intervene to prevent rape or sexual harassment of volunteers who conform to cultural norms of modest dress and body language.

Where There is No 9-1-1

Volunteers must keep in touch with their nearest Peace Corps office and notify staff members when they leave their posts. Each country of service has an emergency action plan, which volunteers receive as part of their training. The plan advises volunteers on preparing for and responding to emergencies such as wars, earthquakes, and hurricanes. During an emergency, Peace Corps officials will notify volunteers and assist them in getting to safe areas.

What to Watch Out for When You are in...

- **Africa**: Mugging, robbery, and carjacking occur often in cities and at the beach. Vandalism, burglary, armed robbery, and theft is also common.

- **Caribbean**: Burglary is a common problem. Rape, murder, armed robbery, and assault occurs infrequently.

- **Eastern Europe and Central Asia**: Visitors should beware of carjacking, theft, fights with firearms, assault, harassment, mugging, and credit card fraud. Terrorism occurs infrequently.

- **Asia**: Rape, robbery, theft, armed robbery, fraud, and kidnapping are among the crimes foreigners have experienced. Terrorism occurs infrequently.

- **Central America and Mexico**: Rape, murder, assault, kidnapping, theft, and carjacking are causes for concern.

- **Middle East**: The region has a low rate of violent crime. Rape, sexual harassment, and theft are among the more prevalent crimes.

- **Pacific Islands**: The region has a low crime rate. Robbery, burglary, petty theft, harassment, and simple assault are among the commonly reported crimes.

- **South America**: Murder, carjacking, rape, kidnapping, assault, and weapons trafficking are among the crimes visitors must be aware of.

CHAPTER 8

Medical Concerns

Medical Statistics

The Peace Corps publishes an annual report of illnesses and injuries that trainees and volunteers experience. To calculate rates of illness and injury, Peace Corps staff members divide the number of new cases of disease or incidents of injury by the number of service years each volunteer has contributed.

Stomach and intestinal ailments topped the most recent list of common complaints with a rate of about 75 per 100 volunteer/trainee (v/t) years. Teeth trouble occurred at a rate of approximately 24 per 100 v/t years. Contagious skin problems occurred at a frequency of approximately 24 per 100 v/t hours. Injuries happened at a rate of about 20 per 100 v/t years. Mental health problems happened at a frequency of about 19 per 100 volunteer years. Volunteers reported gynecological infections at a rate of about 16 per 100 v/t years, and sexually transmitted diseases happened at a rate of about four per 100 v/t years.

HIV/AIDS

Using condoms every time you have sex is wise regardless of the country in which you serve. Peace Corps nurses will offer in-depth information on sexually transmitted diseases. Condoms are sometimes for sale in the host country, but they are always available from the Peace Corps nurse's office and in volunteer health kits. Volunteers should be sure their sexual partners are tested for HIV, but they should not assume that negative screening results make safe-sex practices unnecessary.

Relationships with Locals

Peace Corps volunteers who become pregnant may continue their service if adequate maternity and post-natal care is available, and their parental duties would not prevent them from doing their jobs. The country director must approve continued service. Volunteers may be eligible for maternity and child care benefits through the Peace Corps. Volunteers who decide to terminate a pregnancy do so at the expense of the Peace Corps in countries where the procedure is safe and legal; they then return to their posts after their doctors release them to travel. Volunteers who become fathers while serving may continue their work provided their parental duties do not interfere with their jobs. The Peace Corps will pay for maternity care.

The Peace Corps does not encourage or discourage volunteers from dating or marrying host-country nationals or other PCVs. But volunteers must not let their personal relationships interfere with their work. Volunteers who plan to marry must receive the approval of the country director to continue their service.

Medical Care

There is a Peace Corps medical officer in every country of service, typically in the capital. Free medical care is a benefit of joining the Peace Corps, and workers compensation can cover treatment at the end of service if an injury or illness occurred while serving as a PCV. If a volunteer is too sick or injured to get to the office of the doctor, medical care will be provided. Medical evacuation to another country with better health care, is also available in case of emergencies that cannot be treated in-country. Following the advice of the Peace Corps doctor and the nurse who conducts pre-service training is essential to preventing illness. *For more information on preventive practices in specific countries of service, see Appendix B.*

The manual "Where There is No Doctor: A Village Health Care Handbook" by David Werner, Carol Thuman, and Jane Maxwell offers advice for volunteers who live far away from the Peace Corps health care provider. The book is available as a PDF at **www.hesperian.info.** Although the primary audience for "Where There is No Doctor" is health workers, advice on such topics as homemade casts, practices that prevent parasitic infections ,and how to correctly identify illnesses could be helpful to volunteers.

At the close of pre-service training, volunteers will receive a health kit, which includes pain relievers, syringes, condoms, and antiseptics. PCVs in countries in which malaria is prevalent will also receive anti-malarial drugs and medicine to treat the disease.

The Peace Corps requires volunteers to take a variety of preventive medicines, depending on the diseases that are prevalent in their countries of service. Recreational drugs are off-limits to PCVs.

Eating Safely

Health, safety, and hygiene instruction is tailored to each nation, but some advice applies across many countries of service.

Volunteers should remember that the consequences of injury and illness are sometimes more grave in Peace Corps countries of service because posts are often remote, thus reaching medical care takes more time than in the United States.

The tap water in many countries is not suitable for drinking because it carries parasites or microbes. Peace Corps volunteers must drink bottled water or use purification kits. Making sure that food is cooked thoroughly is another health warning that will serve volunteers well regardless of their country of service.

For more information on health and safety, refer to Appendix B.

What to Watch Out for When You are in...

- **Africa**: AIDS, hepatitis A, diarrhea, typhoid fever, malaria, meningococcal meningitis, tuberculosis, schistosomiasis, and avian flu.

- **Caribbean**: AIDS, hepatitis A, hepatitis B, typhoid fever, and diarrhea.

- **Eastern Europe and Central Asia**: AIDS, hepatitis A, hepatitis B, typhoid, rabies, malaria, tick-borne encephalitis, and avian flu.

- **Asia**: Common diseases include ciguatera poisoning, histoplasmosis, bubonic plague, measles, influenza, felariasis, AIDS, hepatitis A, typhoid, dengue fever, malaria, Japanese encephalitis, avian flu, diarrhea, Crimean Congo hemorrhagic fever, malaria, leptospirosis, and chikungunya.

- **Central America and Mexico**: Dengue fever, diarrhea, leishmaniasis, Chagas disease, AIDS, typhoid, rabies, hepatitis A, hepatitis B, and malaria.

- **Middle East**: AIDS, hepatitis A, hepatitis B, typhoid fever, rabies, diarrhea, leishmaniasis, West Nile virus, measles, and avian flu.

- **South America**: AIDS, diarrhea, hepatitis A, hepatitis B, typhoid fever, dengue fever, malaria, yellow fever, rabies, leptospirosis, altitude sickness, rabies, and Oroya fever.

CHAPTER 9

Packing and Training

Cramming more than two year's worth of gear into luggage with an 80-pound weight limit might seem like an impossible task, but that is only the beginning.

The Peace Corps will provide a country-specific packing list, but less is best in order to prevent back strain. Luggage should be sturdy but portable and lightweight so that you can carry it long distances by yourself. A camping mat and sleeping bag will come in handy in many countries of service.

Tape, plastic bags, earplugs, and a knife with a can-opener attachment are some of the more obscure recommendations from RPCVs. Blogs written by current and returned volunteers offer advice on clothing and other items to pack. The Web site **http://forest.mtu.edu/pcforestry/about/whattobring.html** offers packing advice from volunteers by country of service.

Games are important items to include because the entertainment options in host countries will likely be limited. Shortwave radios, CDs, and books are the tried-and-true boredom busters. Video games and MP3 players can be brought, but be aware that you may have limited access to electrical outlets to recharge such devices. PCVs should buy a shortwave radio and electricity converters before leaving the United States to ensure quality.

Pictures of loved ones and friends can be conversation starters with members of your host family, neighbors, and colleagues. RPCV Mark Kohn cautions against bringing irreplaceable pictures on your service tour. Kohn, who served in the Federated States of Micronesia from 1979 to 1981, said salt air ruined his beloved pictures. From a practical standpoint, it is best to leave your most cherished mementos behind to prevent them from being stolen, and on an emotional level, it makes the transition to your host country easier. "The less you bring from home, the easier it will be to make the new country your home," Kohn said.

Take it or Leave It?

Basic toiletries are available in most host countries. Feminine hygiene products sometimes differ, so pack some and have some sent as care packages.

Do not dump your wardrobe into your suitcase. Do bring a few professional outfits, quality cold-weather gear — if geographically appropriate — and several pairs of well-made boots and shoes. For most casual wear, wait until you reach your country of service and buy the appropriate clothing.

Peace Corps staff will process your applications for a visa and a PCV passport, for which you do not have to pay a fee. The PCV passport is only valid for three months after your service.

Learning the Language and Culture

Language classes in the Peace Corps are unique and, regardless of how little experience volunteers have with the language of their host country, they will begin to have conversations with a teacher who is a native speaker as soon as class begins. Talking to native speakers gives volunteers the chance to develop practical communication skills they can build on during their two years of service. Language trainers also teach volunteers how to adapt to the culture of their host countries and adjust to the local technology.

Returned volunteers often give Peace Corps language training high marks for helping them hit the ground running in their assignments. After five weeks of training in Nepali, RPCV Darren Miller left with the confidence to travel, get around his village, and teach math, science, and English to high school students.

Practical Guidance and Technical Training

Part of the goal of pre-service training is to help volunteers communicate and develop the practical skills they will need to thrive in their new environments.

Training helps PCVs understand health, safety, and hygiene, as well as the basics of cooking and keeping house. Volunteers typically enter the Peace Corps with educational or work experience in the fields in which they will be serving, but through lectures, interactive activities, and demonstrations, they will receive technical training that prepares them for the position they will hold in their host country.

Volunteers spend about half the time in technical training where they practice skills related to their work assignments. They learn the fundamentals of their jobs first and progress to more advanced skills. The technical trainers are usually PCVs who have served in relevant capacities. Tutoring is available for anyone who has difficulty with technical training. After volunteers have served for a year, they participate in a weeklong technical training workshop with lectures, demonstrations, and discussions with volunteers who have finished their terms.

Technical training gives volunteers the confidence to handle the unexpected with humor and flexibility. One returned agricultural generalist recalls applying his rudimentary knowledge of animal husbandry in a surprising situation.

On the island of Kosrae, one of the federated states in Micronesia, PCV Kohn was able to help a family new to caring for livestock. After consulting an animal husbandry textbook, Kohn decided that the family's pig was ill, so he gave the creature an injection of penicillin. The following day, the healthy sow contentedly suckled her newborn piglets.

"So for about two minutes, I was a hero," said Kohn. He explained that there was no correlation between the penicillin shot and the successful pig's delivery — the sow and nature had done all the work.

CHAPTER 10

Living In-country

The thought of living in a foreign country in a community where you may be the only American and the only person who speaks English likely leaves you with many questions and anxieties. Or, perhaps it leaves you completely thrilled to embark. Whichever you are feeling, you will undoubtedly have a lot of questions. The following sections are meant to answer some of your most basic questions about living in your host country. While living arrangements are different for each volunteer, depending on the country you travel to and whether you are located in a large city or small village, this chapter aims to ease some of your anxieties.

You can also find details about living in-country from PCVs by visiting the Peace Corps' Web site at **www.peacecorps.gov/index.cfm?shell=learn. whatlike**. This site includes helpful information such as volunteer journals, video FAQs, photo galleries, volunteer stories, and interactive features.

Housing Arrangements

Volunteers may choose to live alone in a house or in the home of a host family. Nowadays, most PCVs houses have electricity, but it is unreliable, as is the system for running water. Internet access at home is rare, as are land-based telephones. Cell phones are common in many Peace Corps countries.

Most PCVs live alone. Sharing a house or compound with a host family gives volunteers an opportunity to practice the language and become more immersed in the culture. Some volunteers live in temporary housing when they first arrive and move to their permanent homes after taking a few months to get used to their new surroundings.

Doing the Dirty Work

Volunteers often hire residents of their host communities to help them with the laundry. In some cases, the PCV might have to carry the water for doing the laundry; in some host countries, there might be running water. Neighbors are usually eager to help PCVs with laundry, cooking, and cleaning because the money they earn enables them to feed their families.

Corps Cuisine

Peace Corps volunteers encounter striking differences in areas ranging from kitchen technology to dining etiquette and economic constraints on food security. Insight into the cultural significance of food and the opportunity to build relationships by sharing meals with host-country nationals are among the rewards to remaining open to rethinking long-held attitudes toward eating.

Like many other aspects of life, mealtime in the Peace Corps depends on the country and the level of development in which a volunteer works. Volunteers may live in houses with stoves and refrigerators, while other might not have electricity or running water. PCVs who do their own cooking soon learn the value of improvisation. Techniques such as using wine bottles as rolling pins and baking muffins in tuna cans come to seem second nature. A refrigerator might seem like less of a necessity to PCVs who have grown accustomed to keeping their vegetables cool in wet sand. For more tips on culinary improvising, check out the cookbook, *Where There Is No Restaurant* by former volunteers Aimee Clark and Meghan Greeley.

Vegetarianism

Just as volunteers adapt to different kitchen tools, their palates adjust to new tastes, and their minds to new food philosophies.

Seeing animals slaughtered and possibly participating in a slaughter is often part of the Peace Corps experience. Vegetarians are welcome, but depending on the country, they might have difficulty getting enough nourishment from available food sources, and cultural attitudes might impede volunteers from remaining vegetarian. Host-country nationals often would not think of giving a guest a meal without meat, and refusing food is considered rude.

Eating habits reflect resident's views of nature and their outlook on relationships between hosts and guests. Cooks in host countries rely heavily on in-season vegetables, which can make meals more predictable.

Absorbing new culinary customs and mealtime rituals are fun aspects of learning about another culture, but discovering the economic constraints with which some host-country nationals cope is often much more sobering.

While eating lunch in the home of a mother of ten in the Haitian community in which he served, Richard Ireland (RPCV 1998 to 2001), noticed he was being watched. "All of a sudden, I realized all the kids were there, and they were very quiet," Ireland said. Eventually, one of the children, who ranged in age from 1 to 17, spoke up and said that none of them had eaten that day. Ireland immediately stopped eating and decided to hire the children's mother to cook for him, which helped her provide for her family.

Pets

The Peace Corps does not allow volunteers to bring pets, but to ease the loneliness and help with adjustment, many PCVs take in stray animals after arriving in their countries of service.

Connecting with Your Host Community

When RPCV Donna Statler (Belize 1989-1991) returns to the village in her country of service, people wave and call out, "Miss Donna!" At the local high school, there is a scholarship in Statler's name. Statler, who has red hair and fair skin, did not initially feel as though she fit into the village, but during two years of work at the local school, she developed friendships that have lasted 19 years, and she has helped several Belizeans attend school in the United States. Interpersonal relationships are key to working effectively, and volunteers should not underestimate the importance of building rapport with their counterparts.

Society is more communal in many countries of service, and residents are happy to welcome volunteers into their extensive circles of friends.

Ireland found residents of his community of service sympathetic to his social needs. When word got around that Ireland lived alone in a house country where about a dozen relatives usually live, community members stepped in to ease some of the loneliness that they assumed he felt.

Volunteers, who include non-working residents, often develop relationships and friendships that lead to lifelong international friendships. Sharing a home with a host family is another excellent way to develop ties. Volunteers who live alone can establish regular contact with residents by paying to eat a meal with a family near their post, according to RPCV Julie Bradley (Belize 1989-1991). Once ties have been established, residents will invite volunteers to community events such as dances, weddings, and festivals.

CASE STUDY: FINDING FRIENDS AMONG STRANGERS

C. Joe Andrews
Falalop, Ulithi of Yap State
Peace Corps Micronesia 2005-2007

"One of my greatest accomplishments during my service in the Peace Corps was learning to cut *tuba* ('tooba'). At least, that is what we called it on my island. 'Tuba,' 'palm wine,' or 'toddy' has many different names by those who enjoy it around the world. It is the fermented sap of a coconut tree and was a cultural keystone at my post on the almost mile-wide island of Falalop, Ulithi, in the Federated States of Micronesia.

In the evenings on Falalop, I was invited to join the 'drinking circle' — a gathering of community leaders discussing current events around the world and the planning of upcoming events around the atoll. It took me over a year to realize that rather than arrive at the circle as a guest, bringing no tuba of my own, I could learn how to make tuba and contribute to the evening's drink supply. When I began bringing my own tuba to our drinking circle, word quickly spread that I was no longer a helpful American visitor from California, but rather that I had become a local Ulithian.

My tuba-making skills aside, I was involved in numerous successful community projects and had an incredibly fulfilling assignment teaching science and English at Outer Islands High School, which serves students from neighboring islands as far as 500 miles away. I am very proud of these technical aspects of my service, but they pale in comparison to the perspective gained and the joy I felt through the friendships I made as I became a fixture in a once completely foreign community."

"This is why I value my experience in the Peace Corps over all others thus far. I was given the opportunity to fully integrate into a new culture and, in doing so, experienced a new life.

From the outset of the application process, the idea of flexibility and patience were drilled into me. A consistent line of questioning during my interview involved adaptability and strategies to cope with stress. I also recall thinking that perhaps the seven months that I had to wait before getting an assignment was a test of my dedication and desire for service.

The real skills that a PCV needs to be successful vary based on many factors, including where he is posted, whom he is surrounded by, and who he is at the outset of his service. Conventional classroom lessons can only teach so much, and I would argue that the majority of lessons I learned were the result of mistakes that I made, or by venturing out from my comfort zone. The process was facilitated by my training staff of locals and other experts who spent two days explaining many aspects of the host family's Pohnpeian culture.

The main value of my training was rooted in my opportunity to apply the advice I received in our daily eight-hour training sessions — directly to the family and community where I lived. Each session began with a group of 28 trainees sharing the experiences they had had with their host families the day before and any lessons, wisdom, or good laughs that came from them.

The biggest skill that I took away from training was the understanding that in the two years to follow, it was inevitable that I would make mistakes. With this, I learned that I had nothing to fear by diving into my assignment. My overall confidence continued to grow as my new Micronesian friends and family supported me and fed my appetite to become part of my new community around me.

In the 26 months that I lived on Falalop, Ulithi, I learned what it is to be an Ulithian — not just how to speak the language and the significance of the greeting 'Ho buddoh mongoay' (come and eat!). I got to experience lying on my back singing songs with friends under star-packed skies, joining the men on fishing trips, learning the destructive nature and blissful fun of small-island gossip, and knowing the joy of dancing like a fool at the occasional 'fun night' village-wide dance.

The majority of Americans who are familiar with the Peace Corps recognize it as an organization solely devoted to the training of the nationals of developing countries. Although the work and projects that I was involved in were significant, they are not the sole experiences that have forever changed my heart and overall perspective on life. I had the opportunity to not just arrive at my circle of friends as a guest, but to bring my own *tuba* and live each day as a fellow islander."

Peace Corps Paychecks

If your country of service has a working banking system, volunteers will be paid by electronic deposit. If the banks are unreliable, checks are delivered by mail or courier. Payday will be every month or every three months. According to **www.peacecorpswiki.com**, each volunteer receives a $1,000 spending account to draw from for work-related expenses during their entire term of service.

If the banking system functions well, open an account and keep your money as you would in the United States. If you do not trust the banks in your country of service, you can arrange to travel to the nearest Peace Corps office to claim a portion of your pay. Your country director or other Peace Corps staff in the area should be able to offer guidance on how to handle your money. If there are individual in your community whom you trust to discuss money matters with, ask them their opinions of the banking system before depositing your money.

Volunteers will have enough money for basic living expenses and modest forms of entertainment. Volunteers often supplement their Peace Corps living allowance by bringing traveler's checks and cash from home.

You can receive wire transfers in most countries of service. But if you have Internet access, PayPal charges lower fees than most wire services. See **www.paypal.com**.

Technology

Volunteers can use their cherished devices for many of the same purposes they do at home, but in the Peace Corps, these gadgets can be an extra burden because the more electronics you have, the greater the risk of burglary or the possibility that they will not survive your term of service.

Many Peace Corps countries have Internet access, but residential and business service can be spotty. You are most likely to be able to get online at an Internet cafe or the Peace Corps office. Volunteers often do not have the option to connect at home or at work.

A laptop could help you work faster and more efficiently, and also enable you to watch your favorite DVDs. You might consider insuring your laptop; jolting buses and sweltering velds are not laptop-friendly.

The Peace Corps provides cell phones in many countries of service, or you could buy one in-country. To increase your chances of getting reception, buy a multi-band cell phone. To ensure that you can use the SIM card of the local service provider in your host country, opt for a phone that is unlocked.

A camera enables you to give your loved ones back home an online glimpse of your surroundings and new friends. Take a camera you can afford to replace, because the wear and tear of using it in your host country will likely shorten its life. Taking a digital camera will lower your per-photo cost, but finding a shop to handle repairs will be easier if you take a film camera. Packing an MP3 player is not a good idea; also take a device with speakers so you can share your favorite music with guests.

Connecting With Other PCVs

Depending on where volunteers are serving, they might see other PCVs daily, or only once every few weeks. Volunteers who work in cities tend to have more contact with their counterparts than PCVs in remote areas.

While teaching in Addis Ababa, Richard Lipez (RPCV 1962 to1964), was rarely lonely because he worked in the same city as about 50 other volunteers. RPCV Darren Miller (Nepal 1991-1993), by contrast, occasionally walked several hours through the breathtaking Nepali countryside to visit the closest PCV. Making brownies with someone else who understood his craving for them was well worth the trek, Miller said.

Volunteers who have persistent trouble fending off loneliness should speak to their supervisors, who could move them to a less isolated work site or visit them more often, according to Lipez.

Affairs of the heart

The Peace Corps does not encourage or discourage volunteers from dating or marrying host-country nationals or other PCVs. Volunteers must prevent their personal relationships from interfering with their work.

Volunteers who plan to marry must receive the approval of the country director to continue their service.

Keeping in Touch With Loved Ones at Home

Mail

Many nations in which PCVs work have slow and unreliable postal service. Mail often takes several months to travel to and from countries of service.

Once packages arrive in-country, prying hands in the Customs Office often steal goodies from boxes with return addresses in the United States. Try to arrange for hand-delivery by visitors to other Peace Corps volunteers near your post; visitors can also mail your stamped letters after they return to the United States. Aerograms — or air letters — are available in most stationery stores, are lightweight, and are more likely to arrive unharmed than other forms of mail. Aerograms are thin pieces of foldable paper for writing a letter for transit via airmail, in which the envelope and letter are the same piece of paper.

The U.S. Postal Service (USPS) offers airmail "M" bags that allow people to send up to 66 pounds of reading materials overseas at a discount. For details about M bags, visit the USPS Web site at **www.usps.gov.** Although volunteers can sometimes use the diplomatic mail pouch at the U.S. Embassy in their country of service, it is best to not count on access to it.

For more information on staying in touch with you family, visit **www. peacecorps.gov/index.cfm?shell=resources.faf.staying.** The Peace Corps also offers a resource guide for families of PCVs called "On the Homefront." Your can access this resource for free from the previously listed Web site as well.

Phone and e-mail

Many countries of service have cafes where customers can access the Internet for an hourly fee, or make international phone calls. Volunteers can use phone cards or pay the proprietor cash after calling.

Some volunteers purchase cellular phone plans, but they are often prohibitively expensive. Hostels frequented by Peace Corps volunteers sometimes offer international phones. Volunteers can bring laptops, but not all posts are equipped to facilitate Internet connection.

In case of an emergency at home, family and friends can call the Peace Corps' Office of Special Services at 1-800-424-8580, ext. 1470.

Traveling

Volunteers often travel within their countries of service and to other nations in their region. PCVs might not take a vacation during the first three months or the last three months of service. For every month of service, volunteers earn two vacation days.

Volunteers' passports indicate they are in the Peace Corps; volunteers are not eligible for diplomatic passports.

CASE STUDY: FINDING YOUR PLACE BACK IN THE STATES

Richard Ireland
Haiti
1998-2001

A deeper understanding of a different culture and lasting ties to his community of service are some of the most treasured aspects of Richard Ireland's years as a PCV in Haiti. Haitians live more communally than many people in the United States, and they were eager to help Ireland become part of their society. "In Haiti, people live outdoors. So you sit on the front porch, and you're a part of everybody's life," Ireland said.

Through close relationships with neighbors and his knowledge of French Creole, Ireland grew to understand Haitian attitudes toward everything from personal space to their ability to control their own lives. Haitians tend to assume that other people want attention and company, so their interactions sometimes surprise Americans, where people place a higher value on privacy and solitude. "I'd be sitting in my room and I'd look up, and there'd be somebody standing there staring at me who I'd never seen before," Ireland said.

Ireland's job was to help residents find a job or start a business, but the 75 percent unemployment rate made it impossible for him to keep up with the constant requests for assistance. Having worked as a community service group organizer, a massage therapist, and a body-centered psychotherapist, Ireland knew the emotional rewards of helping others solve their problems. Recognizing that he could help some, but not all, who asked for his aid was one of the most stressful aspects of service. Residents' deep financial deprivation showed on a daily basis. Ireland knew a woman who did not know from day to day whether she would be able to feed her family dinner. "It would be in the evening and there was nothing she could do, so she'd start singing," Ireland said.

Ireland compared the experience of returning to the United States to attempting to merge onto the freeway at 25 mph when traffic is moving at 80 mph. "When you come back, you have had this incredible experience, and it's hard to tell people about it," Ireland said. Ireland did adjust to being back in the United States, but he has kept a deep emotional connection to Haiti. "I feel like whenever I go back, it's homecoming," Ireland said.

CHAPTER 11

Working In-country

Punching the Peace Corps Time Clock

Most of a volunteer's waking hours are spent working and building social ties with members of their host community. Volunteers typically have considerable control over their work schedule. Scheduling flexibility enables volunteers to respond to the evolving demands of their project. Some projects, such as running an AIDS testing clinic or teaching elementary school, require more regular hours.

Becoming Your Own Boss

PCVs should be self-motivated, independent learners who can set goals and develop timetables without guidance. Supervision is minimal and resources are scarce. The Peace Corps periodically monitors the progress of PCVs' projects, but volunteers are accountable for designing their daily routines.

Frequently Asked Questions

The following are questions asked by many potential PCVs regarding working in their host country.

Will I have American embassy amenities?

PCVs will generally have access to the U.S. Embassy's American Club, which is a recreational facility featuring familiar food, sports facilities, television, and movies — but other embassy amenities are not available.

How long are PCVs' workdays?

The length of workdays varies significantly, depending on the assignment and the culture of the host country. Teachers' schedules, for instance, are structured according to the hours that school is in session. In some locations, the hours that PCVs work on projects depend upon when their counterparts in the host country are free from agricultural duties.

How much vacation time do PCVs get?

PCVs receive two days of vacation time for every month they serve. Volunteers cannot take vacation during their first three or last three months of service. There are Peace Corps-sanctioned parties, trips, and functions to take part in as well.

How can PCVs change assignments?

To change assignments, volunteers must have the approval of their country directors and of the host-country authorities who requested a PCV.

How can PCVs change countries?

If PCVs fulfill all their training obligations but cannot sufficiently grasp the language of the country of service or the skills of their job, country directors can transfer them to other countries. Other reasons to transfer volunteers include finishing their projects before the end of two years; the Peace Corps leaving a particular country of service; or staff deciding to end PCVs assigned projects. Beyond this, it usually takes an emergency for the Peace Corps to allow a PCV to switch countries.

What stipends do PCVs receive?

The Peace Corps offers a living allowance to cover lodging, meals, and transportation. The stipend enables volunteers to afford at least the same standard of living as host-country nationals. Medical and dental care is free to volunteers. Airfare to and from the country of service is covered. Volunteers receive a readjustment stipend of $225 per month of service after they finish their term in the Peace Corps. This stipend amounts to just over $6,000 toward your transition to life back home and can be used in whatever way you wish.

How can PCVs end their service early?

Volunteers can resign at any time, before or after leaving the United States. To leave, PCVs must notify their supervisors and fill out a resignation form. Supervisors typically work with volunteers to help them resolve the circumstances that motivated their desire to resign. Some potential changes include arranging for more support from colleagues and moving volunteers to other positions. The Peace Corps' global average is usually around 10 percent of volunteers who typically quit before their two years are over.

Medical separation occurs when a volunteer's illness becomes so severe that he or she cannot be treated in-country. Medically separated volunteers return to the states at the expense of the Peace Corps, and they can receive workers compensation. Volunteers have the right to appeal their medical separation through the field nurse, who will ask for an assessment by the director of medical services.

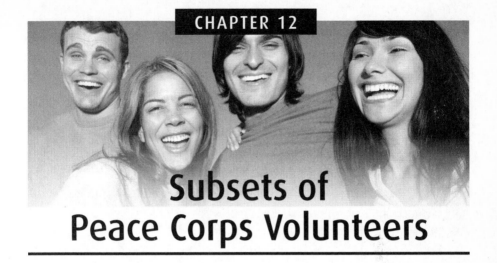

CHAPTER 12

Subsets of Peace Corps Volunteers

Who Volunteers?

This chapter offers a look at the makeup of PCVs. Some of this information has been included in other sections of this book. This chapter provides all the information in a single reference and answers some of the most basic questions you might have about who PCVs are.

What are the current statistics for Peace Corps' volunteers?

- Men: 40 percent
- Women: 60 percent
- Unmarried: 93 percent
- Married: 7 percent
- Caucasians: 84 percent
- Asian-American: 5 percent
- Hispanic/Latinos: 5 percent
- African-American: 3 percent
- Mixed ethnicity: 3 percent
- American Indian: <1 percent

What is the average age of Peace Corps volunteers?

The average age is 28.

What is the attitude of Peace Corps staff members toward lesbian, gay, bisexual, and transgender volunteers?

Lesbian, gay, bisexual, and transgender (LGBT) applicants and volunteers are protected under federal Equal Employment Opportunity laws. Peace Corps staff members are typically equally supportive of volunteers regardless of sexual orientation.

What is the attitude of host-country nationals toward same-sex relationships?

Laws in countries of service range from Jamaica, which make it a crime for men to have sex with each other, to South Africa, which guarantees the right to same-sex marriage.

Many residents of countries in which PCVs serve view same-sex relationships as aberrations, so LGBT volunteers may choose to not discuss the sexuality openly.

How can LGBT volunteers network in-country?

"Volunteers should begin gathering information during the segment of pre-service training devoted to cultural attitudes toward race, gender, sexuality, and other identity issues," said RPCV and site editor Mike Learned, on the Lesbian, Gay, Bisexual, and Transgender U.S. Peace Corps Alumni Web site (**www.lgbrpcv.org**). The Peace Corps medical officer and current PCVs are other potential sources of information, according to Learned.

What support is available to LGBT applicants before they leave the United States?

The Lesbian, Gay, Bisexual, and Transgender U.S. Peace Corps Alumni site offers a mentoring program that pairs potential volunteers with RPCVs. The group also provides a ListServ for applicants. To subscribe to the ListServ or request a mentor, visit the organization's Web site at **www.lgbrpcv.org**.

What can female volunteers do to reduce their risk of experiencing anti-woman crimes?

Women serving in the Peace Corps can request pre-service or in-service self-defense training, said RPCV Julie Bradley (Belize 1989-1991). Female volunteers can also form ties with older residents of their communities of service who will intervene to prevent harassment and assault, if possible. Female volunteers might also feel safer living with a host family than they would if they lived alone.

Women should refrain from going anywhere alone with a group of men, regardless of how familiar they have become, said RPCV Donna Statler (Belize 1989-1991).

Female volunteers should avoid the gestures and styles of dress that indicate sexual availability in their host countries. Women should remain in groups when walking at night in most host countries.

How do host-country nationals react to older volunteers?

Old age signifies wisdom in many host countries, so volunteers who are past their 20s often find it easy to gain respect.

What rules govern religious expression?

Volunteers may not evangelize, but may observe their own religious practices. Proselytizing — attempting to convert others — results in dismissal.

What is the attitude of Peace Corps' staff toward volunteers who are of non-European descent?

Federal law prohibits Peace Corps staff from discriminating based on race or ethnicity. PCVs in their second year of service facilitate racial diversity trainings for new volunteers.

How do host-country nationals react to volunteers whose ancestors came from continents other than Europe?

Some host-country nationals do not see non-Caucasians as "true Americans" and occasionally target them for verbal harassment. Host-country nationals in African countries do not acknowledge any ethnic similarity with African-American PCVs.

What accommodations are available to PCVs with disabilities?

The Peace Corps provides accommodations that enable volunteers with disabilities to work at their assigned projects and participate in the community in which they serve, according to the Web site Mobility International USA (**www.miusa.org**). Examples of accommodations include shipping a Braille machine and constructing a ramp to make a host-family's home wheelchair-accessible.

How do host-country nationals react to volunteers with disabilities?

The people with whom volunteers live and the supervisors they work for have agreed to host PCVs with disabilities and generally have accepting attitudes, according to Camacho. Reactions among other HCNs vary.

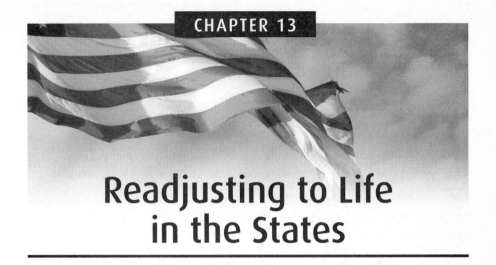

CHAPTER 13

Readjusting to Life in the States

Common Stresses of Readjustment

A common feeling among RPCVs is a sense of isolation when they return home. For two years they have had to live and work in a country void of many of the amenities in the United States. Another area that causes stress for RPCVs is resuming relationships between family and friends. All parties have lived with the stress of separation for two years, and adjustment can be difficult.

Storytelling seems a natural way to re-establish a sense of common experience, but enthralled listeners are sometimes in short supply. "Most people just wanted the 30-second version, and that was difficult," said Julie Bradley (RPCV 1989 to 1991).

Affluence and an abundance of choices are other common sources of stress. Some communities of service do not have electricity, so returning to a country in which stores typically offer dozens of electrical appliances can be disconcerting. Similarly, the contrast between an outdoor market in a developing country and a supermarket in the United States can be hard to bear. "Grocery stores and toy stores just seemed really obnoxious," Bradley said.

To counteract the social isolation and reverse culture shock that comes with returning from the Peace Corps, Bradley suggests keeping in touch with other volunteers from your service country. She also recommends joining RPCV organizations to have people with whom to share the intense experience of two years of Peace Corps service. Bradley suggests that volunteers allow three to four months of transition time.

Keeping in Touch With Other RPCVs

The National Peace Corps Association Web site **www.peacecorpsconnect. org** has links to local organizations for returned volunteers. Local RPCV organizations hold potluck dinners, film screenings, and workshops on international business opportunities.

Continuing service offers more opportunities for RPCVs to get to know each other. Returned volunteers mentor teenagers, discuss their Peace Corps experience in public school classrooms, coordinate museum exhibits, and host bon voyage parties for departing PCVs.

The Peace Corps Web site offers information to help RPCVs stay in touch. On their site, you can update your personal information in the Peace Corps records, receive past and current issues of "RPCV Update," the newsletter just for RPCVs, submit a story about your time with the Peace Corps, learn about joining the National Peace Corps Association, and find how to get copies of your Peace Corps records. You can find all this information and more by visiting **www.peacecorps.gov/index.cfm?shell=resources.returned.staycon**.

Keeping in Touch With Locals

Many RPCVs develop lifelong friendships with host-country nationals that they maintain by e-mail, telephone, and periodic visits. Former volunteers often find that their former neighbors welcome them warmly, despite decades apart. RPCVs sometimes host residents of their service communities and even sponsor the visas for those who want to study in the United States. Keeping in touch with host-country residents helps returned volunteers transition back to life in the states by providing a forum in which they can preserve and share their memories of Peace Corps service.

After Settling

Once returned volunteers have weathered their readjustment, they are ready to use their Peace Corps service to further their professional development.

RPCVs find that employers are often impressed with Peace Corps service even if returned volunteers did not work in programs that relate directly to the jobs for which they are applying. As part of an interview for a position training Hewlett-Packard employees to use company computers, RPCV Darren Miller did a demonstration lesson of long division with bamboo sticks — something he learned from his time in Nepal. Several years later, when Miller asked why he had been given the job over others, Miller's supervisor said his unusual bamboo stick lesson set him apart.

The National Peace Corps Association allows returned volunteers to post their cover letters and résumés for free in the job seeker's section of its Web site. Returned volunteers can also search job listings in the United States and worldwide.

Some returned volunteers find that their service inspires them to become memoir writers, others expand their professional ambitions to include working abroad, and still others become Peace Corps staff members, according to John Coyne (RPCV 1962 to 1964).

Regardless of where on their career path volunteers enter the Peace Corps, almost all of them find that the experience alters their work goals. "Regardless of when you go into the Peace Corps, it will change your life," Coyne said.

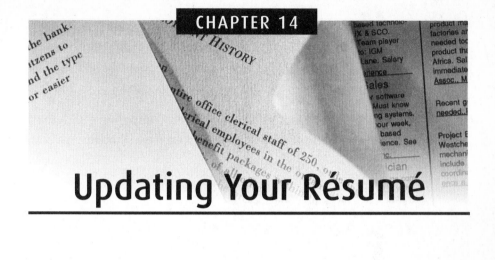

CHAPTER 14

Updating Your Résumé

How will the Peace Corps Help You Get Your Foot in the Door?

PCVs gain valuable skills and experience that will help in any career path. You can use the skills and experiences you gain during your time with the Peace Corps to help build a career in virtually any sector of our society. The Peace Corps Web site offers a resource for RPCVs who need career assistance. On this site, you can research graduate school programs that give special consideration to RPCVs, view a quick overview of job search basics, view a schedule of upcoming career events, find a list of job search Web sites, and order or download manuals on careers or graduate school. You can find this information and more by visiting **www.peacecorps.gov/index.cfm?shell=resources.returned.carres**.

The following sections describe how the Peace Corps can help you in the career of your choice after you return home from your service time.

By helping you learn a second language

Knowledge of high-demand languages can help prepare volunteers for a career in linguistic research, teaching, translation, or intelligence. Instruction in high-demand languages is seldom available in the states, so joining the Peace Corps offers a special learning opportunity.

Serving in the Peace Corps can also help returned volunteers find work by enabling them to learn languages that are more common in the U.S. The ability to speak Spanish, for instance, can increase an RPCV's chances of finding work in teaching, social work, medicine, library science, and a host of other fields.

Peace Corps volunteers have a chance to immerse themselves in a foreign language for two years, which helps them develop a greater proficiency than those who only study in the classroom.

By enabling you to develop character and confidence

Interviewers often ask candidates for examples of times when they have demonstrated characteristics that could likely help them on the job. RPCVs can offer compelling stories to illustrate resourcefulness, leadership, tenacity, and confidence. PCVs who are new graduates or are changing careers will often take on much more responsibility than they would in an entry-level state job. The experience gained as a volunteer enables candidates to present themselves as more competent than their competitors.

Two years of self-motivation, discipline, and creativity also prepares returned volunteers to start their own businesses or non-profits. The flexibility, risk tolerance, and creativity Peace Corps volunteers must use to complete their service projects can help them become successful entrepreneurs.

The challenges volunteers overcome and the skills they gain also broaden their idea of the jobs for which they are qualified. After returning from the Peace Corps, volunteers often apply for jobs that require travel abroad or that require them to transcend obstacles they might previously have considered insurmountable.

By giving you job search resources and a new professional network

Returned volunteers can draw on the job search resources of the National Peace Corps Association, which helps RPCVs connect with each other. The NPCA Web site allows returned volunteers to seek positions by specialty and locale.

RPCVs can also post their résumés and request e-mail alerts of jobs for which they might want to apply.

The Peace Corps publishes a newsletter twice a month that lists positions for which employers would prefer to hire returned volunteers. RPCVs can also find job listings and reference materials at the office of their Peace Corps recruiter.

Fellow RPCVs who work in the same field after returning to the U.S. can keep each other abreast of who is hiring and advise you on how to set yourself apart from other candidates. Returned volunteers who collaborated while serving can also use each other as professional references.

By making it easier to get a federal job

Returned volunteers need not be the highest qualified candidates to be hired for federal jobs; they only need to meet the minimum qualifications of the job descriptions. Those with non-competitive eligibility are considered federal employees and are therefore eligible for positions that are typically filled by promoting from within. If you work at a federal job that requires you to use experience gained in the Peace Corps, you will qualify to begin at a higher level on the pay scale. Your two years of service will also count toward the accrual of retirement benefits and vacation time.

Getting into Grad School with Your Peace Corps Experience

The Master's International program allows returned volunteers to apply the concepts they have learned in the Peace Corps in their graduate classes. As a Master's International student, two years of Peace Corps service comes after a year of course work and before your thesis. About 60 schools offer Master's International programs in a long list of disciplines, including agriculture, child/family policy, education, divinity, environmental management, public health, peace and conflict resolution, psychology, science, urban planning, and writing. Students who have returned from the Peace Corps bring diverse experiences to their academic work and can demonstrate a strong grasp of the practical applications and limitations of their research.

Candidates must submit separate applications to the Peace Corps and to their graduate schools of choice. Getting into a graduate school that has a Master's International program does not guarantee that an applicant will get into the Peace Corps. Likewise, acceptance into the Peace Corps does not guarantee entry into a university. Universities have different requirements for acceptance, but a bachelor's degree and strong GRE scores are typically among them.

Through the Fellows/USA program, returned volunteers can do their graduate work at a reduced cost. Forty U.S. graduate schools accept students into degree programs in geography, English, environmental studies, science, philosophy, nursing, and public health, to name a few fields. As part of the two-year Fellows/USA program, fellows use their Peace Corps background through internships in economically disadvantaged communities. Internships can lead to long-term jobs.

Applicants must take the GRE, GMAT, or NTE, depending on the program they would like to enter. To apply, RPCVs must also provide their descriptions of service, documents that list their work responsibilities, language proficiency, and Peace Corps education. Each school has its own criteria for evaluating applicants, and returned volunteers should contact the institutions in which they are interested.

Even RPCVs who do not enroll in the Master's International or Fellows/USA program find that their years of service enhance their graduate school applications. Applicants who can draw on international volunteer work when writing their personal statements can tell compelling stories that differentiate them from other applicants. Applicants can refer to their Peace Corps service to illustrate their flexibility and tenacity — all qualities that make them well-suited to the rigors of graduate school. Willingness to spend two years abroad in challenging circumstances offers evidence that applicants are dedicated to the fields in which they intend to pursue advanced degrees.

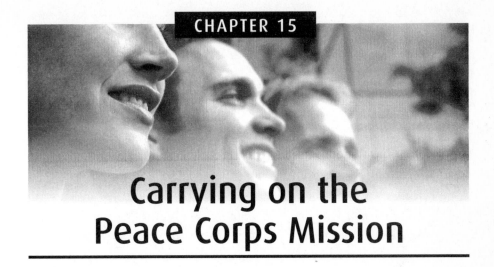

CHAPTER 15

Carrying on the Peace Corps Mission

Returned volunteers often make service a lifelong pursuit. Volunteer opportunities are plentiful, and it should be easy to find several organizations that suit your interests and time constraints.

Here are a few Web sites to guide your search for places to serve:

- **www.idealist.org** lists volunteer openings at home and abroad that allow you to use the skills gained in almost any profession. You can narrow your search by location, discipline, and type of organization.

- At **www.serve.gov,** you can find service positions at national parks and historic sites across the country.

- If you entered the Peace Corps after retiring, check out Senior Corps at **www.seniorcorps.gov**. Senior Corps can connect you with organizations in your hometown that need someone with your professional background. Through the Senior Corps, you can also be a foster grandparent or a friend to elders with physical limitations.

Here are a few projects that you might find especially interesting:

- If you are looking for domestic volunteer work with an international focus, try the International Rescue Committee. The IRC helps refugees and people waiting for political asylum. Volunteers help asylum seekers learn English, mentor new arrivals, and distribute donated goods.

• You might also consider mentoring newly returned RPCVs through the National Peace Corps Association. RPCV mentors serve as sounding boards for people going through the early stages of re-settling.

• The Third Goal of the Peace Corps promotes Americans' understanding the people and cultures of other countries. RPCVs can use their creativity to promote the Peace Corps' Third Goal by engaging in activities such as giving classroom or community talks, writing your local newspaper, giving interviews to local radio and TV stations, taking part in Peace Corps Week, celebrating the Peace Corps' 50th anniversary, or organizing a community event. You can find out more about the Peace Corps' Third Goal by visiting **www.peacecorps.gov/ index.cfm?shell=resources.returned.thirdgoal.whatis**.

CASE STUDY: ADJUSTING TO POST-PEACE CORPS LIFE

Darren Miller
Education
Nepal
1991-1993

A childhood spent in Egypt set the stage for a lifelong appreciation of international adventure for Darren Miller.

When his college career services office advertised an internship with the Peace Corps in Nepal, Miller could not wait to apply. As Miller waited for word on his acceptance, he became more fascinated by the natural beauty of the country and enchanted by the warmth of its inhabitants. When he learned that the Peace Corps had accepted his application and had assigned him to serve as a secondary school teacher in a village that was a seven days' walk from the nearest paved road, Miller was overjoyed.

In spite of his affinity for the country and its people, Miller recalls feeling out of place when he first arrived. Seventeen years later, Miller remembers the moment the Peace Corps Jeep dropped him off. "It was a mix of loneliness, and then excitement about this big adventure," Miller said.

The loneliness began to abate soon after he arrived when his host family welcomed him into their home and the villagers welcomed him into their social lives. Dancing, drumming, rice, and incense were hallmarks of the eight weddings Miller attended during his first month in the village. Nepalese noticed the differences of religion and wealth between them and Miller, but reacted to the disparities with tolerance and humor. Miller sometimes attended a Christian church established by missionaries, and members of his Hindu host family asked friendly questions about his faith.

When a friend from the village saw Miller's seven pairs of underwear drying on the balcony, he teased Miller about his expensive, extensive wardrobe. "So one of those is for you. What are the other six for?" the friend asked.

Not only did Nepal's economy differ from the United States by being less consumption-oriented, it also differed by being more agrarian. Social expectations differed from those in industrialized countries because farming was central to the economy. On Miller's first day at school, he found only the headmaster present. Home and farm obligations had delayed the arrival of the students and faculty.

A relaxed attitude toward delay and inconvenience permeated Nepali culture. Nepalese would respond to problems with a calmness that would leave an American fuming. The driver of a bus on which Miller was riding stopped the coach, got off, and left for an hour and a half; when he returned, he was carrying a bag of laundry. Although the driver had not announced the reason for the stop, the passengers waited patiently in his absence.

Succeeding as a Peace Corps volunteer often depends on a willingness to adapt cheerfully to the unfamiliar. Prospective volunteers should emphasize their ability to keep an open mind regarding people who grew up outside the United States, and they should cite any cross-cultural volunteer work they have done.

To succeed in post-Peace Corps life, Miller suggests keeping in touch with other returned volunteers to share stories and struggles. RPCVs should continue internationally oriented volunteer work, such as donating time to a refugee assistance project, to help with the transition. Soon after returning, Miller and a friend from the Peace Corps took a bike tour during which they spoke to students about their service. The warm welcome Miller received reminded him of the kindness he experienced in Nepal, and it also made him glad to be home. "It renewed my faith in America," Miller said.

Once your wanderlust returns, consider these possibilities:

- With a background in fine arts, you could join the ArtCorps, which places artists with non-governmental organizations in Central America for stints of nearly one year. The artists work to inspire residents to keep pursuing their goals for societal change. Find out more at **www. artcorp.org**.

- If you have a head for business, you could help the Coffee Quality Institute (**www.coffeeinstitute.org**) aid growers in developing countries raise better beans and command better prices. CQI accepts volunteers for two-week trips.

- You can also re-join the Peace Corps for a shorter period through Peace Corps Response. Peace Corps Response recruits returned RPCVs for projects in AIDS education, natural disaster response, and postwar reconstruction in various countries of service. To apply, visit the official Peace Corps Web site at **www.peacecorps.gov/index. cfm?shell=resources.returned.response**.

- Consider becoming a United Nations Volunteer (UNV). Volunteers usually have substantial work experience in developing countries. UNV recruits volunteers with specialized, technical skills. Unfortunately, teachers and individuals with generalist backgrounds are seldom accepted into the program. UNV does not offer short-term overseas work camp, internship, or residency opportunities. Currently, there are over 7,000 UNVs from around the world serving in developing countries. To learn more about becoming a UNV, visit **www. peacecorps.gov/index.cfm?shell=resources.returned.unvol** or **www. unv.org**.

CASE STUDY: THE GRAND SCHEME OF THINGS

Julie Bradley
Education
Belize
1989-1991

Potential applicants should pay attention to even the smallest inklings that they might want to join the Peace Corps and recognize the variety of locations for service. Posts vary according to degree of remoteness and level of development, so applicants can ask to be placed in a country where they would feel at home for two years.

Prospective applicants should not be daunted by the length of time the Peace Corps asks them to serve. "Two years is not long at all in the grand scheme of things," said Bradley, who joined the Peace Corps in response to a recruiting film at the University of Northern Iowa, where she was studying elementary education.

Offering Belizeans a chance to get to know an American and developing friendships in the town in which she served were some of the most important results of Bradley's service, she said. The children in the agricultural community where Bradley served could identify with her childhood on a farm. Family is so central to Belizean society that residents of Bradley's host community were shocked that she would voluntarily spend two years away from her relatives. "I really liked the fact that I got the chance to dispel some of the myths about the United States," Bradley said.

In addition to myths about the United States, Bradley tried to dispel myths about women's abilities. Bradley went to Belize as a teacher trainer, but the principal initially refused to allow her to hold instructional sessions for the faculty.

"In my school, the principal was pretty chauvinistic — and I was pretty young — and he couldn't imagine that I would know anything more than he did," Bradley said. Her initial reaction was anger, but Bradley realized that had he not requested a Peace Corps volunteer, she would not have had a position at his school.

Bradley began by teaching English as a second language and eventually held a teacher training conference on reading instruction. Bradley continued her career in education after leaving the Peace Corps by teaching in Colorado and later in Bolivia. Employers were impressed with the strength of her Peace Corps service. "I think it automatically makes people say, 'Wow, she must be really dedicated and really adventurous,' " Bradley said.

Conclusion

The Peace Corps experience offers volunteers a wide variety of benefits. It can provide opportunities to further your career in the field of education when you return to the United States and perhaps land a government position to the ability to learn about foreign cultures, languages, and people. It can allow you to acquire skills you did not think were possible for you to undertake, thus the Peace Corps is a giant step toward living independently while also working with others to solve common goals and support outreach efforts. RPCVs come home as different people, with different attitudes about their former lives — and a different approach to solving societal issues.

The process of preparing to embark on your Peace Corps tour of duty can be long and cause many feelings of anxiousness — whether from readiness to leave or terror of what to expect. Once you arrive in your host country, you are immediately thrown into a period of training where an unfamiliar language and culture are presented to you. After training, you will arrive in your community of service, where you may or may not be the only American or person who speaks English in the area. The first year of service can be isolating. You are not yet able to communicate with your host family or the people with whom you work. You are learning to eat new foods and trying to become acquainted with new living quarters. You may feel you are not making the impact you had hoped to make at the start of your journey.

In your second year, you suddenly begin to adapt to your surroundings. You find yourself forming friendships with people you were unable to communicate with a year ago. You determine you like the food in your host country even more than you like pizza. And you finally begin to see progress being made in your job sector, whether it involves teaching an entire class of 9-year-olds to read a book written in English or working with an entrepreneur to establish a Web site for his business. And then, suddenly, your two years are over. You find yourself saying goodbye to new friends and looking forward to seeing old ones. You begin thinking about which graduate school you will attend or what you will do with your time during the rest of your retirement.

You leave your host country knowing that you may never return to this place again, and that you will likely never see your host family again. On the plane home, you think about the impact this experience has had on you as a person. You feel ready to move on to the next stage of your life, using these experiences to help others understand a place and a culture they may never know.

This is the experience so many PCVs before you have undergone, and one you will as well if you choose to apply for the "toughest job."

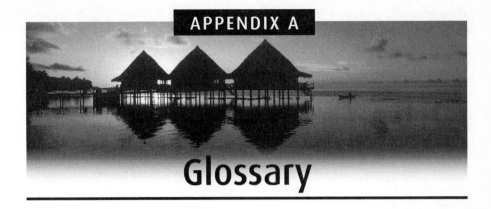

Glossary

Administrative Separation –
When the Peace Corps director
terminates the service of a PCV.

Associate Peace Corps Director
– Staff member who reports to the
country director. Among other
tasks, the APCD is responsible for
helping with the supervision of
staff and volunteers. The APCD
also assists with the design and
assessment of programs.

Completion of Service –
End of the two-year period
to which a Peace Corps
Volunteer committed.

Country Director – Staff
member who oversees the
program, staff, volunteers, and
budget in a country of service.

Country of Service – Country in
which volunteers work.

Health Status Review Form –
Document in which applicants
describe their medical histories
and current health conditions.

Home-of-record – A Peace Corps
Volunteer's permanent residence.

Host-country National – Citizen
of a country of service.

In-service Training – Technical
training workshop offered after
volunteers have been in the Peace
Corps for one year.

Invitation – Information package
successful applicants receive after
submitting their medical papers
and undergoing their interviews.

Medical Evacuation –
Transportation to another country
to be treated for a medical
condition that is too severe for

medical professionals in the host country to address.

Medical Kit – Container of first-aid supplies, syringes, medicines, etc. that Peace Corps Volunteers receive before reaching their posts.

Medical Separation – Early termination of Peace Corps service due to injury or illness.

Nomination – A recruiter's suggestion of the program and region in which a recruiter should serve.

Non-competitive Eligibility – Preferential treatment given to returned Peace Corps Volunteers who apply for federal jobs. Non-competitive eligibility also enables RPCVs, who already work for the federal government, to be promoted and retire sooner than they otherwise could.

Peace Corps Medical Officer – Medical professional who cares for the health of Peace Corps Volunteers.

Peace Corps Volunteer Leader – Supervisor of volunteers who

helps them adjust to their country of service and interact with their co-workers.

Pre-departure Orientation – Three-day training in the United States that PCVs undergo before leaving for their countries of service.

Pre-service Training – Three months of in-country education in the language and culture of the host country combined with training in the jobs volunteers will perform. Pre-service training offers an opportunity to stay with a host family for linguistic and cultural immersion.

Settling-in – Refers to the time after PCVs arrive in their host country when new volunteers set up their living quarters and ease into their jobs.

Staging – Refers to the pre-departure orientation session that PCVs attend before leaving for their host country.

Overview of
Countries of Service

To save you some legwork in gathering basic information on your potential countries of service, what follows is a thumbnail sketch of each country in which the Peace Corps is currently active. Each description contains the contact information for the nation's embassy in the United States and the embassy in the country of service so you can request more information. The information in this appendix was active as of January 2010. You can also find out additional, updated information by visiting the CIA's Web site and view *The World Factbook* at **https://www.cia.gov/library/publications/the-world-factbook**. To find specific health-related information, visit the CDC's Web site at **http://wwwnc.cdc.gov/travel/destinations/list.aspx**. To find safety and security information regarding your host country, visit the U.S. Department of State's Web site at **http://travel.state.gov/travel/travel_1744.html**.

Africa

Benin

Overview of geography, climate, and population

Benin borders the Bight of Benin, and is to the west of Nigeria. It is approximately the size of Pennsylvania.

Most of the country is flat, though some sections have hills and small mountains. The climate ranges from tropical in the south to partially arid in the north. Parching winds blow in the north from December through March. Drinking water is scarce. Approximately 8.7 million people live in Benin.

Religion, ethnicity, and language in a nutshell

The Beninese are Christians, Muslims, and adherents of Vodoun, more commonly known as Voudou or Voodoo. The major ethnic groups are Fon, Adja, Bariba, and Yoruba. Benin is officially a francophone country, but the Beninese also speak Fon, Yoruba, and at least half a dozen tribal tongues.

Brief political history and today's government

Benin was part of the African kingdom of Dahomey in the 1600s when slave traders constituted the first European contact. France claimed Benin as a colony in 1872, and it became independent in 1960. Several military regimes ruled post-colonial Benin until 1972 when a socialist government came to power. The country became a republic in 1991. The president is Thomas Yayi Boni, who was elected by the public. The National Assembly constitutes the legislature; members are popularly elected. A Constitutional Court, Supreme Court, and High Court of Justice make up the judiciary, which oversees a legal system based on French civil law.

Economic snapshot

Agriculture, cotton, and trade with nearby countries are the pillars of Benin's economy. The government is seeking to lure more international investors and increase tourism.

Peace Corps programs

- Business
- Education

Health

HIV/AIDS, diarrhea, hepatitis A, typhoid fever, malaria, yellow fever, and meningococcal meningitis are among the diseases and illnesses volunteers should be aware of in Benin.

Visitors should carry with them any medicines they take regularly because Benin lacks well-stocked pharmacies. Doctor's offices and hospitals are inadequate by U.S. standards. Malaria is a significant risk.

Safety

The State Department advises against crowds of any kind, walking in cities after dark, and going to the beach alone or at night. Instead of taking along passports, travelers should carry photocopies of their passports that have been stamped by a notary.

Mugging, robbery, and carjacking are common in urban areas and on beaches. Visitors should avoid carrying anything expensive when they visit the beach. Drowning in the ocean is common. Travelers should not use ATMs or credit cards because fraud is rampant. False checkpoints and robbery are problems at the border with Nigeria.

Calling home

Benin has one land telephone line per 100 occupants. The country has four cell phone providers and 798 Internet service providers.

Diplomatic contact in the United States

Ambassador Cyrille Segbe Oguin
2124 Kalorama Road NW, Washington, DC 20008
Phone: (202) 232-6656 • Fax: (202) 265-1996

Diplomatic contact from the United States

Ambassador Gayleatha B. Brown
Embassy: Rue Caporal Bernard Anani, Cotonou
01 B. P. 2012, Cotonou
Phone: (229) 21-30-06-50 • Fax: (229) 21-30-03-84

Botswana

Overview of geography, climate, and population

Botswana is a landlocked, partially arid nation in southern Africa in which the Kalahari Desert is located. It has occasional droughts and is warm to hot throughout the year. The country is a little smaller than Texas. Botswana has 1.9 million inhabitants.

Religion, ethnicity, and language in a nutshell

The majority of those who live in Botswana are Christians, while others practice Badimo, and many are non-religious. Most residents are of Tswana descent with Kalanga, Baswara, Kgalagadi, and Caucasian accounting for the other ethnicities. English is the official language, but only about 2 percent of the population speaks it. Setswana is the most commonly spoken language; other tongues include Kalanga and Sekgalagadi.

Brief political history and today's government

The Tswana began to populate Botswana about a millennium ago. Britain claimed the country as a protectorate in the 19th century. The country gained independence in 1966. Khama Ian Khama is the president of Botswana, which is a parliamentary republic. The parliament includes the House of Chiefs, made up of the heads of major tribes, and the National Assembly, members of which are elected by the public. The legal system draws from Dutch and Roman law as well as tradition. The judiciary consists of the High Court, Court of Appeal, and the Magistrates' Courts.

Economic snapshot

Botswana is a moderate-income country with an economy supported by diamond mines, tourism, finance, and agriculture.

Peace Corps programs

- AIDS prevention
- Assisting children orphaned whose parents have died of AIDS

Health

HIV/AIDS, bacterial diarrhea, hepatitis A, typhoid fever, and malaria are among the diseases and illnesses volunteers should be aware of in Botswana.

Medical care that is adequate by Western standards is available in Gaborone. Other areas do not have sufficient health care. Private ambulances are available throughout the country, but only for patients who prove in advance that they can pay for emergency transportation.

Ambulance service is often delayed in remote areas, and emergency air rescue only occurs during the day due to poor lighting at airports. Visitors can generally get common medicines in Gaborone. Those who plan to visit the north of Botswana should be vaccinated against malaria. Visitors to Botswana often go to South Africa for hospital care. Travelers should be tested for tuberculosis before and after visiting Botswana.

Safety
Travelers should avoid crowds of any kind, as well as walking alone in cities. Western visitors should avoid Kgale Hill in Gaborone because violent criminals often target foreigners there. Theft and other petty crimes are common. Burglaries, vandalism, theft from cars, and knife-point robberies are significant risks. Visitors are particularly vulnerable to crime when talking on cell phones in public and walking in cities at night. Stealing from bags is a common problem at the Johannesburg and Cape Town International Airports. Visitors should keep packing lists and should refrain from packing expensive items in their checked bags.

Calling home
Botswana has eight land telephone lines and 80 cell phones per 100 inhabitants. There are 5,820 Internet hosts.

Diplomatic contact in the United States
Ambassador Lapologang Caesar Lekoa
1531-1533 New Hampshire Avenue NW, Washington, DC 20036
Phone: (202) 244-4990 • Fax: (202) 244-4164

Diplomatic contact from the United States
Ambassador Stephen J. Nolan
Embassy: Embassy Enclave (off Khama Crescent), Gaborone
Embassy Enclave, P. O. Box 90, Gaborone
Phone: (267) 395-3982 • Fax: (267) 395-6947

Burkina Faso

Overview of geography, climate, and population

Burkina Faso is a landlocked tropical country, which is primarily flat with some hills. Burkinabe cope with periodic droughts. About 15.7 million people live in Burkina Faso.

Religion, ethnicity, and language in a nutshell

Half of Burkinabe are Muslim, 40 percent adhere to traditional faiths, and a small minority is Christian. Nearly half of the Burkinabe are of Mossi descent; other ethnic groups include Gurunsi, Senufo, Bobo, Fulani, Mande, and Lobi. The official language is French, and 90 percent of Burkinabe speak indigenous African tongues.

Brief political history and today's government

Burkina Faso was part of the Mossi Empire until the early 1600s. France claimed the country as a colony in 1919, and it became independent in 1960. Several coups d'etat occurred during the 1970s and 1980s. The President is Blaise Compaore, who took office in a coup in 1987. Burkina Faso is a parliamentary republic of which the legislative branch is a popularly elected national assembly. The judicial branch includes a Supreme Court and Appeals Court, which are part of a legal system based on French law.

Economic snapshot

Lack of natural resources and industrial development make Burkina Faso extremely poor. Cotton is the major crop, and other types of farming are also important. The government would like to encourage foreign investment.

Peace Corps programs

- Health care
- Promoting education of females
- Secondary and university education
- Business

Health

HIV/AIDS, diarrhea, hepatitis A, typhoid fever, malaria, schistosomiasis, avian flu, and meningococcal meningitis are among the diseases and illnesses volunteers should be aware of in Burkina Faso.

Health care and emergency response capacities are extremely scarce but are most common in Ouagadougou. Visitors should carry with them any prescription drugs they require for as long as they plan to be in the country. Malaria is a significant concern, as is meningitis. Travelers should keep away from bird farms and fowl vendors to avoid contracting avian flu.

Visitors should cook poultry completely before eating and avoid touching birds, whether living or dead.

Safety

Political protests that seem non-violent sometimes turn aggressive, so visitors should avoid crowds of any kind. Muggings as well as public theft of handbags, jewelry, wallets, and electronics equipment are quite common. Visitors are particularly vulnerable to crime during public events in the capitol city of Ouagadougou. Sections of the capitol that are especially dangerous for foreigners include those close to the U.N. Circle, Avenue Kwame N'Krumah, and what used to be the Central Market. Travelers should avoid walking alone, especially in the dark. Visitors should refrain from traveling between cities at night when highway robbery and killings, including those on buses, is more likely to occur. Travelers should take care to avoid fraudulent trade in precious metals and ancient artifacts initiated via e-mails requesting fees to cover the cost of transferring ownership of the items. Other frauds involve e-mails asking recipients to transfer money to war refugees or relatives of rulers.

Calling home

Less than 1 percent of residents of Burkina Faso have land-based telephones. While cell phone use is increasing, it remains low. There are 1,951 Internet hosts.

Diplomatic contact in the United States

Ambassador Paramanga Ernest Yonli
2340 Massachusetts Avenue NW, Washington, DC 20008
Phone: (202) 332-5577 • Fax: (202) 667-1882

Diplomatic contact from the United States

Ambassador (vacant): Charge d'Affaires Samuel C. LAEUCHLI
Embassy: 602 Avenue Raoul Follereau, Koulouba, Secteur 4
01 B. P. 35, Ouagadougou 01; pouch mail — US Department of State, 2440
Ouagadougou Place, Washington, DC 20521-2440
Phone: (226) 50-30-67-23 • Fax: (226) 50-30-38-90

Cameroon

Overview of geography, climate, and population

Cameroon borders the Bight of Biafra, and its climate ranges from tropical to semiarid. Approximately 18 million people live in Cameroon.

Religion, ethnicity, and language in a nutshell

About 40 percent of Cameroonians follow traditional religions; approximately the same percentage adheres to Christianity, and 20 percent believe in Islam. About a third of the country's inhabitants are descendants of Cameroon Highlanders, and about 20 percent are of Equatorial Bantu lineage. Other ethnic groups include Kirdi, Fulani, Northwestern Bantu and Eastern Nigritic. English and French are the official languages; Cameroonians also speak at least two-dozen African languages.

Brief political history and today's government

Cameroon was part of the Kanem Empire at around 800 C.E. First recorded European contact was with the Portuguese in the 15th century. Germany claimed Cameroon as a protectorate in 1884. After the First World War, France and Britain divided and governed the country. The independent country known as Cameroon, with its current boundaries, came to exist in 1961. The nation is a republic with a variety of political parties. The president is Paul Biya, and the prime minister is Ephraim Inoni. The legislative branch consists of the National Assembly. The judiciary consists of the Supreme Court and the High Court of Justice. The National Assembly elects the judges of the High Court of Justice.

Peace Corps programs

- Education
- Agroforestry
- Business
- Conservation education
- Public health

Health

HIV/AIDS, diarrhea, hepatitis A, hepatitis E, typhoid fever, malaria, yellow fever, schistosomiasis, rabies, and meningococcal meningitis are among the diseases and illnesses volunteers should be aware of in Cameroon.

The health care system is inadequate by Western standards, even in major urban centers. Sanitation is lacking, instruments are obsolete, and health workers are poorly trained. Patients must typically pay cash before receiving treatment. Remote areas often have no medical personnel, facilities, or medicines. Visitors should bring their own prescription and over-the-counter drugs. The medicine chloroquine does not always kill the strain of malaria prevalent in Cameroon. Visitors should use mefloquine, doxycycline, or atovaquone/proguaril before arriving in-country. Some wild ducks are infected with avian flu, but no people have come down with it. Humans have been infected with avian flu across the border in Nigeria.

Safety

Violent demonstrations occurred in early 2008 and remain a risk. Visitors should avoid traveling outside urban centers at night. Scams involving the Internet are on the rise. Fraudulent requests for money often centered around adopting children, hiring domestic help, or buying pets. Thefts of items left in cars, larceny, armed robbery, and attacks on highway users are common. Drivers should beware of fake checkpoints at which thieves sometimes steal dozens of cars at a time. Visitors should keep secure notarized photocopies of their drivers' licenses, passports, residence cards, and car registration papers and carry the originals. Security staff might ask for bribes in exchange for allowing drivers to pass through checkpoints uninjured.

Calling home

Less than 1 percent of the population has phones with landlines. About 15 percent of Cameroonians use cell phones. There are 512 Internet hosts.

Diplomatic contact in the United States

Ambassador Joseph foe-atangana Mendouga
2349 Massachusetts Avenue NW, Washington, DC 20008
Phone: (202) 265-8790 • Fax: (202) 387-3826

Diplomatic contact from the United States

Ambassador Janet E. Garvey
Embassy: Avenue Rosa Parks, Yaounde
Branch office(s): Douala

Cape Verde

Overview of geography, climate, and population

Cape Verde is a rocky, volcanic island chain in the Atlantic Ocean off the coast of Senegal. The country is a little bigger than Rhode Island. The climate is temperate and dry. As of 2009, about 429,000 people lived in Cape Verde.

Religion, ethnicity, and language in a nutshell

Many Cape Verdeans practice a version of Roman Catholicism combined with traditional views; others are Protestant. Nearly three-quarters of the residents of Cape Verde are Creole, a little less than 30 percent are African, and 1 percent is of European descent. Cape Verdeans speak Portuguese and Crioulo, which combines Portuguese and West African tongues.

Brief political history and today's government

No one lived in Cape Verde when the Portuguese claimed it as a colony in the 1600s. The country became independent in 1975. Cape Verde is a multi-party republic of which Pedro Verona Pires is president and Jose Maria Pereira Neves is prime minister. The legal system stems from Portuguese law. The judiciary consists of the Supreme Tribunal of Justice.

Economic snapshot

Tourism and transportation are pillars of Cape Verde's service-based economy. Agriculture is difficult due to location and climate.

Peace Corps programs

- Teacher training
- Business •
- Education for females
- AIDS prevention

IT

Health

HIV/AIDS and malaria are among the diseases and illnesses volunteers should be aware of in Cape Verde.

Clinics, hospitals, and medicines are in short supply. Praia and Mindelo have hospitals. Brava and Santo Antao islands do not have working airports, so patients cannot be airlifted from them in response to emergencies. Most malaria infections occur on Santiago island. July through December is the period when visitors are at greatest risk of contracting malaria.

Safety

Criminals often target rich international visitors. Travelers are particularly vulnerable to crime when they are in crowds. Burglary and minor theft occur frequently. Groups of unsupervised children often commit minor violent crimes against foreigners on the street.

Potentially lethal, strong currents are also a concern for those who plan to use the ocean. The island of Fogo has an active volcano, which means that visitors should be prepared for natural disasters such as eruptions and earthquakes.

Calling home

Cape Verde has 71,600 land telephone lines and 108,900 cell phones. There are 344 Internet hosts.

Diplomatic contact in the United States

Ambassador Fatima Lima Veiga
3415 Massachusetts Avenue NW, Washington, DC 20008
Phone: (202) 965-6820 • Fax: (202) 965-1207

Diplomatic contact from the U.S.

Ambassador Marianne M. Myles
Embassy: Rua Abilio Macedo n6, Praia
C. P. 201, Praia
Phone: (238) 2-60-89-00 • Fax: (238) 2-61-13-55

Ethiopia

Overview of geography, climate, and population

Ethiopia is a landlocked country almost twice the size of Texas. The climate is tropical with monsoons and varied terrain. Ethiopians deal with earthquakes, erupting volcanoes, and droughts.

Religion, ethnicity, and language in a nutshell

More than half of Ethiopians are Christian, about 30 percent are Muslim, and about 5 percent follow indigenous faiths. Ethiopians are ethnically Oromo, Amara, Tigraway, Somalie, Guragie, Sidama, and Welaita. They speak Amarigna, Oromigna, Tigrigna, Somaligna, Guaragigna, Sidamigna, Hadiyigna, and English.

Brief political history and today's government

The Ethiopian empire existed since before the common era. Italy occupied the country during World War II. Ethiopia became a federal republic in 1974 and split from Eritrea in 1993. The border between Ethiopia and Eritrea is still disputed. The nation's legal system evolved out of civil law and consists of federal and regional courts.

Economic snapshot

Agriculture is the basis of Ethiopia's economy, though drought frequently wreaks havoc with farming. Coffee is an essential export, although growers usually do not receive high prices for their crop.

The International Monetary Fund forgave Ethiopia's debt in 2005.

Peace Corps programs

- AIDS prevention
- Caring for orphans whose parents have died of AIDS
- Palliative care for patients with HIV

Health

HIV/AIDS, diarrhea, hepatitis A, hepatitis E, typhoid fever, malaria, meningococcal meningitis, rabies, and schistosomiasis are among the diseases and illnesses volunteers should be aware of in Ethiopia.

Medical care in the capital is below Western standards and is very poor in other areas. Most doctors have good training. In hospitals throughout the country, medicines are scarce and equipment is obsolete. Visitors should bring their own medicines and doctors' written descriptions of the pharmaceuticals. Those who must bring more of a drug than one person would typically use must get a permit from the Ministry of Health.

Travelers might experience altitude sickness with symptoms that include difficulty breathing, tiredness, insomnia, upset stomach, and headache.

Parasites infest most bodies of water, so visitors should avoid swimming.

Safety

Visitors should be warned of violent political rallies and civil upheaval. Visitors to the border between Ethiopia and Eritrea, as well as the 30-mile-deep corridor of land along the frontier, should beware of war and land mines. To avoid kidnappers and highway robbers, the State Department recommends that foreigners refrain from traveling within 30 miles of the border between Ethiopia and Eritrea between the town of Adigrat to the border between Ethiopia and Sudan. Throughout the country, drivers should caravan and travel only during the day. Visitors should also avoid kidnappers and robbers who target foreigners by refraining from travel between 60 miles east of the town of Adigrat and the border between Ethiopia and Djibouti. Travelers should also avoid the Afar Region near the Eritrean frontier. The town of Axum is relatively safe, although it lies within an area in which foreigners are prone to kidnapping. Visitors should avoid traveling in the Somali region due to the threat of attacks by insurgents. The Gambella area in the west is the site of periodic tribal fighting.

Pickpockets and purse snatchers target pedestrians in Addis Ababa, particularly in the outdoor market in Addis Ababa. Travelers should store their passports and other valuables, rather than carrying them when they go to the city.

Calling home
Ethiopia's telecommunications system is rudimentary; there are only enough cell phones and land-based telephones for fewer than two people in a hundred. There are 136 Internet hosts.

Diplomatic contact in the United States
Ambassador Samuel Assefa
3506 International Drive NW, Washington, DC 20008
Phone: (202) 364-1200 • Fax: (202) 587-0195

Diplomatic contact from the United States
Ambassador (vacant): Charge d'Affaires Roger A. Meese
Embassy: Entoto Street, Addis Ababa
P. O. Box 1014, Addis Ababa
Phone: (251) 11-517-40-00 • Fax: (251) 11-517-40-01

The Gambia

Overview of geography, climate, and population

The Gambia borders the Atlantic Ocean and is almost twice the size of Delaware. The climate is tropical, with a wet season from June to November and a dry season from November to May. As of 2009, 1.78 million people lived in the Gambia.

Religion, ethnicity, and language in a nutshell

Ninety percent of Gambians are Muslim, about 10 percent are Christian, and 1 percent follow traditional religions. Forty-two percent of Gambians are Mandinka, 18 percent are Fula, 16 percent are Wolof, 10 percent are Jola, 9 percent are Serahuli, 4 percent are other Africans, and 1 percent are non-African. English is the official language, and Gambians also speak Mandinka, Wolof, Fula, and other languages.

Brief political history and today's government

The Gambia was part of the Mali Empire in the 1500s. The Gambia became independent from Britain in 1965. President Yahya A. J.J. Jammeh is president, having seized power in 1994. The Gambia became a republic in 1997. The legislature consists of a national assembly, with most members elected by the public and a few selected by the president. The Supreme Court comprises the judiciary. The legal system draws on English, Islamic, and traditional law.

Economic snapshot

Three-fourths of Gambians are farmers. Other industries include tourism as well as processing nuts, seafood, and animal skins.

Peace Corps programs

- Education
- Public health
- Environmental conservation
- Community development

Health

HIV/AIDS, diarrhea, hepatitis A, typhoid fever, malaria, schistosomiasis, meningococcal meningitis, and rabies are among the diseases and illnesses volunteers should be aware of in the Gambia.

Medical care is sparse. Some medicines are not available, so visitors should bring their own supplies with proof of prescriptions. Emergency care is not dependable. Malaria is a particular concern.

Safety

Pickpocketing and other minor street crimes are common. Visitors should avoid leaving their baggage unattended to prevent theft. Travelers should avoid strangers who offer assistance without being asked. Drivers should keep windows up and doors locked to prevent theft from cars stopped in traffic jams. Visitors planning to stay in the Gambia over a long period should hire security guards for their homes. Female travelers should avoid solitary walks after dark, particularly on the beach and in areas popular with tourists. Women should avoid strangers who offer their services as tour guides because such initial contact is often a precursor to crime. To avoid becoming victims of fraud, U.S. citizens should be wary of any requests to invest in businesses, disclose their financial records, or transfer money.

Calling home

There are about 52,000 land-based telephones and approximately 400,000 cell phones in the Gambia. There are six Internet hosts.

Diplomatic contact in the United States

Ambassador (vacant)
Suite 905, 1156 15th Street NW, Washington, DC 20005
Phone: (202) 785-1379 • Fax: (202) 785-1430

Diplomatic contact from the United States

Ambassador Barry L. Wells
Embassy: Kairaba Avenue, Fajara, Banjul
P. M. B. No. 19, Banjul
Phone: (220) 439-2856, 437-6169, 437-6170 • Fax: (220) 439-2475

Ghana

Overview of geography, climate, and population

Ghana is almost as large as Oregon and is home to the planet's biggest artificial lake. The climate is tropical, and it varies from one part of the country to another. The southeast is mostly dry while the southwest is moist. The north is hot and dry. Dusty winds sweep Ghana from January through March. Droughts are also common. About 23.8 million people live in Ghana.

Religion, ethnicity, and language in a nutshell

Approximately 70 percent of Ghanaians are Christians, about 15 percent practices Islam, slightly more than 8 percent adhere to traditional faiths, and about 7 percent have no religion. About 45 percent of Ghanaians are of Akan lineage, approximately 15 percent are of Mole-Dagbon extraction, around 11 percent are Ewe, a little more than 7 percent are Ga-Dangme, 4 percent are Guan, approximately 4 percent are of Gurma lineage, and approximately 2 percent are Grusi, Mande-Busanga account for 1 percent of the population, as do other tribes. About 8 percent of Ghanaians are not members of any tribe. English is the official language. Ghanaians also speak Asante, Ewe, Fante, Boron and Dagomba, Dangme, Dagarte, Akyem, Ga, and Akuapem.

Brief political history and today's government

North Africans began to occupy Ghana in the 13th century, and the Portuguese came in the 15th century. Britain claimed the country as a colony in the 1800s, and it gained independence in 1957. Ghana is a constitutional democracy with a publicly elected parliament. The president is John Kufuor. The Supreme Court comprises the judiciary.

Economic snapshot

Agriculture is essential to Ghana's economy as are gold and cocoa exports. A significant amount of foreign aid supports the country's economy.

Peace Corps programs

- Education
- Environmental education
- AIDS prevention
- Business
- Public health

Health

HIV/AIDS, diarrhea, hepatitis A, typhoid fever, malaria, yellow fever, schistosomiasis, meningococcal meningitis, and avian flu are among the diseases and illnesses volunteers should be aware of in Ghana.

Clinics in Accra are more adequate than those outside the capital, but medical care across the country falls below Western standards. Pharmacies are not well stocked, so visitors should carry supplies of prescription and over-the-counter drugs. Visitors must be vaccinated against yellow fever in order to legally enter the country.

Safety

Demonstrations are likely to turn violent, so visitors should avoid them. Pickpockets, handbag thieves, and fraudulent business people particularly target foreigners who frequent public markets, parks, beaches, and tourist areas. Visitors should remain in groups, avoid traveling at night, refrain from wearing jewelry, and hide their cash. If attacked, visitors should try to avoid physical injury by not resisting.

Pickpockets, purse thieves, and perpetrators of financial scams often target international visitors. To reduce the risk of armed robbery, visitors should travel in groups and refrain from going outside at night. Travelers should not share taxis with strangers. Credit card fraud is increasingly prevalent, so visitors should avoid charging purchases. Before purchasing precious metals, visitors should check vendors' licenses by contacting the Precious Metals and Mining Commission. Most business deals that include exporting gold dust are fraudulent.

Visitors should be careful when swimming in the ocean because rough surf frequently leads to drownings.

Calling home

The land-based telephone system, which includes 356,000 lines, is not reliable. About one-quarter of Ghanaians have cell phones.

Diplomatic contact in the United States

Ambassador (vacant): Charge d'Affaires Adolphus K. Arthur
1156 15th St. NW #905, Washington, DC 20005
Phone: (202) 785-1379 • Fax: (202) 785-1430

Diplomatic contact from the United States

Ambassador Donald G. Teitelbaum
Embassy: 24 4th Circular Rd. Cantonments, Accra
P. O. Box 194, Accra
Phone: (233) (21) 741-000 • Fax: (233) (21) 741-389

Guinea

Overview of geography, climate, and population

Guinea, a West African nation almost as large as Oregon, borders the Atlantic Ocean. Guinea is sultry, with monsoons likely from June through November.

The country is dry from December through May with dusty winds. Along the sea sides, the terrain is flat. The center of the country has hills and mountains. About 10 million people live in Guinea.

Religion, ethnicity, and language in a nutshell

Eighty-five percent of Guineans are Muslim, 8 percent are Christian, and 7 percent practice traditional faiths. Forty percent of Guineans are Peuhl, 30 percent are Malinke, 20 percent are of Soussou descent, and 10 percent are of other ethnicities. French is the official language, and each ethnic group has its own tongue.

Brief political history and today's government

The land now called Guinea was part of the Songhai, Mali, and Ghana empires from the 1100s to the 1600s. The Portuguese sold enslaved Guineans beginning in the 15th century. Guinea came under French control in the 1800s and gained independence in 1958. The country is now a republic headed by President Lansana Conte. The prime minister is Lansana Kouyate. The legislative branch consists of the national assembly, some members are chosen by the public while others are selected by their political parties. The judiciary includes the Court of the First Instance, Court of Appeal, and Supreme Court. The legal system stems from customary and French civil law.

Economic snapshot

Mineral mining is central to Guinea's economy; the country contains much of the earth's bauxite. Guinea also has iron ore, uranium, diamonds, and gold.

Peace Corps programs

- Education
- Public health
- Environmental conservation
- AIDS prevention, business

Health

HIV/AIDS, diarrhea, hepatitis A, typhoid fever, malaria, yellow fever, schistosomiasis, Lassa fever, and meningococcal meningitis are among the diseases and illnesses volunteers should be aware of in Guinea.

Health care is sparsely available, even in cities. Some private clinics offer more treatment options than public ones but still fall far below Western standards. Most medicine is not readily available. Equipment is often not sterile. Emergency rooms are very rare, and there are no ambulances or other forms of emergency transportation.

Visitors should drink only bottled or distilled water, as almost all other water is contaminated. Malaria is a serious concern.

Safety

Visitors should avoid crowds because of ongoing civil violence. Travelers should avoid military facilities, the Presidential Palace, and government offices. Travelers should consult the State Department's travel warnings before visiting the areas near the borders with Liberia, Sierra Leone, or the Ivory Coast. Purse snatching and pickpocketing is common. Thieves often target foreigners because they appear rich. Foreigners are especially vulnerable near international hotels, in restaurants popular with tourists, at the airport, and in outdoor markets. Thieves often initially approach their victims by offering to help with their baggage, so travelers should arrange to have hotel staff or others assist with their luggage. Perpetrators of fraudulent business schemes often target foreigners, usually by sending an e-mail regarding money.

Calling home

There are two land-based telephones and cell phones per 100 people. There are 173 Internet hosts.

Diplomatic contact in the United States

Ambassador Mory Karamoko Kaba
2112 Leroy Place NW, Washington, DC 20008
Phone: (202) 483-9420 • Fax: (202) 483-8688

Diplomatic contact from the United States

Ambassador (vacant): Charge d'Affaires Elizabeth Raspolic
Embassy: Koloma, Conakry, east of Hamdallaye Circle
B. P. 603, Transversale No. 2, Centre Administratif de Koloma, Commune de Ratoma, Conakry
Phone: (224) 65-10-40-00 • Fax: (224) 65-10-42-97

Kenya

Overview of geography, climate, and population

Kenya borders the Indian Ocean and is almost twice as large as Nevada. The coasts are tropical, and the center is dry. Residents number 39 million.

Religion, ethnicity, and language in a nutshell

About 45 percent of Kenyans are Protestant, around 30 percent are Roman Catholic, 10 percent follow Islam, and 10 percent adhere to traditional faiths. Two percent of the population follows other religions. English and Kishwahili are the official languages; Kenyans speak many other African languages. Nearly three quarters of Kenyans are Kikuyu, 14 percent are Luhya, 13 percent are Luo, 12 percent are Kalenjin, 11 percent are Kamba, 6 percent are Kisii, 6 percent are Meru, 15 percent are of other African ethnicities, and 1 percent are non-African.

Brief political history and today's government

People have lived in what is now Kenya since at least 8,000 years before the Christian era. The Portuguese claimed territory in Kenya in the 16th century. In the 1700s, the country came under Arabic control. Kenya became a British colony in 1920 and gained independence in 1963. Mwai Kibaki is the president of Kenya, which is now a republic. The legislative branch consists of the National Assembly, of which some seats are filled by public election and others by presidential selection. The judiciary includes a court of appeal and a high court. The legal system stems from tribal, Kenyan, and English law.

Economic snapshot

Kenya's economy relies heavily on agriculture, with tea, coffee, and sugarcane figuring prominently. The petroleum, grain, and sugar industries are also important.

Peace Corps programs

- Business
- Public health
- IT
- Education

Health

HIV/AIDS, diarrhea, hepatitis A, typhoid fever, schistosomiasis, malaria, cholera, Ebola, Rift Valley fever, and anthrax are among the diseases and illnesses volunteers should be aware of in Kenya.

Clinics in the capital offer health care that is adequate by Western standards, but facilities outside Nairobi are less reliable.

Safety

Travelers are warned of terrorism and crime. The U.S. Embassy in Nairobi was bombed by terrorists in 1998, and a hotel was attacked in 2002. Terrorists are likely to target tourist magnets and civilian areas. Travelers should avoid crowds, especially political demonstrations, because some have turned violent. Protests often take place near government offices, universities, and parks. Police often use force against demonstrators. Inter-tribal violence is a concern in the countryside. Americans are particularly vulnerable to kidnapping in the Kiwayu Island tourist section. Armed robbery and tribal conflict are concerns, particularly in the northern section of the country and near the game parks. Drivers traveling to the Northern Kenya should caravan in case of mechanical problems. Residents of villages in which children have been abducted have sometimes attacked foreign and domestic strangers they suspected of the kidnappings. The crime rate in Kenya is high, especially in beach towns. Attackers carrying weapons often target visitors. Travelers should avoid carrying valuables for fear of pickpockets and purse snatchers. Visitors should avoid walking alone after dark. Burglaries, carjackings, and other violent crimes are common. Carjackers often target mass transit vehicles because they carry more passengers than regular cars. To reduce the risk of injury, victims of carjackings should avoid resisting the attackers.

Criminals often impersonate police officers, so visitors who encounter apparent members of law enforcement should ask for identification. Thefts from cars stopped in traffic are common, so drivers should keep their doors locked and their windows up. Foreigners should buy items only from established shops, rather than from street vendors.

Calling home

Kenya has about 293,000 land-based telephones and 6.4 million cell phones. There are 2,120 Internet hosts.

Diplomatic contact in the United States

Ambassador Peter Rateng Oginga Ogego
2249 R Street NW, Washington, DC 20008
Phone: (202) 387-6101 • Fax: (202) 462-3829

Diplomatic contact from the United States

Ambassador Michael Ranneberger
Embassy: U.S. Embassy, United Nations Avenue, Nairobi; P. O. Box 606 Village Market, Nairobi 00621
Box 21A, Unit 64100, APO AE 09831
Phone: (254) (20) 363-6000 • Fax: (254) (20) 363-410

Lesotho

Overview of geography, climate, and population

Lesotho is a landlocked nation a little smaller than Maryland. It has a temperate, drought-prone climate and a hilly, mountainous terrain. The population is 2.1 million.

Religion, ethnicity, and language in a nutshell

Eighty percent of residents are Christian, while 20 percent hold traditional beliefs. More than 99 percent of the inhabitants of Lesotho are of Sotho lineage, while the rest are European and Asian. English is the official language; residents also speak Sesotho, Zulu, and Xhosa.

Brief political history and today's government

In the early 19th century, Chief Moshoeshoe began a Basuto kingdom in the area that is now Lesotho. The kingdom became a British territory in the late 19th century and gained independence in 1966, according to the *Kingfisher Reference Atlas*. Lesotho is a constitutional monarchy governed by Prime Minister Pakalitha Mosisili. The royal couple, King Letsie III and Queen MaSenate Mohato Seeiso, are primarily figureheads, according to the official Web site of Lesotho. English common law and Roman-Dutch law influenced Lesotho's legal system. A high court, court of appeal, magistrate courts, and a traditional court comprise the judiciary.

Economic snapshot

The backbone of Lesotho's economy consists of fees exacted from citizens who work in South Africa's mines, as well as payments from the Southern Africa Customs Union. Clothes-making accounts for much of the manufacturing that occurs in Lesotho. Other industries include the processing of agricultural products.

Peace Corps programs

- Education
- Business economic development
- AIDS prevention

Health

HIV/AIDS, dengue fever, filariasis, leishmaniasis, river blindness, African tick bite fever, rickettsial infection, African sleeping sickness, schistosomiasis, tuberculosis, and polio are among the diseases and illnesses volunteers should be aware of in Lesotho. HIV/AIDS affects more than 30 percent of the population.

There are no ambulances in Lesotho. Health care facilities are sparse, but better medical services are available in Bloemfontein, South Africa. Visitors should bring medicines and photocopies of their prescriptions because drugs are in short supply.

Safety

Robbers and murderers often target foreigners. Weapon-wielding gangs are prevalent. Burglaries and carjackings also occur frequently, especially in the capital. International visitors have been crime victims while using pedestrian walkways and frequenting well-known restaurants. Visitors should avoid crowds and should not walk in the capital, even by day. Violent crimes are common even during the day, but are even more frequent at night. Police are unable to respond adequately to all calls. Baggage theft is frequently a problem at the Johannesburg International Airport, which travelers use to reach Lesotho. Travelers changing planes and those flying on small airlines are especially vulnerable. Airline passengers should avoid packing valuables in their checked luggage and should use the plastic-wrapping service at the airport.

Calling home

Lesotho has 48,000 land-based telephones and 249,800 cell phones. There are about 15 cell phones per one hundred people. There are 66 Internet servers.

Diplomatic contact in the United States

Currently Ambassador David Mohlomi Rantekoa
2511 Massachusetts Avenue NW, Washington, DC 20008
Phone: (202) 797-5533, 797-5534, 797-5535, 797-5536 • Fax: (202) 234-6815

Diplomatic contact from the United States

Ambassador Robert Nolan
Embassy: 254 Kingsway, Maseru West (Consular Section)
P. O. Box 333, Maseru 100, Lesotho
Phone: (266) 22 312666 • Fax: (266) 22 310116

Liberia

Overview of geography, climate, and population

Liberia is located in Western Africa and borders the North Atlantic Ocean, between Cote d'Ivoire and Sierra. Liberia is mostly flat with rolling coastal plains rising to rolling plateau and low mountains in northeast. The climate is tropical, hot, and humid. It has dry winters with hot days and cool to cold nights, and wet, cloudy summers with frequent heavy showers. The population is 3.4 million.

Religion, ethnicity, and language in a nutshell

In Liberia, 40 percent of residents are Christian, 20 percent are Muslim, and 40 percent have indigenous beliefs. Ninety-five percent of residents are indigenous Africans (including Kpelle, Bassa, Gio, Kru, Grebo, Mano, Krahn, Gola, Gbandi, Loma, Kissi, Vai, Dei, Bella, Mandingo, and Mende), 2.5 percent are Americo-Liberians (descendants of immigrants from the U.S. who were slaves), 2.5 are Congo People (descendants of immigrants from the Caribbean who had been slaves). English is the official language, and 20 percent of residents speak it. Some 20 ethnic group languages are also spoken, few of which can be written or used in correspondence.

Brief political history and today's government

Liberia has a dual system of statutory law based on Anglo-American common law for the modern sector and customary law based on unwritten tribal practices for the indigenous sector.

Economic snapshot

Civil war and government mismanagement destroyed much of Liberia's economy, especially the infrastructure in and around the capital, Monrovia. Many businesses fled the country, taking capital and expertise with them, but with the conclusion of fighting and the installation of a democratically elected government in 2006, some have returned. Richly endowed with water, mineral resources, forests, and a climate favorable to agriculture, Liberia had been a producer and exporter of basic products — primarily raw timber and rubber. Local manufacturing, mainly foreign owned, had been small in scope. President Johnson Sirleaf, a Harvard-trained banker and administrator, has taken steps to reduce corruption, build support from international donors, and encourage private investment. Embargos on timber and diamond exports have been lifted, opening new sources of revenue for the government. The reconstruction of infrastructure and the raising of incomes in this ravaged economy will largely depend on generous financial and technical assistance from donor countries and foreign investment in key sectors, such as infrastructure and power generation.

Peace Corps programs
- Education
- HIV/AIDS
- Health

Health
Bacterial and protozoal diarrhea, hepatitis A, malaria, yellow fever, schistosomiasis, Lassa fever, rabies, and typhoid fever are among the diseases and illnesses volunteers should be aware of in Liberia.

Hospitals and medical facilities in Liberia are very poorly equipped and are incapable of providing many services. Emergency services comparable to those in the U.S. or Europe are non-existent, and the blood supply is unreliable and unsafe for transfusion. Americans with serious medical problems travel or are medically evacuated to the United States, Europe, or South Africa. Medicines are scarce, often beyond expiration dates, and generally unavailable in most areas. As there is neither an effective garbage removal service nor a functioning sewer system, the level of sanitation throughout urban areas is very poor, which increases the potential for disease. Upper respiratory infections and diarrhea are common, as well as more serious diseases such as typhoid and malaria. All travelers to Liberia must be vaccinated against yellow fever and should carry a supply of all prescription medication, including anti-malaria medication, adequate for their entire stay. A typhoid vaccination is also recommended.

Safety
The Department of State urges U.S. citizens to plan proposed travel to Liberia carefully and to exercise caution when traveling in Liberia. Neither public transport nor taxis are available at the international airport, which is located 40 miles outside of Monrovia; therefore, before traveling to Liberia, Americans are urged to make arrangements for transportation from the international airport into the city center. Americans traveling to Liberia are also urged to ensure that they have confirmed reservations at a reputable hotel, as rooms can be scarce and difficult to find without advance plans.

Americans who travel to or reside in Liberia should realize that Liberia's police force is in the process of being rebuilt. There is a UN Mission in Liberia (UNMIL), but its mandate is to ensure political stability in Liberia. Americans who travel around Liberia must realize that the role of UN Police (UNPOL) officers is to serve as advisors to the Liberia National Police. Accordingly, they do not have the authority to arrest or detain, and they are unarmed. The Liberia National Police, for its part, has a limited presence in Monrovia, and even less of a presence outside of Monrovia. In addition, police officers can be a source of problems for visitors as well as a source of aid or assistance. Although problems with corruption have improved, travelers may be detained by police officers who solicit bribes. Americans are encouraged to carry a photocopy of their passports with them at all times so that, if questioned by local officials, proof of identity and U.S. citizenship is readily available. If detained or arrested, U.S. citizens should always ask to be allowed to contact the U.S. Embassy.

U.S. citizens in Liberia should be aware of their surroundings at all times and use caution when moving around, especially at night. The U.S. Embassy recommends that American citizens observe a suggested curfew of 2:00 a.m.-6:00 a.m. Travel outside of Monrovia after dark is strongly discouraged, as roads are in poor condition and thus dangerous to navigate at night. U.S. citizens should avoid crowds, political rallies, and street demonstrations and should maintain security awareness at all times.

The crime rate in Liberia is high and is exacerbated by the high rate of unemployment. Theft, assault, sexual crimes, and murder are problems, and they occur more frequently after dark. Foreigners, including U.S. citizens, have been targets of street crime, robbery, and sexual assault. Women have been attacked on deserted beaches. Residential armed break-ins have occurred. The police are ill-equipped and largely incapable of providing effective protection or investigation. Criminal activity has been reported in both urban and rural areas.

Petty corruption is rampant; poorly paid government officials are not immune from the temptation to collect fees for doing their job. The result is that travelers may be asked for bribes and inconvenienced for not paying them.

Calling home
The limited services available are found almost exclusively in the capital Monrovia. Fixed line service is stagnant and extremely limited, with the mobile-cellular subscription base growing and teledensity exceeding 20 per 100 persons. There are five Internet hosts.

Diplomatic contact in the United States
Ambassador Milton Nathaniel Barnes

5201 16th Street NW, Washington, DC 20011
Phone: (1) (202) 723-0437 • Fax: (1) (202) 723-0436

Diplomatic contact from the United States

Ambassador Linda Thomas-Greenfield
Embassy: 111 United Nations Drive, P. O. Box 98, Mamba Point,
1000 Monrovia, 10
Phone: (231) 7-705-4826 • Fax: (231) 7-701-0370

Madagascar

Overview of geography, climate, and population

Madagascar is an island nation of 20.6 million off the coast of Mozambique. It is nearly twice the size of Arizona. The country's climate ranges from sultry to mild to hot and dry.

Religion, ethnicity, and language in a nutshell

More than half of the residents of Madagascar — called Malagasy — hold traditional religious beliefs. About 40 percent are Christian and 7 percent are Muslim. French, English, and Malagasy are the official languages. Malagasy also speak Antanosy, Bara, Sakalava, and Betsimisaraka. Some Malagasy are of Malayo-Indonesian descent; others have a combination of African, Malayo-Indonesian, and Arab lineage. Other residents of the island trace their ancestors to France and India.

Brief political history and today's government

The Portuguese arrived in Madagascar in the 16th century, according to the *The Kingfisher Reference Atlas.* The country came under French control in the late 19th century and became independent in 1960. Marc Ravalomanana is the president of the republic. The legislature includes the National Assembly and the Senate. The public chooses assembly members. Senators come from regional assemblies and are appointed by the president. The judiciary includes the Supreme Court and the high constitutional court. Madagascar's legal system draws from Malagasy and French law.

Economic snapshot

Madagascar's economy relies on farming, harvesting seafood, and forestry. The economic system was socialist before the 1990s, when some industries became privately owned.

Peace Corps programs
- Education
- Environment
- Health

Health

Plague, malaria, chikungunya, HIV/AIDS, various sexually transmitted diseases, schistosomiasis, typhoid fever, hepatitis A, diarrhea, and dengue fever are among the diseases and illnesses volunteers should be aware of in Madagascar.

Medical care falls far below Western expectations. Foreign specialists in the capital of Antananarivo have more expertise than their Malagasy counterparts but are still not well-trained by American standards. The quality of medical care outside Antananarivo is even worse than in the capital. Some medicines are available in the capital, but visitors should bring prescriptions that include their medicine's generic name. Outside the capital, medicine is scarcer, so visitors should bring enough of their own pharmaceuticals to last until the end of their stay.

Before arriving, visitors should take medicine to prevent malaria. After arriving, travelers should use insect repellent and clothing that fully covers their arms and legs. Rabies transmitted by stray animals is a concern, so visitors should be vaccinated before leaving the United States.

Visitors should assume all non-bottled water is not potable. Bottled water is common in the capital. In other areas, visitors will need to use a purifier or purification tablets.

Safety

Visitors should beware of pickpockets and purse snatchers. Thieves who target homes and cars are also cause for concern. Violent crimes are particularly dangerous when victims resist the assailants. Pedestrians have been targets of armed robberies. Criminals target foreigners even in well-lit, well-traveled areas, so visitors should go out in groups and avoid wearing fine jewelry. Travelers should not leave property in parked cars. Visitors should avoid walking outside at night, even in groups and near international hotels. Ex-convicts and former members of the military and police force have formed gangs that kidnap people and break into homes. The threat of crime is greater in cities than in the countryside. The police lack the resources to respond effectively to crime.

Calling home

Madagascar's telephone system is more reliable than that of many African countries. However, just seven people in 100 have telephones. There are 9,734 Internet hosts.

Diplomatic contact in the United States

Ambassador Jocelyn Bertin Radifera
2374 Massachusetts Avenue NW, Washington, DC 20008
Phone: (202) 265-5525, (202) 265-5526 • Fax: (202) 265-3034

Diplomatic contact from the United States

Ambassador R. Niels Marquardt
Embassy: 14-16 Rue Rainitovo, Antsahavola, Antananarivo 101
B. P. 620, Antsahavola, Antananarivo
Phone: (261) (20) 22-212-57, 22-212-73, 22-209-56 • Fax: (261) (20) 22-345-39

Malawi

Overview of geography, climate, and population

Malawi is a landlocked country not quite as big as Pennsylvania. Its climate is subtropical; the rainy season runs from November to May, and the dry season lasts from May through November. Malawi's terrain includes plateaus, plains, and mountains. The population of Malawi is 14.2 million.

Religion, ethnicity, and language in a nutshell

About 80 percent of Malawians are Christian, approximately 13 percent are Muslim, 3 percent practice another religion, and 4 percent do not adhere to any faith. Malawians are of Chews Nyana, Tumbuka, Yao, Lomwe, Sena, Tonga, Ngoni, Ngonde, Asian, and European descent. The majority of the country's inhabitants speak the official Chichewa language. About 13 percent use the Chinyanja tongue, approximately 10 percent speak Chiyao, about 10 percent speak Chitumbuka, 3 percent use the Chisena tongue, approximately 2 percent speak Chilomwe, 2 percent speak Chitonga, and 4 percent speak other tongues.

Brief political history and today's government

Approximately two millennia ago, a Bantu kingdom existed in the region now known as Malawi. The country was preceded by Nyasaland, a protectorate of Great Britain, which came into existence in 1891. After independence in 1964,

Malawi adopted a republican form of government in 1966, according to *The Kingfisher Reference Atlas.* Today the president is Bingu wa Mutharika, who was elected in 2004. The legislature includes a publicly elected National Assembly. The judiciary consists of the Supreme Court of Appeal, the High Court, and the magistrate's courts.

Economic snapshot

The economy of Malawi relies heavily on agriculture and aid from the World Bank and the International Monetary Fund.

Peace Corps programs

- Health
- Environment
- AIDS prevention
- Education

Health

HIV/AIDS, hepatitis A, typhoid fever, diarrhea, malaria, plague, schistosomiasis, giardiasis, African sleeping sickness, tuberculosis, tetanus, rabies, and cholera are among the diseases and illnesses volunteers should be aware of in Malawi.

Many health care professionals have limited English proficiency. Clinics are inadequate by Western standards. Travelers can obtain better care by crossing the border into South Africa. Medicines are often in short supply. Before arriving, visitors should buy insurance to cover medical examinations. Some medical providers require payment in advance of treatment. Visitors should refrain from drinking tap water, using ice cubes, and eating raw produce. Bottled water should be used for drinking and cooking. Travelers should take anti-malaria medicines before leaving the United States. After arriving, visitors should wear clothing that completely covers their arms and legs. The risk of contracting tuberculosis increases in crowded buildings. Travelers should be vaccinated against typhoid, tetanus, and rabies before arriving. Cholera is most common in villages without well-developed sanitation systems but does not often occur in cities.

Safety

Travelers should avoid crowds to avoid being injured in civil upheavals. Foreigners are more likely to be victims of property crimes than violent crimes. Carjacking and burglary are prevalent. Burglars sometimes target hotels as well as homes. Street robbery and pickpocketing are common. Visitors should avoid walking anywhere after dark, even in large groups, to reduce the risk of being mugged or assaulted. Walking is potentially dangerous even by day.

Calling home

Latest figures show about 429,000 cell phones in Malawi, mostly in or near the cities, and approximately 102,000 land-based telephones. There are 59,700 Internet hosts.

Diplomatic contact in the United States

Ambassador Hawa Ndilowe

1156 15th Street, NW, Suite 320, Washington, DC 20005

Phone: (202) 721-0270 • Fax: (202) 721-0288

Diplomatic contact from the United States

Ambassador Peter W. Bodde

Embassy: 16 Jomo Kenyatta Road, Lilongwe 3

P. O. Box 30016, Lilongwe 3, Malawi

Phone: (265) (1) 773 166 • Fax: (265) (1) 770 471

Mali

Overview of geography, climate, and population

Mali is a generally flat, landlocked country almost twice as big as Texas. Its climate ranges from nearly tropical to arid. In February to June, the weather is typically hot and dry. During June to November the approximately 12.6 million residents usually experience sultriness and rain.

Religion, ethnicity, and language in a nutshell

Ninety percent of Malians follow Islam, 1 percent are Christian, and 9 percent hold traditional religious beliefs. Half of Malians are Mande, 17 percent are Peul, 12 percent are Voltaic, 6 percent are Songhai, 10 percent are Tuareg and Moor, and 5 percent have another ethnicity. French is the official language. Eighty percent of Malians speak Bambara, and many African tongues are prevalent.

Brief political history and today's government

People have populated the area now known as Mali since before the dawn of recorded history. The Mali Empire controlled the region from the years 300 to 1500 of the Christian era. Moors controlled the country beginning in the late 16th century. France took control of Mali in 1880. The nation became self-governing in the 1960s.

The country is a republic governed by President Amadou Toumani Toure. The legislature consists of a National Assembly, members of which are popularly elected. The judiciary includes the Supreme Court, which presides over a legal system that stems from customary and French civil law. The judiciary has the power to review laws created by the National Assembly.

Economic snapshot

Cotton and gold are Mali's most important exports. Farming and fishing provide most of the country's jobs.

Peace Corps programs

- Agriculture
- Public health
- Environment
- Business
- Sanitation

Health

Bacterial and protozoal diarrhea, HIV/AIDS, hepatitis A, malaria, schistosomiasis, meningococcal meningitis, and typhoid fever are among the diseases and illnesses volunteers should be aware of in Mali.

Medical facilities in Mali are limited, especially outside of the capital, Bamako. Psychiatric care is non-existent. The U.S. Embassy in Bamako maintains a list of physicians and other health care professionals who may see U.S. citizen patients. The Embassy cannot guarantee these services or specifically recommend any physicians.

The U.S. Department of State is unaware of any HIV/AIDS entry restrictions for visitors to, or foreign residents of, Mali.

Many American medicines are unavailable; French medications are more easily found. Available medications can be obtained at pharmacies throughout Bamako and are usually less expensive than those in the United States. Travelers should carry with them an adequate supply of needed medication and prescription drugs, along with copies of the prescriptions, including the generic names for the drugs. Caution should be taken to avoid purchasing potentially dangerous counterfeit medications when buying on the local market in Mali.

Safety

The U.S. Embassy in Bamako strongly advises American citizens against traveling to the northern regions of Mali as the terrorist group Al Qaeda in the Islamic

Maghreb (AQIM) continues to use northern Mali as a safe haven and platform from which to conduct operations. AQIM has been designated as a terrorist organization by both the United States and the European Union and has declared its intention to attack Western targets. In October 2008, AQIM released two Austrian tourists in northern Mali who had been kidnapped in February 2008 in Tunisia. In December 2008, AQIM kidnapped two Canadian diplomats in Niger. AQIM kidnapped four European tourists on January 22, 2009, along the Mali-Niger border near the northern Malian town of Anderamboukane. AQIM subsequently released the Canadian hostages and two of the four European tourists in northern Mali in April 2009.

Violent crime in Mali is infrequent, but petty crimes, such as pickpocketing and simple theft, are common in urban areas. Passports and wallets should be closely guarded when in crowded outdoor areas and open-air markets. Individuals traveling on the Bamako-Dakar railroad are advised to be vigilant, especially at night. Criminals will not hesitate to use violence if they encounter resistance from victims. There are sporadic reports of nighttime robberies on the roads outside of the capital; tourists should not drive outside of Bamako at night. Travelers should stay alert, remain in groups, and avoid poorly lit areas after dark.

Sporadic banditry and random carjacking have historically plagued Mali's vast desert region and its borders with Mauritania and Niger. While banditry is not seen as targeting U.S. citizens specifically, such acts of violence cannot be predicted.

Calling home
The telephone system is not reliable. There are 82,500 land-based telephones and 1.5 million cell phones in Mali.

Diplomatic contact in the United States
Ambassador (vacant): Charge d'Affaires Mohamed Ouzouna MAIGA2130 R Street NW, Washington, DC 20008
Phone: (202) 332-2249, (202) 939-8950 • Fax: (202) 332-6603

Diplomatic contact from the United States
Ambassador Gillian A. Milovanovic
Embassy: located off the Roi Bin Fahad Aziz Bridge west of the Bamako central district
ACI 2000, Rue 243, Porte 297, Bamako
Phone: (223) 270-2300 • Fax: (223) 270-2479

Mauritania

Overview of geography, climate, and population

Mauritania borders the Sahara and the Atlantic Ocean. The country is mostly flat. It has a desert climate, and sandstorms are common in March and April. Mauritanians cope with recurring droughts. The country is about three times as large as New Mexico. About 3 million people live in Mauritania, and most of the population is in the south.

Religion, ethnicity, and language in a nutshell

Mauritania is a Muslim country. Forty percent of the population are of mixed Arab and African lineage. Thirty percent of Mauritanians are Arabic and about another third are African. The country's official language is Arabic but inhabitants also speak Soninke, Pulaar, French, Hassaniya, and Wolof.

Brief political history and today's government

The Mali and Ghana empires ruled Mauritania from the 300s to the 1500s. Arabic rule began in the 1600s. France claimed Mauritania as a protectorate in 1903 and a colony in 1920. Mauritania won independence in 1960. Mauritania is a democratic republic and the court system reflects French and Islamic influences. The president is Sidi Ould Cheikh Abdellahi, and the prime minister is Zeine Ould Zeidane. The public elects the president who chooses the prime minister. A Senate, elected by town officials, and a national assembly, elected by the public, comprises the legislature. The judiciary consists of a Supreme Court, Court of Appeals, and a variety of lesser courts.

Economic snapshot

About 50 percent of Mauritanians are farmers. Forty percent of the country exports are of iron ore. Mauritania's income from exports is one-third of the amount of the debt it owes other countries.

Calling home

There are 34,900 land telephones and 1 million cell phones. Mauritania has 14 Internet hosts.

Peace Corps programs

- Education
- Business
- Health
- Agriculture

Health

Medical care is scarce. The capital and major cities have modern clinics, but there are almost none in the countryside. Pharmacies are not well-stocked so visitors should bring their own medicine. Visitors should protect themselves from Malaria by taking mefloquine, doxycycline, or atovaquone. Insect repellent also helps prevent infection.

Safety

Alleged terrorists fatally shot four foreign tourists and injured another in 2007. Terrorists also attacked a military base near the borders with Algeria and Mali. Travelers should not go into the Sahara without an official guide, plenty of provisions and rugged vehicles. Bandits and smugglers are at work in the countryside. Visitors should beware of land mines near the Western Sahara. Travelers should carry their identification every time they go out. Any crowd could turn into a demonstration, which could turn violent, so visitors should avoid large groups.

Diplomatic contact in the United States

Ambassador (vacant)
2129 Leroy Place NW, Washington, DC 20008
Phone: (202) 232-5700, (202) 232-5701 • Fax: (202) 319-2623

Diplomatic contact from the United States

Ambassador Mark M. Boulware
Embassy: 288 Rue Abdallaye, Rue 42-100 (between Presidency building and Spanish Embassy), Nouakchott
BP 222, Nouakchott
Phone: (222) 525-2660, 525-2661, 525-2662, and 525-2663 • Fax: (222) 525-1592

Mozambique

Overview of geography, climate, and population

Mozambique is a country of about 21.6 million that is almost twice as large as California. Its climate is tropical and subtropical. The country's terrain ranges from low country to mountains and is prone to droughts, cyclones, and floods.

Religion, ethnicity, and language in a nutshell

Slightly more than 20 percent of Mozambicans are Catholic, about 18 percent are Muslim, approximately 18 percent are Zionist Christian, and around 18 percent follow other religions.

Nearly 100 percent of residents are of African lineage, including those of the Makhuwa, Tsonga, Lomwe, and Sena tribes. Europeans account for .06 percent of the population, .2 percent of residents are of mixed European and African lineage, and .08 percent are Indians.

Portuguese is the official language. About 8 percent of the population speaks Portuguese as a first language, and nearly 30 percent use it as a second language. About 26 percent of Mozambicans speak Emakhuwa, approximately 11 percent are Xichangana speakers, and nearly 8 percent speak Elomwe. About 7 percent speak Cisena, approximately 6 percent communicate in Echuwabo, and 32 percent use other Mozambican tongues. Nearly 2 percent of the population speaks unspecified tongues or other non-Mozambican languages.

Brief political history and today's government

The Portuguese claimed Mozambique as a colony in the 1400s; the country became independent in 1975. Mozambique was under Marxist rule until 1989. Armando Emilion Guebuza is the president. The legislature consists of an Assembly of the Republic, members of which are publicly elected. The judiciary includes the Supreme Court — some judges of which assembly members elect, others of which the president appoints — an administrative court, customs courts, maritime courts, courts martial, and labor courts. The legal system draws on customary and Portuguese civil law.

Economic snapshot

The economy relies heavily on farming and foreign aid, but most Mozambicans are impoverished. Much of Mozambique's international debt has been canceled. The country has a significant trade deficit.

Peace Corps programs

- Education
- Health

Health

HIV/AIDS, diarrhea, hepatitis A, typhoid fever, malaria, plague, and schistosomiasis are among the diseases and illnesses volunteers should be aware of in Mozambique.

Health care is inadequate by Western standards. In some areas outside the capital, there is no medical care available. Other areas outside Maputo have only rudimentary medical facilities. Medical professionals typically do not speak English proficiently. Pharmacies are not well stocked. Some medical facilities require payment in advance of treatment. In all cases, patients must pay before leaving the facility.

Safety

Carjacking is a significant risk, so driving at night is not advisable. Emergency services are rare, and road maintenance is poor. Drivers on major highways between Mozambique and South Africa should beware of car thieves and robbers. Drivers should caravan even during the day. Reportedly, pedestrians sometimes intentionally fling themselves in front of foreigners' cars and try to collect payment for injuries. Drivers should restrict their trips to often-used roads to avoid the land mines that remain underneath less well-traveled thoroughfares. Visitors should avoid demonstrations, which sometimes turn violent. Mugging, purse snatching, and pickpocketing are prevalent in the capital and other cities. Visitors should only walk in well-traveled areas and should be especially careful when going out at night, even in popular sections of town. Travelers should securely store all valuables and avoid taking them along when they go out. The police generally do not respond quickly to reports of crime.

International flights often require passengers to change planes at the Oliver Tambo International Airport in Johannesburg, South Africa, where theft from baggage is common. Visitors should not put valuables in their checked bags and should keep detailed packing lists. Travelers should also use the wrapping service offered at the airport.

Calling home

The telephone system is fairly reliable but has one land-based line for every 100 people. There are about 3 million cellular phones. There are 15,231 Internet hosts.

Diplomatic contact in the United States

Ambassador Amelia Matos Sumbana
1525 New Hampshire Avenue, Washington, DC 20036
Phone: (202) 293-7146 • Fax: (202) 835-0245

Diplomatic contact from the United States

Ambassador (vacant): Charge d'Affaires Todd C. Chapman
Embassy: Avenida Kenneth Kuanda 193, Maputo
P. O. Box 783, Maputo
Phone: (258) (21) 492797 • Fax: (258) (21) 490114

Namibia

Overview of geography, climate, and population

Namibia is a hot, dry country about half as big as Alaska. It contains the Namib and Kalahari deserts, but most of the terrain is a plateau. About 2.1 million people live in Namibia.

Brief political history and today's government

Germany claimed what is now Namibia as a colony in the mid-1800s. South Africa entered Namibia as an occupying force during World War I and took it as a territory in the late 1940s. Namibia became independent in 1990. Hifike-punye Phambe is the president of the republic. The legislative branch includes the national council, members of which come from regional councils, and the national assembly, members of which are publicly elected. The judiciary includes the Supreme Court, justices of which are seated by presidential appointment at the suggestion of the Judicial Service Commission. The legal system stems from Roman-Dutch law and the constitution.

Religion, ethnicity, and language in a nutshell

Between 80 to 90 percent of Namibians are Christians, and 10 to 20 percent hold traditional beliefs.

Approximately 50 percent of Namibians are part of the Ovambo tribe, 9 percent are members of the Kavangos tribe, 7 percent are of the Herero tribe, 7 percent are Damara, 5 percent are Nama, 4 percent are Caprivian, 3 percent are Bushmen, 2 percent are Baster, and .5 percent are Tswana. Six percent of Namibians are of European lineage, and approximately 7 percent are of Euro-African heritage.

English is the official language, and 7 percent of the population speaks it. Almost everyone of African lineage speaks Afrikaans, and 60 percent of people descended from Europeans do. About 30 percent of Namibians speak German, and 1 percent speaks African languages such as Herero, Nama, and Oshivambo.

Economic snapshot

Mineral extraction and export form the backbone of the economy. Subsistence farming is also essential. The value of the Namibian dollar rises and falls with the value of South Africa's rand.

Peace Corps programs

- Education
- Public health
- AIDS prevention

Health

Bacterial diarrhea, HIV/AIDS, hepatitis A, malaria, schistosomiasis, and typhoid fever are among the diseases and illnesses volunteers should be aware of in Namibia.

Windhoek has a small number of private medical hospitals and clinics capable of providing emergency care and performing many routine procedures. Doctors, both general practitioners and specialists, as well as dentists, generally have training and facilities that are comparable to U.S. standards. Facilities outside the capital vary widely. Several large towns have well-equipped facilities similar to those available in Windhoek, while smaller towns generally do not. Malaria is prevalent only in the north of the country. Malaria prophylaxis is not required in Windhoek, but is suggested for travel to the north.

Safety

Crime is a serious concern in Namibia, but visitors who employ common-sense preventive measures normally enjoy an incident-free stay. Incidents of violent crime directed specifically against Americans or other foreigners are rare, but the number of overall incidents continues to increase. The most common crimes are property-motivated crimes of opportunity, including pickpocketing, purse snatching, vehicle theft, and vehicle break-ins. Taxi drivers have robbed several American passengers; if taxis must be used, radio taxis that display the NABTA logo (Namibia Bus and Taxi Association) are the most reliable. Violent crimes are less frequent than non-violent incidents. Common sense measures such as being alert to one's surroundings, avoiding isolated areas of town, not leaving valuables in parked cars, keeping car doors locked and windows up while driving, and safeguarding purses, wallets, and especially cellular phones are the best deterrents against becoming a victim. Drivers should exercise caution at rest stops outside of towns or away from gasoline stations.

Wild animals may pose some danger. Travelers are advised that, even in the most serene settings, animals are wild and can pose a threat to life and safety. Travelers are cautioned to observe all local or park regulations and heed all instructions given by tour guides. In addition, tourists are advised that potentially dangerous areas sometimes lack fences and warning signs. Appropriate caution should be used in all unfamiliar surroundings.

Calling home

Namibia has a good communication system with a combined fixed-line and mobile-cellular teledensity of about 55 per 100 persons. There are 17,840 Internet hosts.

Diplomatic contact in the United States

Ambassador Patrick Nandago
1605 New Hampshire Avenue NW, Washington, DC 20009
Phone: (202) 986-0540 • Fax: (202) 986-0443

Diplomatic contact from the United States

Ambassador Gail Dennise Mathieu
Embassy: 14 Lossen Street, Windhoek
Private Bag 12029 Ausspannplatz, Windhoek
Phone: (264) (61) 295-8500 • Fax: (264) (61) 295-8603

Niger

Overview of geography, climate, and population

Niger is a landlocked country almost twice the size of Texas. Most of the nation is arid with a tropical section in the south. The terrain is mostly desert with some hills and plains. The land is prone to drought. About 15.3 people live in Niger.

Religion, ethnicity, and language in a nutshell

Eighty percent of residents are Muslim. The remaining 20 percent adhere to Christianity or indigenous faiths. About 55 percent of Nigeriens are of Haoussa lineage, and a little more than 20 percent are of Djerma Sonrai ancestry. Approximately 9 percent of inhabitants are Touareg, about 8 percent are Peuhl, around 5 percent are Kanouri Manga, and about 1 percent are of other lineage. French is the official language. Residents also speak Hausa and Djerma.

Brief political history and today's government

Niger gained independence from France in 1960. Between independence and the early 1990s, the country was under military rule in the 15th and 16th centuries; the area that is now Niger was part of the Songhai Empire. What is now Niger was under French control beginning in 1922. Niger gained independence in 1960. Between independence and the early 1990s, the country was under military rule. In 1993, Niger became a democracy. Colonel Ibrahim Bare took power in a coup d'etat.

Another military coup d'etat deprived Bare of power in 1999. Those who instigated the coup established a democracy later in 1999. Mamadou Tandja was elected president in 1999 and re-elected in 2004. The country's legal system is based on French civil law and traditional law. The legislature includes the national assembly, members of which are publicly elected. The judiciary consists of a state court and court of appeals.

Peace Corps programs

- Business
- Education

Health

Bacterial and protozoal diarrhea, hepatitis A, malaria, schistosomiasis, rabies, meningococcal meningitis, and typhoid fever are among the diseases and illnesses volunteers should be aware of in Niger.

Health facilities are extremely limited in Niamey, and urban centers and completely inadequate outside the capital. Although physicians are generally well trained, even the best hospitals in Niamey suffer from inadequate facilities, antiquated equipment, and shortages of supplies, particularly medicines. Emergency assistance is limited. Travelers must carry their own properly labeled supplies of prescription drugs and preventative medicines.

Malaria is prevalent in Niger. Plasmodium falciparum malaria, the serious and sometimes fatal strain found in Niger, is resistant to the anti-malarial drug chloroquine. The CDC has determined that a traveler who is on an appropriate anti-malarial drug has a greatly reduced chance of contracting the disease. Other personal protective measures, such as the use of insect repellents, also help to reduce malaria risk. Travelers who become ill with a fever or flu-like illness while traveling in a malaria-risk area and up to one year after returning home should seek prompt medical attention and tell the physician about their travel history and the anti-malarial drugs they have been taking.

Tap water is unsafe to drink throughout Niger and should be avoided. Bottled water and beverages are safe, although visitors should be aware than many restaurants and hotels serve tap water. Ice made from tap water is also unsafe to consume.

Safety

U.S. citizens are urged to avoid travel along the border between Niger and Mali, as neither government is able to provide security in this area. On December 14, 2008, two United Nations officials, former Canadian diplomats, were kidnapped by the terrorist group Al Qaeda in the Islamic Maghreb (AQIM) while returning to Niamey after a visit to a Canadian-operated gold mine. The officials were subsequently smuggled across the border to a remote desert region of Mali, where they were released in April 2009. On January 22, 2009, four Europeans were abducted by AQIM operatives along the Mali-Niger border as their tour group was returning from a cultural festival in the Malian town of Anderamboukane. The payment of ransom in these and other kidnapping cases has increased the risk of similar abductions.

U.S. citizens are advised to avoid street demonstrations and maintain security awareness at all times. These demonstrations tend to take place near government buildings, university campuses, or other gathering places such as public parks. Although demonstrations can occur spontaneously, large student demonstrations typically begin in January and February and continue through May. American citizens are, therefore, urged to be particularly vigilant at these times. During previous student demonstrations, NGO and diplomatic vehicles bearing "IT" or "CD" plates have been targeted by rock-throwing demonstrators. Many past demonstrations have featured rock throwing and tire burning, especially at key intersections in the city of Niamey.

Crime is at a critical level, primarily due to thefts, robberies, and residential break-ins. Foreigners are vulnerable to attempts of bribery and extortion by law enforcement authorities. Thefts and petty crimes are common during the day or night; however, armed attacks are normally committed at night by groups of two to four persons, with one assailant confronting the victim with a knife, while the others provide surveillance or a show of force. Tourists should not walk alone around the Gaweye Hotel, the National Museum, or on or near the Kennedy Bridge at any time and should avoid the Petit Marché after dark, as these areas are especially prone to muggings. Walking at night is not recommended as street lights are scarce, providing criminals the protection of darkness to commit their crimes. Recent criminal incidents in Niger have included carjackings, sexual assaults, home invasions, and muggings. In December 2000, an American was killed in a carjacking incident in Niamey, and another American was gravely wounded in a carjacking incident outside of Niamey in 2004. In 2007, two American citizens were raped and two others attacked with a machete. More recently, a World Bank employee was mugged while walking in downtown Niamey on a weekend morning; local bystanders did not intervene. Travelers should keep expensive new electronics out of sight and always keep their doors locked and windows rolled up when stopped at stoplights.

Calling home

The communication system in Niger is inadequate, with a combined fixed-line and mobile-cellular teledensity of only 13 per 100 persons with cellular subscriber-ship increasing rapidly from a small base. There are 253 Internet hosts.

Diplomatic contact in the United States

Ambassador Aminata Djibrilla Maiga Toure
2124 Kalorama Road NW, Washington, DC 20008
Phone: (202) 232-6656 • Fax: (202) 265-1996

Diplomatic contact from the United States

Ambassador Bernadette M. Allen
Embassy: Rue Des Ambassades, Niamey
B. P. 11201, Niamey
Phone: (227) 20-72-26-61 through 64 • Fax: (227) 20-73-31-67

Rwanda

Overview of geography, climate, and population

Rwanda is a landlocked developing country in central Africa, east of Democratic Republic of the Congo. Rwanda is made up of mostly grassy uplands and hills; relief is mountainous, with altitude declining from west to east. The climate is temperate; there are two rainy seasons (February to April and November to January); the climate is mild in mountains with frost and snow possible. The population is 10.4 million.

Religion, ethnicity, and language in a nutshell

In Rwanda, 56.5 percent of residents are Roman Catholic, 26 percent are Protestant, 11.1 percent are Adventist, 4.6 percent are Muslim, 0.1 percent are of indigenous beliefs, and 1.7 percent are non-religious. Eighty-four percent of residents are Hutu (Bantu), 15 percent are Tutsi (Hamitic), and 1 percent are Twa (Pygmy). French, Kinyarwanda, and English are the official languages of Rwanda and universal Bantu vernacular and Kiswahili (Swahili) are also used.

Brief political history and today's government

The legal system is based on German and Belgian civil law systems and customary law; there is a judicial review of legislative acts in the Supreme Court.

Economic snapshot

Rwanda is a poor rural country with about 90 percent of the population engaged in (mainly subsistence) agriculture. It is the most densely populated country in Africa and is landlocked with few natural resources and minimal industry. Primary foreign exchange earners are coffee and tea. The 1994 genocide decimated Rwanda's fragile economic base, severely impoverished the population — particularly women — and eroded the country's ability to attract private and external investment. However, Rwanda has made substantial progress in stabilizing and rehabilitating its economy to pre-1994 levels, although poverty levels are higher now. GDP has rebounded, and inflation has been curbed. Despite Rwanda's fertile ecosystem, food production often does not keep pace with population growth, requiring food imports. Rwanda continues to receive substantial aid money and obtained IMF-World Bank Heavily Indebted Poor Country (HIPC) initiative debt relief in 2005-06. Rwanda also received Millennium Challenge Account Threshold status in 2006. The government has embraced an expansionary fiscal policy to reduce poverty by improving education, infrastructure, and foreign and domestic investment and pursuing market-oriented reforms, although energy shortages, instability in neighboring states, and lack of adequate transportation linkages to other countries continue to handicap growth.

Peace Corps programs

- Health
- HIV/AIDS

Health

HIV/AIDS, diarrhea, hepatitis A, malaria, rabies, and typhoid fever are among the diseases and illnesses volunteers should be aware of in Rwanda.

Medical and dental facilities are limited, and some medicines are in short supply or unavailable. Travelers should bring their own supplies of prescription drugs and preventive medicines. In Kigali, Americans may go to King Faisal Hospital, a private facility that offers limited services and dental facilities. There is also a missionary dental clinic and a few private dentists.

American-operated charitable hospitals with some surgical facilities can be found in Kibagora, in southwestern Rwanda, in Ruhengeri, near the gorilla trekking area, and in Rwinkavu, near the entrance to Akagera National Park.

Safety

There are currently no travel restrictions in place within Rwanda, but travelers should use caution crossing the border into Burundi and eastern Democratic Republic of the Congo (DRC).

The Congo-based Democratic Forces for the Liberation of Rwanda (FDLR), including ex-Rwandese Armed Forces, Interahamwe, and other extremists who participated in the 1994 genocide, remain in eastern Congo. A joint Congolese-Rwandan military operation against the FDLR began in January 2009 inside Congo. The FDLR does not pose a serious security threat inside Rwanda. Twice in 2008, the FDLR launched mortar rounds into Rwanda, near the border town of Gisenyi, and in a separate incident, FDLR cadre crossed the border and killed a local official in the same area. These appear to be isolated incidents.

Pickpocketing in crowded public places is common, as is petty theft from cars and hotel rooms. Although violent crimes such as carjacking, robbery, and home invasion occur in Kigali, they are rarely committed against foreigners. Americans are advised to remain alert, exercise caution, and follow appropriate personal security measures. Although many parts of Kigali are safe at night, walking alone after dark is not recommended because foreigners, including Americans, have occasionally been the targets of robbery.

Calling home

Rwanda has a small, inadequate telephone system primarily serving businesses and the government. The capital, Kigali, is connected to the centers of the provinces by microwave radio relay and, recently, by cellular telephone service. Their combined fixed-line and mobile-cellular telephone density is only about 13 telephones per 100 persons. There are 81 Internet hosts.

Diplomatic contact in the United States

Ambassador James Komonyo

1714 New Hampshire Avenue NW, Washington, DC 20009

Phone: (1) (202) 232-2882 • Fax: (1) (202) 232-4544

Diplomatic contact from the United States

Ambassador W. Stuart Symington

Embassy: 2657 Avenue de la Gendarmerie, Kigali

B. P. 28, Kigali

Phone: (250) 596-400 • Fax: (250) 596-591

Senegal

Overview of geography, climate, and population

Senegal is almost as big as South Dakota, with plains and foothills. The climate is tropical with a rainy season from May to November and a dry period from December to April. Strong winds accompany the rainy season. Hot winds mark the dry season. About 13.7 million people live in Senegal.

Religion, ethnicity, and language in a nutshell

Ninety-four percent of Senegalese are Muslim, 5 percent are Christian, and 1 percent follow traditional faiths. A little more than 40 percent of Senegalese are Wolof, slightly more than 20 percent are of Pular descent, while 15 percent are Serer, approximately 4 percent are of Jola ancestry, and 3 percent are Mandinka. A little more than 1 percent are Soninke, 1 percent are European and Lebanese, and just over 9 percent are of other ethnicities. French is the official language of Senegal. Senegalese also speak Wolof, Pulaar, Jola, and Mandinka.

Brief political history and today's government

The French claimed Senegal as a colony in 1887. The country became independent in 1960. France consolidated its colonies Senegal and French Sudan in 1959. The two colonies, called the Mali Federation, became independent in 1960. In 1982 Senegal and Gambia partnered to create Senegambia, which broke up in 1989. Separatists have been waging a low-intensity war for more than 20 years but have not seceded. From independence to 2000, Senegal had a socialist government.

The republic is now governed by President Abdoulaye Wade. The prime minister is Cheikh Hadjibou Soumare.

The cabinet consists of a Council of Ministers, members of which are appointed by the prime minister and the president. The president is publicly elected and is responsible for appointing the prime minister. The parliament includes the National Assembly, 90 members of which are elected by the public directly and 60 members of which are elected through a party-based system of proportional representation.

The judiciary includes a constitutional court, council of state, Court of Final Appeals, and Court of Appeals.

Economic snapshot

Senegal is part of the West African Economic and Monetary Union and is seeking to intertwine its economy more with those of the countries around it. Senegal depends on foreign aid but has received some debt relief from the IMF. Foreign investors have agreed to mine iron, zircon, and gold.

Peace Corps programs

- Agriculture
- Environment
- Business
- Public health

Health

HIV/AIDS, hepatitis A, typhoid fever, diarrhea, Crimean-Congo hemorrhagic fever, dengue fever, malaria, Rift Valley fever, yellow fever, schistosomiasis, and meningococcal meningitis are among the diseases and illnesses volunteers should be aware of in Senegal.

Medical facilities in Dakar provide a range of treatment, but hospitals fall below Western standards. Outside the capital, health care is rudimentary. American medicines are scarce, but French equivalents are often available, particularly in the capital and other tourist destinations. Visitors should bring their own prescription and over-the-counter medicine, as well as copies of prescriptions. Malaria is prevalent and before leaving the United States, travelers should consult their doctors regarding preventive medicine. Travelers should drink only boiled or filtered water and wash produce in diluted bleach.

Safety

For fear of violence, visitors should avoid the demonstrations that often occur on Friday afternoons in Dakar and outside the capital. Travelers should be especially alert around the Pink Lake because they are vulnerable to crime on its isolated beaches. Volunteers should not visit the lake alone and should avoid it after dark. Highway robbery occurs frequently at night on well-traveled roads, particularly the National Road from Ndioum to Kidira and from Kidira and Tambacounda.

Convicts who escaped from a prison in Guinea in 2007 are possibly at large near the border. Due to land mines and war between rebels and the Senegalese armed forces, volunteers should refrain from visiting the Casamance region west of Kolda unless they fly directly into the Cap Skirring resort or Ziguinchor. Attacks by bandits are on the rise and sometimes occur during the day on main highways.

While the rate of violent crime is relatively low, petty crime occurs often. Visitors are especially vulnerable to pickpockets and purse snatchers in crowds and near tourist attractions. Beggars and street vendors sometimes distract victims to facilitate theft.

Volunteers should avoid solitary walks on beaches and in other remote places and should refrain from walking in poorly-lit areas even with others. Travelers should avoid mass transit. Drivers should keep doors locked and windows closed. Volunteers should carry notarized copies of their passports and other identity papers. Visitors should only carry credit cards immediately before making purchases. Crime rates typically spike before significant holidays. Travelers are especially vulnerable to crime in major cities and in crowds. Avoid wearing jewelry and displaying cash.

Violent crime is rare, but some international visitors have been the victims of armed robberies while walking in small groups. Visitors should seek to avoid injury by immediately complying with robbers or other violent criminals.

Fraudulent business deals are common, and perpetrators often target U.S. citizens. Volunteers should be wary of e-mails discussing money transfers, sale of valuables, or assistance for refugees. Other scams involve requests for citizens' bank account numbers or offers of gold for sale at a bargain.

Calling home

The telephone system in Senegal is fairly reliable. It includes 282,600 land-based telephones and 2.9 million cell phones. There are 199 Internet hosts.

Diplomatic contact in the United States

Ambassador Amadou Lamine Ba

2112 Wyoming Avenue NW, Washington, DC 20008

Phone: (202) 234-0540 • Fax: (202) 332-6315

Diplomatic contact from the United States

Ambassador Marcia S. Bernicat

Embassy: Avenue Jean XXIII at the corner of Rue Kleber, Dakar

B. P. 49, Dakar

Phone: (221) 33-829-2100 • Fax: (221) 33-822-2991

Sierra Leone

Overview of geography, climate, and population

Sierra Leone is in Western Africa, bordering the North Atlantic Ocean between Guinea and Liberia. It is slightly smaller than South Carolina. The country has a coastal belt of mangrove swamps, wooded hill country, upland plateau, and mountains in the East. The climate is tropical, hot, and humid, with a summer rainy season (May to December) and winter dry season (December to April). The population is 6.4 million.

Religion, ethnicity, and language in a nutshell

The inhabitants of Sierra Leone are Muslim (60 percent), Christian (10 percent), and of indigenous beliefs (30 percent.) There are 20 African ethnic groups that make up 90 percent of the population, and 10 percent are refugees from Liberia's recent civil war. There are also small numbers of Europeans, Lebanese, Pakistanis, and Indians. English is the official language, but regular use is limited to a literate minority. Mende is the principal vernacular in the south, and Temne is the principal vernacular in the north. Krio — English-based Creole — is also spoken.

Brief political history and today's government

The legal system is based on English law and customary laws indigenous to local tribes.

Peace Corps programs

- Education

Health

HIV/AIDS, bacterial and protozoal diarrhea, hepatitis A, malaria, yellow fever, schistosomiasis, Lassa fever, and typhoid fever are among the diseases and illnesses volunteers should be aware of in Sierra Leone.

The U.S. Department of State is unaware of any HIV/AIDS entry restrictions for visitors to or foreign residents of Sierra Leone.

There are medical conditions and illnesses in Sierra Leone that are rarely seen in the Western world or that are difficult to treat locally. Emergency medical care in Freetown is poor and limited by both the services available and flight schedules.

Medical facilities in Sierra Leone fall critically short of U.S. and European standards. There is no ambulance service in Sierra Leone, trauma care is extremely limited, and local hospitals should only be used in the event of an extreme medical emergency. Many primary health care workers, especially in rural areas, lack adequate professional training. Instances of misdiagnosis, improper treatment, and the administration of improper drugs have been reported. Quality and comprehensive medical services are very limited in Freetown and are almost nonexistent for all but most minor treatment outside of the capital. Medicines are in short supply and, due to inadequate diagnostic equipment, there is a lack of medical resources, limited medical specialty personnel, and a low availability of complex diagnosis and treatment. Life-threatening emergencies often require evacuation by air ambulance at the patient's expense.

Visitors with serious health concerns, such as diabetes, heart disease, asthma, or people who are on blood thinners — with the exception of aspirin — are discouraged from traveling to Sierra Leone.

All visitors traveling to Sierra Leone must have current vaccinations prior to arrival in Freetown. These include, but are not limited to, tetanus, yellow fever, polio, meningitis, typhoid, hepatitis A and B, and rabies. The cholera vaccine is not required. The International Certificate of Vaccinations yellow card should be hand-carried as proof of current yellow-fever inoculation.

Visitors should begin taking malaria prophylaxis two weeks prior to arrival and hand-carry enough medication for the duration of their visit. It is mandatory that visitors bring their own supply of medications.

The quality of medications in Sierra Leone is inconsistent, and counterfeit drugs remain a problem. Local pharmacies are generally unreliable. In the event medications are needed, such as over-the-counter medication, antibiotics, allergy remedies, or malaria prophylaxis, travelers may contact the U.S. Embassy's American Citizen Services (ACS) Unit to receive general information about reliable pharmacies.

Gastrointestinal diseases, malaria, and HIV/AIDS pose serious risks to travelers in Sierra Leone. Because sanitary conditions in Sierra Leone are poor and refrigeration is unreliable, caution should be used when eating uncooked vegetables, salads, seafood, or meats at restaurants and hotels. Only bottled water should be consumed.

Safety

Security in Sierra Leone has improved significantly since the end of the civil war in 2002. The United Nations Peacekeeping Mission in Sierra Leone (UNAMSIL) withdrew in December 2005, and Sierra Leone resumed responsibilities for its own security. The Sierra Leonean police are working to improve their professionalism and capabilities, but fall short of American standards in response time, communications, and specialty skills.

Areas outside Freetown lack most basic services. Travelers are urged to exercise caution, especially when traveling beyond the capital. Road conditions are hazardous, and serious vehicle accidents are common. Emergency response to vehicular and other accidents ranges from slow to nonexistent.

There are occasional unauthorized, possibly armed, roadblocks outside Freetown, where travelers might be asked to pay a small amount of money to the personnel manning the roadblock. Because many Sierra Leoneans outside of Freetown speak broken English or Krio, it can be difficult for foreigners to communicate their identity. Public demonstrations are rare but can turn violent. U.S. citizens are advised to avoid large crowds, political rallies, and street demonstrations and maintain security awareness at all times. In addition, American citizens should carry a means of communication at all times (fully charged cell phone with emergency contacts).

Entrenched poverty in Sierra Leone has led to criminality. Visitors and resident Americans have experienced armed mugging, assault, and burglary. Petty crime and pickpocketing of wallets, cell phones, and passports are very common especially on the ferry to and from Lungi International Airport. Law enforcement authorities usually respond to crimes slowly, if at all. Police investigative response is often incomplete and does not provide support to victims. Inefficiency and corruption is a serious problem at all levels within the government of Sierra Leone. Americans traveling to or residing in Sierra Leone should maintain a heightened sense of awareness of their surroundings to help avoid becoming the victims of crime.

Calling home

Sierra Leone has marginal telephone service. The national microwave radio relay trunk system connects Freetown to Bo and Kenema; mobile-cellular service is growing rapidly from a small base. There are 273 Internet hosts.

Diplomatic contact in the United States

Ambassador Bockari Kortu Stevens
1701 19th Street NW, Washington, DC 20009
Phone: (202) 939-9261, 939-9262, and 939-9263 • Fax: (202) 483-1793

Diplomatic contact from the United States

Ambassador June Carter Perry
Embassy: Southridge-Hill Station, Freetown
Phone: (232) (22) 515 000 or (76) 515 000 • Fax: (232) (22) 515 355

South Africa

Overview of geography, climate, and population

South Africa is a primarily semi-arid, drought-prone country almost twice as big as Texas. Its territory includes a central plateau, hills and plains. The central plateau, called the Great Escarpment, contains the High Veld, the Middle Veld, and the Transvaal Basin, as well as the Orange and Limpopo rivers. South Africa does not have an abundance of major rivers or lakes, so water conservation is essential. About 49 million people live in South Africa.

Religion, ethnicity, and language in a nutshell

About 11 percent of South Africans are Zion Christian, approximately 8 percent are Pentecostal/Charismatic, about 7 percent are Catholic, around 7 percent are Methodist, about 7 percent follow the Dutch Reformed faith, and approximately 4 percent are Anglican. A little more than 1 percent of South Africans are Muslim; other sects of Christianity account for 36 percent of the population, and 15 percent follow no religion. Slightly more than 3 percent of residents of South Africa describe themselves as having another religion or declined to specify.

Isi Zulu speakers make up about 23 percent of the population of South Africa; a little more than 17 percent speak Isi Xhosa. About 13 percent of South Africans speak Afrikaans, a little more than 9 percent use the Sepedi tongue, and a little more than 8 percent communicate in English. Slightly more than 8 percent of South Africans speak Setswana, a little less than 8 percent use Sesotho, a bit more than 4 percent are Xitsonga speakers, and around 7 percent use other languages.

Nearly 80 percent of South Africans are black Africans, about 10 percent are white, and a little more than 2 percent are South Asian Indian.

Brief political history and today's government

About two millennia ago, the Bushmen, Hottentots, and Bantu-speaking tribes came to the area now known as South Africa. The Dutch settled the area in 1652. In the early 19th century, the colony fell under British control. South Africa gained independence in 1931. Racial segregation and political repression of blacks began in 1948. The country adopted a republican form of government in 1961 and established four reservations for blacks. The reservations, called homelands, were Bophuthatswana, Ciskei, Transkei, and Venda. In 1989 President F.W. De Klerk took office and began to dismantle apartheid. In 1994, the first integrated elections brought to power Nelson Mandela, an anti-apartheid crusader. The current president is Thabo Mbeki. The president is responsible for appointing the cabinet. The National Assembly is responsible for electing the president. The parliament includes the National Assembly and the National Council of Provinces. The 400 members of the National Assembly are publicly elected. The 90 members of the National Council of Provinces are elected by provincial governments. The judiciary consists of a Constitutional Court, a Supreme Court of Appeals, High Courts, and Magistrate Courts.

Peace Corps programs

- Education
- AIDS prevention
- Development of non-governmental organizations

Health

HIV/AIDS, diarrhea, hepatitis A, typhoid fever, Crimean Congo hemorrhagic fever, malaria, and schistosomiasis are among the diseases and illnesses volunteers should be aware of in South Africa.

Privately-owned clinics in cities and near wildlife reserves are up to Western standards but are sometime less than adequate in remote areas. Visitors can obtain the equivalents of most medicines available in the United States. Malaria is a risk in the provinces of Limpopo and Mpumalanga. Mosquitoes carrying malaria live in the Kruger National Park and other game reserves.

The area north of the Tugela River, except the cities in Richards Bay, also has malarial mosquitoes. The danger of catching malaria is lower from June to September. Before leaving the United States, travelers should take anti-malarial medicines.

Safety

Visitors should avoid crowds, especially political demonstrations. Vehicle break-ins, armed robberies, carjackings, and muggings are common. Criminal gangs frequently follow people home from malls or the Tambo International Airport in Johannesburg and rob them, sometimes using guns. If visitors experience such a robbery, they should cooperate immediately to reduce the risk of injury. To decrease the likelihood of being targeted by such a gang, travelers should appear alert and avoid wearing jewelry, displaying cash, or buying expensive items.

Drivers should hide valuables and keep windows closed and doors locked. Victims of carjackings should comply immediately to reduce the risk of being murdered by the attackers.

More reported rapes occur in South Africa than in any other country. Due to high HIV/AIDS rates, rape survivors should seek testing and anti-retroviral treatment.

Assault, theft, and armed robbery are common near hotels and mass transit centers in densely populated areas. Muggers have attacked foreigners on trains between Pretoria and Johannesburg. Visitors should avoid inviting strangers into their homes because foreigners have sometimes been drugged and robbed after doing so.

Theft of items from luggage is common at the Tambo, Cape Town International, and Johannesburg airports. Passengers changing planes and using small carriers are most vulnerable to thieves who steal from baggage. Visitors should lock their bags, use the plastic wrapping service the airport offers, and avoid packing valuables in checked luggage. Travelers should also keep packing lists.

Gang fights and muggings are common in Cape Town. Visitors should remain alert, walk in groups, and refrain from taking valuables with them.

Robbers frequently target armored cars, particularly in December and January, because stores send more money to banks during those months than at other times of the year.

Perpetrators of frauds involving credit cards, counterfeit money, and check cashing target foreigners. Visitors should avoid accepting help, or assisting others with using cash dispensing machines. Travelers should keep their eyes on their credit cards when shopkeepers process them. Perpetrators of frauds sometimes contact international visitors by e-mail or phone to ask questions about their finances and attempt to persuade them to invest in non-existent businesses.

Calling home
The communication system in South Africa is the best-developed and most modern in Africa, with a combined fixed-line and mobile-cellular teledensity that exceeds 110 telephones per 100 persons. There are 1.73 million Internet hosts.

Diplomatic contact in the United States
Ambassador Welile Augustine Nhlapo
3051 Massachusetts Avenue NW, Washington, DC 20008
Phone: (202) 232-4400 • Fax: (202) 265-1607

Diplomatic contact from the United States
Ambassador Donald Gips
Embassy: 877 Pretorius Street, Pretoria
P. O. Box 9536, Pretoria 0001
Phone: (27) (12) 431-4000 • Fax: (27) (12) 342-2299
Consulate(s) general: Cape Town, Durban, and Johannesburg

Swaziland
Overview of geography, climate, and population
Swaziland is a landlocked, drought-prone country nearly surrounded by South Africa. About 1.1 million people live in Swaziland. The climate ranges from tropical to almost temperate. Swaziland contains mountains, hills, and plains.

Religion, ethnicity, and language in a nutshell
Forty percent of Swazis are Zionist, a faith that combines Judaism with traditional veneration of ancestors. Twenty percent of residents practice Roman Catholicism, 20 percent are Muslim, and 30 percent follow other faiths, including Bahai, Anglican, Methodist, Mormon, and Jewish. Ninety-seven percent of Swazis are African, and 3 percent are European. The Africans are mostly Swazi. English and siSwati are the official languages.

Brief political history and today's government

The kingdom of Swaziland was established in the 18th century. The Boers and the British controlled the kingdom until 1902. The British ruled alone until independence in 1968.

Demonstrations by students and workers led to promises of democracy and reform by King Mswati III in the last decade of the 20th century but many of the changes never materialized. Political parties were long banned but their legality is still undecided. The Prime Minister is Absolom Themba Dlamini. The prime minister selects members of the cabinet who cannot take their seats without the king's approval. The parliament includes the Senate and the House of Assembly. The Senate includes 30 seats, with ten members chosen by the House of Assembly and 20 appointed by the king. The House of Assembly has 65 members, ten of which the king chooses and 55 of which the public elects.

Local councils nominate candidates for the House of Assembly. The judiciary consists of a High Court and a Supreme Court. The king chooses the judges of both courts.

Economic snapshot

The South African rand's fluctuations in value determine those of the lilangeni, Swaziland's currency. Payments from the Southern African Customs Union make up more than half of the national government's income. Remittances from Swazis employed in South Africa supplement governmental revenues.

Peace Corps programs

- Public health
- AIDS prevention

Health

HIV/AIDS, malaria, schistosomiasis, typhoid fever, hepatitis A, diarrhea, yellow fever, cholera, and tuberculosis are among the diseases and illnesses volunteers should be aware of in Swaziland.

Health care is rudimentary across the country. A small clinic in the capital has adequate equipment and personnel for routine treatment. The facilities and staff needed for extensive procedures are available in South Africa. Visitors should bring their own medicines as well as doctor's notes describing them. Many prescription pharmaceuticals are for sale in South Africa.

Safety

Visitors should avoid demonstrations for fear of violence by the army members who are often called in to disperse participants. Visitors are most vulnerable to petty and violent crimes in Mbabane but similar incidents occur outside the capital. Muggings and other crimes can turn lethal, and resisting attackers does not usually dissuade them. Carjacking is prevalent and, if attacked, drivers should comply without delay. Visitors are particularly vulnerable on dark, crowded city streets, but muggers also attack during the day. Many street robberies have occurred while crowds watched. To avoid becoming targets for criminals when in public, travelers should not wear jewelry, use cell phones, or display cash. Visitors should change money only at authorized centers and avoid street vendors.

Calling home

Swaziland has 44,000 land-based telephones and 250,000 cell phones. There are 41,600 Internet hosts in Swaziland.

Diplomatic contact in the United States

Ambassador Ephraim Mandla Hlophe
1712 New Hampshire Avenue, NW, Washington, DC 20009
Phone: (202) 234-5002 • Fax: (202) 234-8254

Diplomatic contact from the United States

Ambassador Maurice S. Parker
Embassy: 2350 Mbabane Place, Mbabane
P. O. Box 199, Mbabane
Phone: (268) 404-2445 • Fax: (268) 404-2059

Tanzania

Overview of geography, climate, and population

Tanzania is a drought-prone country of 41 million — a little bit bigger than twice the size of California. It borders the Indian Ocean. The climate ranges from tropical to temperate, depending on elevation. The terrain includes coastal plains, plateaus in the center of the country, and mountainous regions in the north and south.

Religion, ethnicity, and language in a nutshell

On the mainland, about one third of Tanzanians are Christian, about 35 percent follow Islam, and approximately 35 percent practice indigenous beliefs. Ninety-nine percent of residents of Zanzibar are Muslim. On the mainland, 95 percent of Tanzanians are members of 130 Bantu tribes. About 1 percent of Tanzanians who live on the mainland are Asian, European, and Arab. On Zanzibar, Tanzanians trace their lineage to Arabia and Africa. The official languages are Kishwahili, Swahili, and English. Most Tanzanians speak local dialects.

Brief political history and today's government

The mainland's legislature consists of a National Assembly that has 274 members, 232 of which are publicly elected, 37 are women of the president's choosing, and five are part of the Zanzibar House of Representatives. A Permanent Commission of Enquiry, Court of Appeal, High Court, District Courts, and Primary Courts comprise the judiciary. The nation's legal system evolved out of English common law.

Economic snapshot

Agriculture is the backbone of Tanzania's economy, with farm products comprising 85 percent of exports. Tanzania also relies on aid from the World Bank and the International Monetary Fund. Private sector growth and investment have increased in recent years due to changes in the banking system.

Peace Corps programs

- Education
- AIDS prevention
- Environmental education
- Public health
- Agriculture

Health

Medical facilities are limited, and medicines are sometimes unavailable, even in Dar es Salaam. There are hospitals on Zanzibar that can treat minor ailments. For any major medical problems, including dental work, travelers should consider obtaining medical treatment in Nairobi or South Africa where more advanced medical care is available.

Cholera is prevalent in many areas of Tanzania, and several strains of malaria are endemic. Malaria prophylaxes are advised, and travelers are strongly advised to carry malaria prophylaxes with them. Visitors should consult their physicians before traveling to learn about prophylaxis and the possible side effects of various available medications. In addition, other personal protective measures, such as the use of insect repellents, help to reduce malaria risk. Travelers who become ill with a fever or flu-like illness while traveling in a malaria-risk area and up to one year after returning home should seek prompt medical attention and tell the physician their travel history and what anti-malarial medications they have been taking.

Safety

Terrorist incidents in the recent past highlight the continuing threat posed by terrorism in East Africa and the capacity of terrorist groups to carry out such attacks. On August 7, 1998, terrorists bombed the U.S. Embassies in Dar es Salaam and Nairobi, Kenya. On November 28, 2002, terrorists bombed a hotel in Mombasa, Kenya, approximately 50 miles north of the Kenya -Tanzania border, and unsuccessfully attempted to shoot down an Israeli charter plane departing Mombasa Airport. U.S. citizens should be aware of the risk of indiscriminate attacks on civilian targets, including usual gathering places of tourists and Westerners. At all times, travelers should maintain a high level of security vigilance. They should avoid political rallies and related public gatherings. In the past, peaceful demonstrations have turned violent with little or no warning as riot police clashed with demonstrators.

Crime is a serious problem in Tanzania, and visitors should be alert and cautious. Street crime in Dar es Salaam is common and includes mugging, vehicle theft, "smash and grab" attacks on vehicles, armed robbery, and burglary. Thieves and pickpockets on buses and trains steal from inattentive passengers.

Crime involving firearms is becoming more common. A series of robberies involving increasing levels of violence has occurred along the coast and on Zanzibar. Robbers have held up tour buses and dive boats at gunpoint. In spring 2008, there were a string of armed robberies in hotels along the east coast of Ungunja (the main island) in Zanzibar.

Calling home

There are 169,135 land-based telephones and 6.7 million cell phones. There are 20,757 Internet hosts.

Diplomatic contact in the United States

Ambassador Ombeni Yohana Sefue
2139 R Street NW, Washington, DC 20008
Phone: (202) 939-6125 • Fax: (202) 797-7408

Diplomatic contact from the United States

Ambassador (vacant): Charge d'Affares Lawrence Andre

Embassy: 686 Old Bagamoyo Road, Msasani, Dar es Salaam

P. O. Box 9123, Dar es Salaam

Phone: (255) (22) 266-8001 • Fax: (255) (22) 266-8238, 266-8373

Togo

Overview of geography, climate, and population

Togo is a hot, drought-prone country almost as big as West Virginia. The south of Togo is tropical while the north is dry. The terrain ranges from plateaus in the south to hills in the center to savanna in the north. There are plains along the coasts, which are marked by wetlands and lagoons. About 6 million people live in Togo.

Religion, ethnicity, and language in a nutshell

Twenty-nine percent of Togolese are Christian, 20 percent follow Islam, and 51 percent adhere to indigenous beliefs. Ninety-nine percent of Togolese belong to 37 African tribes including the Ewe, Mina, and Kabre. Less than 1 percent trace their ancestry to Syria and Lebanon. French is the official language. Residents who live in the south speak Ewe and Mina, while those in the north are Kabye and Dagomba speakers.

Brief political history and today's government

Beginning in the late 19th century, Germany claimed Togo as a protectorate. In the early 20th century, Britain and France split the country into British Togoland and French Togo. British Togoland became part of Ghana in 1957; French Togo achieved independence in 1960. In 1967, General Gnassingbe Eyadema took power and was president for about 40 years.

Eyadema's party has ruled most of the time since he took office, and his son, Faure Gnassingbe, took office after he died in 2005. Togo is a republic but is becoming a multi-party democracy. The legislature consists of the National Assembly. Members of the National Assembly are elected by the public. The judiciary includes the Court of Appeal and the Supreme Court. The nation's legal system evolved out of the French tradition.

Economic snapshot

The majority of the population is employed in agriculture, both to feed themselves and to produce crops for sale. About 40 percent of export revenue comes from cotton, coffee, and cocoa. Phosphate is also an important export. For about ten years, the Togolese government has been trying to pique the interest of international investors and reform the economy, with the backing of the International Monetary Fund and the World Bank.

Peace Corps programs

- Education
- Business
- AIDS prevention
- Environment

Health

HIV/AIDS, hepatitis A, typhoid fever, diarrhea, yellow fever, malaria, meningococcal meningitis, avian flu, and schistosomiasis are among the diseases and illnesses volunteers should be aware of in Togo.

Medical facilities are limited, and emergency care is virtually non-existent. Pharmacies are not consistently stocked, so visitors should bring their own medicines in labeled containers. Volunteers should consult their doctors about anti-malarial drugs before leaving the United States.

Safety

Travelers should avoid rallies, which can turn violent. The rate of violent crime has increased across the country. Machete-wielding assailants have attacked victims in dark neighborhoods of the capital. Travelers visiting the capital should avoid the Grand Marché neighborhood, the beach road, and the area near the Ghanaian border. To avoid muggings and theft of handbags, volunteers should refrain from visiting the beach and the market in Lomé. The rate of carjackings has increased. Thieves target passengers in taxis, so visitors should not share cabs with strangers.

Operators of business scams often target foreigners. Frauds typically begin with unexpected e-mails that discuss transferring money or shipping goods out of the country. Criminals will sometimes ask for bank account numbers.

Calling home

The telecommunications system is somewhat reliable. There are 15 land-based telephones and cell phones for every 100 people. The country has 82,000 landlines and 708,000 mobile phones. There are 702 Internet hosts.

Diplomatic contact in the United States
Ambassador Kadangha Limbiya Bariki
2208 Massachusetts Avenue NW, Washington, DC 20008
Phone: (202) 234-4212 • Fax: (202) 232-3190

Diplomatic contact from the United States
Ambassador Patricia McMahon Hawkins
Embassy: 4332 Blvd. Gnassingbe Eyadema, Cite OUA, Lome
B. P. 852, Lome; 2300 Lome Place, Washington, DC 20512-2300
Phone: (228) 261-5470 • Fax: (228) 261-5501

Uganda

Overview of geography, climate, and population
Uganda is a landlocked country of about 32.3 million people and not quite as
large as Oregon. The climate is mostly tropical and usually wet. The northeast
section of the country tends to be hot and dry. Two dry periods typically occur
from December to February and June to August. Uganda's terrain consists of plateaus and mountains. Uganda contains part of Lake Victoria, the largest lake on
the continent. Other lakes include Lake Kyoga, Edward, and Albert.

Religion, ethnicity, and language in a nutshell
About 40 percent of Ugandans are Roman Catholic, and 42 percent follow Prot-
estantism, including Anglicanism, Pentecostalism, and the Seventh-day Adventist
faith. About 12 percent adhere to Islam, 3 percent believe in another religion, and
a little less than 1 percent follow no faith. Approximately 16 percent of Ugandans
are ethnically Baganda, a little less than 10 percent are of Banyakole ancestry,
a little more than 8 percent are of Basoga lineage, approximately 7 percent are
Bakiga, about 6 percent are of Iteso heritage, approximately 6 percent are Langi,
nearly 5 percent are Acholi, more than 4 percent are Basigu, about 4 percent are
Lugbara, and about 3 percent are Bunyoro. Thirty percent describe their ethnicity as "other." The official language is English. Other languages include Ganda
and Luganda. Ugandans also speak Arabic, Swahili, a variety of Niger-Congo
languages, and several Nilo-Saharan tongues.

Brief political history and today's government
Britain claimed Uganda as a protectorate in the late 19th century. Uganda gained
its independence in 1962. Despot Idi Amin governed Uganda in the 1970s. Amin

ordered the killing of about 300,000 citizens who opposed his regime. Milton Obote took office after Amin and is believed to have brought about the deaths of 100,000 Ugandans. Yoweri Museveni has been in power since 1986 and has had a fairly stable government.

The National Assembly comprises the legislature. The National Assembly has 332 members, 215 of whom are publicly elected. Sub-groups of the remaining 104 are chosen by such societal groups as women, military members, people with disabilities, teens, and workers.

The judiciary includes the Court of Appeals and the High Court. The president suggests justices to serve on the Court of Appeal, and the recommendations are subject to the approval of National Assembly members. Customary law and British common law inform the legal system.

Economic snapshot

Agriculture is the keystone of Uganda's economy. Eighty percent of workers are farmers. Coffee is the main export. In recent decades, the Ugandan government has reformed the country's currency, increased export revenues, and given government workers raises. Uganda's economy is steadily growing.

Peace Corps programs

- AIDS prevention
- Public health education on HIV

Health

HIV/AIDS, diarrhea, hepatitis A, typhoid fever, malaria, chikungunya, plague, African sleeping sickness, schistosomiasis, Ebola hemorrhagic fever, Marburg hemorrhagic fever, pneumonic plague, and meningitis are among the diseases and illnesses volunteers should be aware of in Uganda.

Health care is rudimentary, even in the capital. Emergency care is poor, and surgery is largely unavailable. Medicine and equipment are scarce. Visitors should carry their own prescription and over-the-counter pharmaceuticals. Malaria is a significant threat. Visitors should consult their physicians about anti-malarial medicine before leaving the United States.

Safety

Rebels who target Americans for abduction and murder are active near the Sudanese and Congolese borders. Bandits and land mines are also hazards in the north, west, and southwest border regions.

In 2005, the Lord's Resistance Army rebel military group killed a foreigner in the Murchison Falls National Park. The government has increased security at the park since the attack. Nonetheless, when travelers visit the north bank of the Victoria Nile River, which runs through the park, they should remain in the Delta Circuit section west of the Paraa Safari Lodge. The Delta Circuit is also known as the Buligi Circuit.

A band of weapon-wielding men murdered two American missionaries in the Yumbe district in 2004.

Volunteers visiting northern Uganda should be certain of their plans for lodging, travel, and communications before arriving in the region. Travelers risk their safety if they enter the area to visit camps for displaced people without associating with a sponsoring organization.

Karamojong soldiers have frequently attacked vehicles and committed armed banditry in northeastern Uganda. Skirmishes between Karamojong soldiers and the Uganda People's Defense Forces also occur periodically. Volunteers should refrain from traveling to the Karamoja region for fear of violence.

In 2007, a band of Congolese raiders attacked the town of Butogota in the Kanungu District, killing three Ugandans. In 1999, members of the Interahamwe, one of the organizations that perpetrated genocide in Rwanda, killed four Ugandans and eight tourists in Bwindi Impenetrable National Park, which is popular with tourists who wish to see gorillas. The government military now guards the park and security staff escort tourists while viewing gorillas. The Ugandan military has a base at the Ishasha Camp in the Queen Elizabeth National Park.

In 2006 and 2007, the Ugandan military clashed with rebels on the western border with the Democratic Republic of Congo. The government military also fought with Congolese warriors on Lake Albert in western Uganda in 2007. In August 2007, a Briton working for an oil company on the lake died in the cross-fire. In September 2007, an exchange of fire between the Ugandan and Congolese armed forces killed several people.

In February 2008, attackers fatally shot a Belgian tourist climbing Mt. Elgon in the Mt. Elgon National Park. An unknown assailant shot the tourist as she stepped out of her tent at night. Park staff believes that the shooter was a cattle rustler.

Beginning in March 2008, the Ugandan military began massing in the area of Mt. Elgon to remove insurgents from caves on the mountains. Volunteers who plan to climb Mt. Elgon should first determine the degree of danger by contacting the U.S. embassy in Kampala or the Ugandan Wildlife Authority.

Political rallies occur occasionally in the capital and other cities. Demonstrations can turn violent with seemingly no provocation, so visitors should avoid them. Volunteers should listen to news reports to learn of upcoming demonstrations.

Pedestrians should be wary of armed robbers who attack even during the day in well-traveled areas. Pickpocketing and purse snatching are common in all public places, including mass transit vehicles. Thieves looking to steal valuables target cars parked or stuck in traffic. Such thefts have sometimes occurred although the items were hidden in locked vehicles that were parked in areas monitored by security guards. Banditry and carjacking are also risks. Bandits sometimes force cars off the road even during the day. Victims of such attacks should reduce their risk of injury by complying immediately with the assailants. Volunteers should avoid traveling at night, particularly in remote areas.

Burglary and armed robbery are common. The rate of armed robberies in Kampala is on the rise. Many armed robbers have targeted victims as they came home after dark.

Rapists frequently target foreign women, sometimes while the women are riding motorcycle taxis.

Visitors should refuse all food and drink offered by strangers because the items might contain drugs intended to sedate potential victims of rape or robbery. Even food and drink in sealed containers should be considered potentially dangerous. Customers of restaurants and bars should always keep their drinks in sight to prevent criminals from spiking them with sedatives. Patrons of bars and restaurants should remain in groups to decrease their risk of sexual assault.

The frequency of financial fraud is on the rise. Scams often involve credit cards, checks, and wire transfers, so visitors should use money orders and avoid providing bank account information to strangers.

Calling home

The telecommunications system is quite lacking. There are 108,100 land-based telephones and 2.9 million cell phones. There are 546 Internet hosts.

Diplomatic contact in the United States

Ambassador Perezi Karukubiro Kamunanwire
5911 16th Street NW, Washington, DC 20011
Phone: (202) 726-7100 through 7102, (202) 726-0416 • Fax (202) 726-1727

Diplomatic contact from the United States

Ambassador Steven Browning
Embassy: 1577 Ggaba Road, Kampala
P. O. Box 7007, Kampala
Phone: (256) (414) 259 791 through 93, 95 • Fax (256) (414) 258-794

Zambia

Overview of geography, climate, and population

Zambia is a landlocked country of 11.8 million a little bigger than Texas. The climate is tropical with a rainy season occurring from October to April. Tropical storms and droughts are common. Zambia has hills, plateaus and mountains.

Religion, ethnicity, and language in a nutshell

Fifty to 75 percent of Zambians are Christians, about 25 to 50 percent follow Islam and Hinduism, and 1 percent adhere to indigenous beliefs. Almost 99 percent of Zambians are ethnically African, a little more than 1 percent trace their ancestry to Europe, and less than 1 percent are of another lineage. English is the official language.

Other common languages spoken include Bemba, Kaonda, Lozi, Lunda, Luvale, Nyanja, and Tonga. Zambians also speak dozens of other aboriginal languages.

Brief political history and today's government

Zambia became a British protectorate called Northern Rhodesia in the late 19th century after a Scottish explorer surveyed it in the middle of the 1800s. From the early 1950s through the early 1960s, Northern and Southern Rhodesia combined with Nyasaland formed a federation. Zambia broke away from the federation and gained independence from Britain in 1964. Kenneth Kaunda became president following independence and kept the office until 1991. The United National Independence Party was the only political party until 1991, when free elections put Frederick Chiluba of the Movement for Multiparty Democracy into office. Zambians elected another member of the Movement for Multiparty Democracy, Levy Mwanawasa, in 2001 and again in 2006.

The legislature consists of the National Assembly, which has 158 seats. The president chooses eight members of the National Assembly and the rest are elected by popular vote. The judiciary includes the Supreme Court and the High Court. The nation's legal system reflects customary and English common law.

Economic snapshot

Copper exports are essential to Zambia's economy. Copper mines used to be government owned, but private companies took them over in recent years. Copper production has been growing bit by bit since 2004. Zambia's currency is fairly stable and inflation is low.

Peace Corps programs

- Agriculture
- Public health
- Education
- AIDS prevention
- Environment

Health

HIV/AIDS, hepatitis A, typhoid fever, diarrhea, plague, malaria, rabies, and schistosomiasis are among the diseases and illnesses volunteers should be aware of in Zambia.

Public health care facilities are typically short staffed and poorly supplied. Private facilities offer adequate care for non-emergencies. For emergency procedures, patients typically go to South Africa, the United States, or Europe.

Except in large cities, even routine health care is rudimentary. Health care providers typically require patients to pay for services in cash before leaving clinics. To cope with shortages of medicines, volunteers should bring their own pharmaceuticals in labeled containers from the drugstore. Visitors should also carry their doctors' prescriptions for the medicines.

Safety

Congolese militias are a threat in northern Luapula Province and along the border between Zambia and the Democratic Republic of Congo, so travelers should avoid visiting these areas. Land mines are a risk near the eastern, western, and northern borders.

Travelers should avoid rallies because they can suddenly turn violent. Carjacking, theft, mugging, and burglary happen frequently in the capital and other large cities even in the daytime. Crime is most prevalent in city centers and low-income areas. Carjackers typically pull up behind a car that has just entered a driveway or pretend to have car trouble with which they need the victim's help. Thieves sometimes target public and private vehicles stopped in traffic. Criminals have sometimes preyed on victims of car accidents by stealing their belongings while pretending to help them. Drivers should keep windows closed and doors locked, and avoid traveling at night.

Calling home
The telecommunications system is fairly reliable. There are 93,000 land-based telephones and 1.6 million cell phones in Zambia. There are 7,423 Internet hosts.

Diplomatic contact in the United States
Ambassador Inonge Mbikusita-Lewanika
2419 Massachusetts Avenue NW, Washington, DC 20008
Phone: (202) 265-9717 through 9719 • Fax (202) 332-0826

Diplomatic contact from the United States
Ambassador Donald E. Booth
Embassy: corner of Independence and United Nations Avenues, Lusaka
P. O. Box 31617, Lusaka
Phone: (260) (211) 250-955 • Fax (260) (211) 252-225

Asia

Cambodia
Overview of geography, climate, and population
Cambodia is a country of about 14.2 million that is nearly the size of Oklahoma. Cambodia borders the gulf of Thailand; the climate is tropical with monsoons occurring from May to November. The dry season takes place from December through April. Cambodia is prone to drought and flooding.

Religion, ethnicity, and language in a nutshell

Ninety-five percent of Cambodians are Theravada Buddhist and 5 percent follow other religions. Ninety percent of Cambodians are ethnically Khmer, 5 percent trace their ancestry to Vietnam, 1 percent are of Chinese lineage, and 4 percent are of another heritage. Ninety-five percent of the population speaks the official Khmer language, and the remaining 5 percent speak French and English. Sixty-seven percent of Cambodians are of Malay descent. Fifteen percent of the population are of Chinese descent. Six percent of Cambodians are indigenous and 12 percent are of other heritage.

Brief political history and today's government

What is now known as Cambodia was part of the Angkor Empire that was at the height of power between the 900s and the 1200s. The French claimed what is now Cambodia as part of French Indochina in the late 19th century. The Japanese occupied the country during the 1940s and it became independent in 1953. In 1975 the Khmer Rouge took over and was later responsible for the deaths of more than 1 million citizens. Vietnam occupied the country from 1978 to 1988. A civil war overtook the country in 1978 and lasted for 13 years. The U.N. organized elections in 1993, which led to a government that was disbanded in 1997 as a result of civil conflict. Another administration took power in 1998. Some members of the Khmer Rouge are waiting to be tried for crimes against humanity. After elections in 2003, it took a year to form a coalition government due to factional disputes. A new national government is to be elected in the summer of 2008.

The legislature consists of the National Assembly, which has 123 publicly elected members, and the Senate, which consists of 61 members, two appointed by the monarch, and two elected by the National Assembly.

The judiciary includes the Supreme Council of the Magistracy and the Supreme Court.

The nation's legal system includes codes left over from French rule, decrees by the monarchy, legislative acts, customary law, and common law.

Economic snapshot

Cambodia's economy has expanded steadily since the beginning of the 21st century. The garment industry is the backbone of the economy. A bilateral agreement with the United States established that Cambodia would get a guaranteed amount of textile imports in exchange for bettering working conditions. In 2005, a World Trade Organization trade agreement expired and left Cambodian textile manufacturers to compete with China and India. Tourism in Cambodia is growing, and the government is forming ties with the World Bank and the International Monetary Fund. More than half of Cambodians are younger than 21 years and are largely uneducated.

Peace Corps Programs

- English education
- Teacher training

Health

HIV/AIDS, diarrhea, hepatitis A, typhoid, dengue fever, malaria, Japanese encephalitis, and avian flu are among the diseases and illnesses volunteers should be aware of in Cambodia.

Health care across the country falls below Western standards. A few medical facilities in the capital can provide adequate emergency care. There is one clinic in Siem Reap that can take care of patients with minor problems. There is almost no health care outside Phnom Penh.

Volunteers should bring their own medicines because supplies are limited and pharmaceuticals sold in Cambodia are often of poor quality.

Safety

Terrorism targeting U.S. citizens, particularly in popular tourist spots, is a hazard. Examples of potential terrorist targets include hotels, houses of worship, beach resorts, clubs, bars, restaurants, schools, and parks and outdoor concert venues.

Visitors should not take part in rallies and should refrain from joining large crowds.

In 2000, dissidents based in the United States organized violent strikes against official buildings in the capital. In 2003, participants in a civil disturbance attacked the embassy of Thailand as well as businesses with Thai proprietors. In 2006, authorities charged half a dozen suspects with conspiring to bomb targets in the capital during the Water Festival. In 2007, criminals placed three homemade bombs at the Vietnam-Cambodia Friendship Monument in the capital. Only one of the bombs partially exploded, and no one was injured.

For fear of land mines and explosives that have not detonated, visitors should not take woodland walks or venture into rice paddies without a guide who is familiar with the area and its history. Volunteers should avoid any object that appears to be military in nature and should report suspected land mines to the Cambodia Mine Action Center by calling 023-368-841 Travelers who wish to visit the Angor Wat temple and the city of Siem Reap should arrive by plane. If flying is impossible, visitors who take boats or cars should use only major highways and stay in the main temple complex after arriving.

Criminals have access to military-grade weapons and bombs. Armed robbers target international visitors, among others. To reduce the risk of death or serious injury, robbery victims should comply immediately. Police generally do not respond to international visitors' complaints of crime. The police do not patrol rural areas of the provinces. Visitors should avoid solitary walks in Sihanoukville after twilight. The waterside is especially dangerous, and pedestrians have frequently been assaulted.

Visitors are particularly vulnerable to motorcycle-based purse snatchers during major festivals and at tourist attractions in Sihanoukville, Siem Reap, and Phnom Penh.

Travelers should avoid displaying cash, refrain from wearing jewelry, and taking solitary walks at night. To reduce the risk of being targeted by armed robbers or injured in an accident, visitors should use private cars rather than moto-taxis or cyclos. Rapists have attacked foreign women in at least one case on a moto-taxi.

Passports and other identification documents could be stolen or confiscated, so visitors should carry photocopies while securely storing the originals.

Calling home
There are 32,800 land-based phones and 1.14 million cell phones in Cambodia.

Diplomatic contact in the United States
Ambassador Heng Hem
4530 16th Street NW, Washington, DC 20011
Phone: (202) 726-7742 • Fax (202) 726-8381

Diplomatic contact from the United States
Ambassador Carol A. Rodley

Embassy: #1, Street 96, Sangkat Wat Phnom, Khan Daun Penh, Phnom Penh
Box P, APO AP 96546
Phone: (855) (23) 728-000 • Fax (855) (23) 728-600

China

Overview of geography, climate, and population

China is a nation of 1.3 billion people and is a little smaller than the United
States. The climate varies from arid in the northwest to subtropical in the southeast. In the north of China, the summers are warm and the winters are cold.

Religion, ethnicity, and language in a nutshell

China is officially an atheist country, but 3 to 4 percent of Chinese are Christian
and 1 to 2 percent are Muslim. About 92 percent of Chinese are ethnically Han;
approximately 8 percent are of Zhuang, Uygur, Hui, Yi, Tibetan, Miao, Man-
chu, Mongol, Buyi, and Korean ancestry. The Chinese speak Mandarin, Yue, Wu,
Minbei, Minnan, Xiang, Gan, and Hakka.

Brief political history and today's government

China's history has been recorded for 3,500 years. The Qin dynasty established
a powerful centralized government in 221 B.C. The Han dynasty ran from 202
B.C. to 220 A.D. Mongols were in power until the 14th century. The Ming
dynasty ran from 1368-1644. From 1644 to 1912, the Ching dynasty was in
power. In 1912, the country became a republic. The government turned communist and was ruled by Mao Zedong from 1949 to 1976. Deng Xiaoping came
to power in 1978 and began moving China toward a market-based economy.
The legislature consists of a People's National Congress with 2,987 members,
who are selected by provincial, regional, and municipal people's congresses. The
judiciary includes the supreme people's court, local people's courts and special
people's courts. The nation's legal system evolved out of the Soviet and continental civil law tradition.

Economic snapshot

In the past two decades, China's economy has become increasingly open to international trade and foreign investment. In the 1970s, the number of agricultural collectives began to decrease, the financial sector became less centralized,
and both the private sector and stock markets grew. China's government seeks to
continue providing jobs for laid-off workers, migrant employees, and entry-level

laborers. The Chinese energy sector is growing. Energy officials in 2007 started the process of buying five nuclear reactors. A dam across the Yangtze River also produces electricity.

Peace Corps programs

- English education

Health

HIV/AIDS, diarrhea, hepatitis A, typhoid fever, Crimean Congo hemorrhagic fever, Japanese encephalitis, malaria, leptospirosos, and avian flu are among the diseases and illnesses volunteers should be aware of in China.

Health care falls below Western standards. Shanghai, Beijing, and Guangzhou have clinics with internationally-trained doctors. Other large cities have special wards for foreigners, which have modern diagnostic equipment and English-speaking health care providers. Hospital staff usually ask for a deposit to cover treatment. Some hospitals in large metropolitan areas accept credit cards. Although some wards are designated for foreigners, U.S. citizens have frequently had problems with language barriers and other differences between medical care in the United States and China. Foreign patients have sometimes had trouble getting their medical records from health care providers.

Medicine is in short supply, and even pharmaceuticals with the names of those in the United States are not necessarily the same products.

Ambulances have only rudimentary equipment and are often unavailable. In the countryside, only the most basic of health care is available, and medical staff have little training, medicine, or equipment. Employees of rural medical facilities often refuse to treat international visitors regardless of the severity of the emergency.

Clinics often require payment in advance.

Safety

Visitors whose living quarters have gas appliances should note that natural gas does not always have an odor to alert residents to leaks. Visitors should buy carbon monoxide detectors before leaving the United States and install them in their residences. Carbon monoxide detectors are rare in China. Foreigners are subject to government surveillance. Officials are legally allowed to secretly monitor telephone and fax communications and to search foreigners' computers. Taking pictures of anything that could have military or security value could cause conflicts with government officials. Visitors who use high technology in their work are more likely to be monitored by the government.

Very few terrorist and criminal bombings have happened. Attacks have largely been due to disputes over land, business and other issues. Foreigners should be sure they thoroughly understand any leases they sign. Landlords have sometimes evicted tenants without notice and barred them from re-entering buildings to get their possessions.

Officials may prevent foreigners involved in civil suits from leaving the country until the case goes through court, a process that can take years. U.S. citizens should be wary of any Chinese citizen asking for a letter of invitation to come to the United States for any purpose. Chinese nationals who operate human smuggling rings have used such letters to apply for fraudulent visas that help them get their victims out of the country.

Crime is relatively rare in China. Violence against foreigners is especially uncommon but is on the rise. Pickpockets target international visitors, frequently while security guards watch, at tourist attractions, outdoor markets, airports, and shops. Rapists have targeted foreigners, particularly in nightclub districts of cities. Armed robberies are not uncommon in western China and have become more frequent in Beijing. Highway robbers have struck near the China-Nepal border.

The only places to legally exchange money are official change bureaus, banks and hotels. Counterfeiting is rampant in China. Foreigners who buy RMB at unofficial change bureaus risk losing their money. Police investigations into allegations of foreigners committing financial crimes can take months, and the visitors cannot leave China before their cases are solved. Chinese bar patrons sometimes fight with visitors from the United States because of their country of origin. U.S. citizens detained immediately after brawls do not have access to attorney and cannot contact the consulate.

Visitors should pay for taxis with small bills because taxi drivers sometimes use counterfeit money to make change. Travelers should avoid arguing with taxi drivers over fares or routes because police sometimes detain foreigners in such instances.

Volunteers should be wary of strangers who ask them out for tea to practice their English because such invitations sometimes end with foreign visitors being forced to pay an exorbitant restaurant bill. Young women often approach bar patrons for similar purposes.

Male volunteers should avoid women outside hotels in areas frequented by tourists. Chinese women sometimes pretend to be seeking sex or a relationship but are intending to take unsuspecting visitors to remote locations to be robbed.

Travelers arriving at international airports should be wary of strangers who claim to be employees and offer to carry their bags to the departure gate. Such impostors often take visitors to areas of the airport far from the gate and demand an airport tax. Airport taxes are included in ticket prices. Visitors approached by fraudulent bag handlers should call airport security.

Robbers and thieves often target visitors at airports, particularly those in Beijing, Zhengzhou, Shenyang, Dalian, Qingdao, and Taiyuan. Visitors staying in international hotels have been victims of assault and robbery. Visitors should keep their passports on hand but secure from pickpockets. Volunteers who have residence permits should carry them and store their passports securely except when going out of town. Visitors should register with the United States embassy or consulate. Travelers should also photocopy their passports and visas.

Volunteers should be aware that buying or selling pirated items could break municipal laws and that bringing such materials into the United States is illegal.

Calling home
The telecommunications system is developing. Recent figures show 368 million land-based telephones and 461 million cell phones. There are 10.6 million Internet hosts.

Diplomatic contact in the United States
Ambassador Zhou Wenzhong
2300 Connecticut Avenue NW, Washington, DC 20008
Phone: (202) 328-2500 • Fax (202) 328-2582

Diplomatic contact from the United States
Ambassador Jon M. Huntsman, Jr.
Embassy: 55 An Jia Lou Lu, 100600 Beijing
PSC 461, Box 50, FPO AP 96521-0002
Phone: (86) (10) 8531-3000 • Fax (86) (10) 8531-3300

Consulate(s) general: Chengdu, Guangzhou, Shanghai, Shenyang, Wuhan

Mongolia
Overview of geography, climate, and population

Mongolia is a little smaller than Alaska. The climate ranges from desert to continental. The terrain includes steppe, mountains in the southwestern, and western areas. The Gobi Desert is in the center of the southern section. The population is 3 million.

Religion, ethnicity, and language in a nutshell

Ninety percent of Mongolians speak Khalkha Mongol. Residents also use Turkic and Russian. About 95 percent of the population are Mongol, approximately 5 percent Mongolians are Turkic, and one-tenth of a percent of the population traces their ancestry to other countries, including China and Russia. About 50 percent of Mongolians are Buddhist Lamaist; 6 percent are Shamanist and Christian. Four percent are Muslim. Forty percent of Mongolians do not practice any religion.

Brief political history and today's government

The Mongol Empire gained prominence in the 1200s. The Chinese took control in the 1600s, and Mongolia became independent in 1921. A Communist government came to power in 1924 and fell in 1990. The president is Nambaryn Enkhbayar. The legislature consists of the State Great Hural, which has 76 publicly elected members. The legal system is based on continental and civil law. The Supreme Court constitutes the judiciary.

Economic snapshot

Herding and agriculture have historically been central to Mongolia's economy. The industrial sector revolves around copper, coal, gold, molybdenum, fluorospar, uranium, tin, and tungsten. After the collapse of the Soviet Union, which used to provide significant economic aid, Mongolia fell into recession. The private sector has grown, and the economy has moved toward a free market. In the early 2000s, frigid winters and parching summers killed much of the livestock in Mongolia, causing the gross domestic product to stagnate and drop. Later in the decade, growth picked up due to strong markets in precious metals. Inflation is currently quite high. Mongolia is a member of the World Trade Organization, and the government wishes to increase its economic partnerships with other countries in the region.

Peace Corps programs

- English education
- AIDS prevention
- Community development
- Youth development business

Health

HIV/AIDS, hepatitis A, hepatitis B, typhoid, rabies, dengue, filariasis, Japanese encephalitis, leishmaniasis, plague, tick-borne encephalitis, measles, influenza, leptospirosis, plague, meningococcal meningitis, and tuberculosis are among the diseases and illnesses volunteers should be aware of in Mongolia.

Visitors should avoid swimming, except in heavily chlorinated pools, for fear of freshwater parasites. Volunteers should avoid drinking non-bottled water and refrain from using ice cubes made with tap water. Visitors should make sure food is completely cooked and refrain from buying food from those who sell it on the street. Travelers should not eat unpasteurized dairy products.

Most of the clinics are in Ulaanbaatar but outside of the capital, medical care is sometimes unavailable and always scarce.

Health care, including emergency treatment, falls below Western standards. Medicine is in short supply.

Emergencies may require medical evacuation to other Asian countries or to the United States. Before evacuation begins, patients must provide proof of their ability to pay.

Restaurants typically have poor sanitation, especially outside the capital.

Safety

Terrorists and kidnappers do not intentionally target foreigners. Visitors should avoid demonstrations for fear of disorder. Travelers should also refrain from walking alone after dark in urban areas. Crime is especially prevalent in Ulaanbaatar. Pickpockets and purse snatchers often target foreigners. Gangs of thieves often encircle and then choke victims to facilitate stealing the contents of their pockets. Criminals also cut victims' clothes to steal the valuables in their pockets. Visitors should reduce their risk of injury by cooperating immediately with pickpockets if approached by them.

Visitors should be especially careful on mass transit, in outdoor markets, at the Gandan Monastery, and at the Central Post Office. Volunteers arriving at or leaving from the Chinggis Khan International Airport in Ulaanbaatar should be especially careful of gangs seeking to rob them or pick their pockets. Groups of thieves seeking to pick tourists' pockets often target victims at the entrances, exits and elevators of the State Department Store as well as in the vicinity of the establishment. Gangs of robbers and pickpockets look for foreign victims at the Naran Tuul Covered Market.

Calling home

There are 158,900 land-based telephones and 775,300 cell phones in Mongolia. There are 298 Internet hosts.

Diplomatic contact in the United States

Ambassador Khasbazaryn Bekhbat

2833 M Street NW, Washington, DC 20007

Phone: (202) 333-7117 • Fax (202) 298-9227

Diplomatic contact from the United States

Ambassador Jonathan Addleton

Embassy: Big Ring Road, 11th Micro Region, Ulaanbaatar,

14171 Mongolia

PSC 461, Box 300, FPO AP 96521-0002; P.O. Box 1021, Ulaanbaatar-13

Phone: (976) (11) 329-095 • Fax (976) (11) 320-776

Philippines

Overview of geography, climate, and population

The Philippines is a little bigger than Arizona. The climate is tropical with monsoon season occurring in the northeast from November to April and in the southwest from May to October. The country is predominantly mountainous with some lowlands. The population is 97.9 million.

Religion, ethnicity, and language in a nutshell

Official languages include Filipino and English. Major dialects include Tagalog, Cebuano, Ilocano, Hiligaynon, Ilonggo, Bicol, Waray, Pampango, and Pangasinan.

About 28 percent of the population are Tagalog. Approximately 13 percent of Filipinos are of Cebuano ancestry. Around 9 percent of Filipinos are Ilocano. A little more than 7 percent are Hiligaynon Ilonggo, 6 percent are Bikol, and a bit more than 3 percent are of Waray heritage. About a quarter of the population is of other heritage.

About 80 percent of Filipinos are Roman Catholic. Approximately 5 percent follow Islam. About 3 percent are Evangelical. A little more than 2 percent of Filipinos belong to the Iglesia Ni Kristo.

Around 2 percent are Aglipayan, and a little more than 4 percent are Christian. About 2 percent follow another faith, .6 percent are of an unspecified faith, and .1 percent follow no religion.

Brief political history and today's government

The Spanish claimed the Philippines as a colony in the 1500s. The Spanish lost them to the United States at the end of the Spanish-American War. The Philippines became self-ruling in 1935 and independent in 1946. Japanese troops held the islands from 1942-1945. Soldiers from the United States and the Philippines fought against the Japanese occupation. The United States kept military bases in the Philippines until the 1990s.

The president is Gloria Macapagal-Arroyo. The legislature includes a Congress, consisting of a Senate and House of Representatives. There are 24 senators and 239 house members. Senators are publicly elected; some house members are popularly elected and others are chosen based on proportional representation.

The legal system stems from Spanish, British, and American law. The judiciary consists of a Supreme Court, Court of Appeals, and a court to try cases of government corruption.

Economic snapshot

Since the beginning of the 21st century, the economy has grown steadily due to government investment, a strong service industry, and money from Filipino expatriates. Government spending on infrastructure as well as declining debt have strengthened the economy.

Peace Corps programs

- Youth development
- Environment
- Education
- Business

Health

HIV/AIDS, diarrhea, hepatitis A, hepatitis B, typhoid fever, dengue fever, malaria, rabies, Japanese encephalitis, typhoid, chikungunya, filariasis, plague, avian flu, schistosomiasis, leptospirosis, and diarrhea are among the diseases and illnesses volunteers should be aware of in the Philippines.

Large urban centers offer medical care that is satisfactory by Asian standards but that falls below Western standards. Health care in the countryside is quite restricted. Patients must typically pay cash deposits to cover projected hospital bills before receiving care. When patients could not pay for procedures or pharmaceuticals that would save their lives, hospital staff have refused to provide them. Hospital staff often hold patients and their medical records until accounts are settled.

Visitors should take mefloquine, atovaquone/ proguanil, doxycycline, and —in rare cases, after G6PD screenings—primaquine to prevent malaria. Chloroquine will not protect travelers against the strains of malaria prevalent in the Philippines. Travelers should avoid taking halofantrine, sold under the brand name Halfan, for malaria because it can cause potentially fatal heart problems. Patients should only accept treatment with halofantrine if doctors have diagnosed them with potentially fatal malaria and there is no other medicine available.

Visitors are not typically in danger of contracting malaria in Manila and other major cities. Malaria is prevalent in sections of the country lower than 1,969 feet above sea level, with the exception of Bohol Island, Borocay Island, Catanduanes Island, and Cebu Island. Volunteers should buy anti-malarial medicines before leaving the United States. Anti-malarial drugs sold in the Philippines are often of poor quality and possibly harmful.

Safety

Terrorism is a danger, especially on the island of Mindanao and the Sulu Archipelago. Central and western Mindanao are the most dangerous. Terrorists have committed bombings that are injurious, lethal, and damaging to property. In 2008, terrorists planted a deadly bomb outside a club in Cotabato City. Terrorists have also placed bombs in mass transit stations and near public buildings, including the House of Representatives in the capital.

Kidnappers hold foreigners for ransom, particularly in the countryside. Visitors should be as vigilant about crime in Manila as they would be in a major city in the United States. Pickpocketing, financial fraud, and confidence schemes are common crimes. To reduce the risk of becoming victims of crime, visitors should avoid strangers who appear overly friendly. Visitors in restaurants and clubs should keep their food and drink in sight at all times to prevent criminals from putting sedatives in them that would make robbery or sexual assault easier to commit. Travelers should refuse food and beverages from those they do not know for fear of drugging.

Visitors in Manila are vulnerable to kidnapping, assault, and armed robberies.

Volunteers should use taxis but should avoid getting in cabs that already have passengers in them. Visitors should not take cabs unless drivers agree to use meters. Travelers should memorize or write down the license numbers of the cabs they take. Drivers should keep doors locked and windows closed. Volunteers should not use trains, buses, or jeepneys because they are unsafe, and passengers are prone to becoming crime victims. Visitors should keep their credit cards in sight to reduce the risk of having criminals use devices to collect personal identification numbers from the magnetic strips. Visitors should be cautious if they encounter people who claim to be selling Federal Reserve notes or U.S. securities. Many such sales in Mongolia are fraudulent.

Buying or selling pirated goods can be illegal under municipal laws. Returning to the United States with items made in violation of others' intellectual property rights is illegal and could lead to fines.

Calling home

There are 3.6 million land-based telephones and 42.86 million cell phones in the Philippines. There are 271,609 Internet hosts.

Diplomatic contact in the United States

Ambassador Willy C. Gaa
1600 Massachusetts Avenue NW, Washington, DC 20036
Phone: (202) 467-9300 • Fax: (202) 467-9417

Diplomatic contact from the United States

Ambassador Kristie A. Kenney
Embassy: 1201 Roxas Boulevard, Ermita 1000, Manila
PSC 500, FPO AP 96515-1000
Phone: (63) (2) 301-2000 • Fax: (63) (2) 301-2399

Thailand

Overview of geography, climate, and population

Thailand is a little bigger than two times the size of Wyoming. The climate is tropical with monsoons occurring in the southwest from May to September and in the northeast from November to March. The south is always hot and humid. The terrain consists of mountains, a central plain, and the Khorat Plateau in the eastern section of the country. About 65.9 million people live in Thailand.

Religion, ethnicity, and language in a nutshell

Languages include Thai and English, as well as dialects that vary according to geography and ethnicity.

Seventy-five percent of the population are Thai; 14 percent are Chinese; and 11 percent are of other lineage.

About 95 percent of the population are Buddhist. Approximately 5 percent of Thais are Muslim, .7 percent are Christian, and 0.1 percent are of other faiths.

Brief political history and today's government

Siam, the country that became Thailand, has existed since the 1300s. Thais changed their government from a traditional kingdom to a constitutional monarchy in 1932. Thailand was a Japanese ally during the Second World War.

The King is Phumiphon Adunyadet. The Prime Minister is Samak Sundavavej. The legislature includes the National Assembly, which has a Senate and a House of Representatives. The Senate has 150 members, some of whom are publicly elected, others of whom are appointed. The legal system is derived from civil and common law. The judiciary consists of the Supreme Court, justices of which are appointed by the monarch.

Economic snapshot

Thailand has a capitalist economy and a strong system of transportation. Exports and tourism are central to the country's economy. In 2006, a military coup d'etat and restrictions on foreign investment led to economic stagnation. Exports, car making, and commercial agriculture have since rallied the economy.

Peace Corps programs

- Education
- Business

Health

HIV/AIDS, diarrhea, hepatitis A, hepatitis B, dengue fever, Japanese encephalitis, malaria, rabies, leptospirosis, typhoid, rabies, diarrhea, filariasis, plague, and avian flu are among the diseases and illnesses volunteers should be aware of in Thailand.

Most medical care is satisfactory by Western standards. Health services are especially advanced in the capital.

Volunteers who will spend time in areas where malaria is prevalent should take atovaquone/proguanil or doxycycline. Malaria is a hazard in the countryside along the border of Cambodia, Laos, and Myanmar. Visitors to Phang Nga and Phuket have a very low risk of contracting malaria. Malaria is not a concern in urban areas or in large resorts. Volunteers need not worry about catching malaria in Bangkok, Chiang Mai, Chiang Rai, Pattaya, Koh Samui, and Koh Phangan.

Volunteers should buy anti-malarial medicines before leaving the United States. Anti-malarial pharmaceuticals sold in Thailand often do not meet Western standards of quality and could harm patients.

Visitors should refuse to take the anti-malarial drug halofantrine, sold under the brand name Halfan, because it can cause fatal heart problems. Travelers should only accept treatment with halofantrine if doctors have diagnosed them with potentially lethal malaria and no other treatment is available.

Safety

Terrorism is a concern in areas popular with international visitors. Terrorists are likely to strike in such places as bars, restaurants, hotels, tourist attractions, clubs, schools, houses of worship, outdoor entertainment sites, parks, and beach resorts.

In September 2007, a bombing took place outside a military office in the capital, harming pedestrians. In May 2007, a bomb went off outside the Chitralada Palace. In January 2007, someone fired grenades in the office of a newspaper in Bangkok and the parking area of a hotel in the same neighborhood, but no injuries or deaths were reported. In December 2006, six bombs were detonated in the capital, killing three Thais and injuring six foreigners as well as several dozen residents. The perpetrators are unknown. U.S. citizens should avoid public crowds in Bangkok.

Attacks by separatists and others occur at least several times a week in southern Thailand. In March 2008, bombs were detonated at the CS Pattani Hotel in Pattani Province, killing two people and injuring 13. In Yala Province, the same day, a bomb took the life of the driver of the car in which it exploded. Government officials are worried that bombings could become more common in Bangkok, especially around national holidays. In September 2006, one U.S. citizen died and another was injured when several bombs exploded in a shopping section of Hat Yai. In August 2006, 28 people were hurt when 22 explosives were detonated in banks in Yala province. In 2005, a bomb in the Hat Yai airport injured two U.S. citizens. Visitors are especially vulnerable to bombings in shopping districts popular with international travelers. Volunteers should avoid visiting southern Thailand, particularly the provinces of Narathiwat, Pattani, Yala, Satun, and Songkhla. Visitors should refrain from traveling to the town of Hat Yai. Government officials have sometimes mandated curfews, unannounced searches of passengers on mass transit and patrols of public spaces by members of the armed forces.

Murderers attacked seven U.S. citizens of Hmong and Laotian descent near the Laos-Thailand frontier between 2004 and 2006. During the same years, many others with Laotian connections were killed in the border region. In 2006, eight people, including a U.S. citizen of Hmong descent, disappeared from Chiang Mai. Police have not arrested suspects in most of the instances. Volunteers who must travel near the border with Laos should consult the Thai police, the U.S. consulate in Chiang Mai, the U.S. embassy in Bangkok, or the U.S. embassy in Vientiane. In 2007, three U.S. citizens of Hmong lineage disappeared after allegedly leaving for Laos on business. Laotian officials said the missing men returned to Thailand, but their relatives in the United States have not heard from them since.

Armed clashes regularly occur at the border between Burma and Thailand between. Dissidents fight with the Burmese armed forces, and Thai police battle with drug traffickers. Drug smugglers, pirates, and bandits are active near the border. War in Burma could spread quickly into Thailand. When traveling in rural areas near the border, volunteers should always take guides who live in the region and know it well. Officials close the Thailand-Burma border frequently, so visitors who go to Burma might find it impossible to return to Thailand on schedule. Before leaving the country, volunteers should ask Thai officials whether the border is open and should cross only at official frontier posts. Visitors should employ certified guides to avoid crossing at the wrong places.

In September 2006, a military junta overthrew the Thai government after numerous rallies in Bangkok and Chiang Mai. Demonstrations have not occurred since the current democratic government was established, but they could resume. Visitors should avoid protests for fear of unpredictable violence. Volunteers should listen to news reports of upcoming protests and avoid the areas in which the rallies are likely to occur.

Bangkok has a lower crime rate than many metropolitan areas in the United States. Burglary, pickpocketing, and theft of handbags are the crimes most commonly committed against foreigners. Volunteers should take particular care when they are in mass transit stations, in crowded areas, or visiting tourist attractions. Thieves at the Chatuchak Weekend Market in Bangkok often slice victims' bags and steal valuables without being detected. Visitors who become victims of theft at the Chatuchak Weekend Market cannot report the crime to police nearby but must go instead to the headquarters of the tourist police.

Violent criminals rarely target international visitors, but a few tourists from other countries were recently murdered on the islands of Phuket and Koh Samui. Travelers to Phuket and Koh Samui should stay in well-populated areas and remain aware of their surroundings.

Taxi drivers, and operators of local three-wheeled cabs called tuk-tuks, often try to charge international passengers significantly more than rides should have cost. Visitors should ask taxi drivers who appear to be operating cabs unsafely to let them out.

Visitors who fly into the airport in Bangkok should take cabs from the taxi stand, airport limousines from official counters, or buses provided by the airport. Volunteers should refrain from entering taxis that are already carrying one or more passengers.

Travelers should not take the advice of cab drivers who recommend jewelers or entertainment spots because such suggestions sometimes lead to international visitors being swindled. Visitors should charge purchases only in well-known establishments and should verify the accuracy of credit card transactions.

International visitors are often victims of elaborate scams involving buying precious stones. An accomplice in the gem scam will typically tell visitors that a tourist attraction — for instance, the Grand Palace or the Jim Thompson House — is closed. The person then advises the traveler to see an attraction that is allegedly open once a year and indicates a cab that has been waiting. The accomplice notes that an annual government jewel sale is supposedly taking place that day. When the visitor reaches the attraction, another accomplice, sometimes from a country other than Thailand, says that an annual gem sale is scheduled for that day. The jewelers convince the tourist to buy thousands of dollars of gems which are actually of very low value. The shop refuses to take the gems back in spite of initial promises of a money-back guarantee. Travelers should know that neither the Thai government nor the royal family own gem stores or hold sales of precious stones. To report a gem scam or other crime, visitors can call the tourist police toll free at 1155.

Staff of bars and other nightspots, particularly in Patpong, sometimes attempt to extort unwary tourists by drastically inflating drink prices and threatening violent attacks as a consequence of refusal to pay. Tourists who encounter such scams should reduce their risk of injury by complying, then reporting the incidents to the tourist police by calling 1155 toll-free. Bartenders and prostitutes sometimes add the sedative scopolamine to the drinks of unsuspecting tourists to facilitate robbery. For fear of drugging, volunteers should refuse any food or drink strangers offer, even if the products are in sealed containers. Some strangers wishing to drug travelers for robbery find victims on mass transit. Visitors should keep food and drink in sight at all times and take others along when visiting establishments with which they are not familiar. Some sightseeing companies provide illicit drugs for their customers, but volunteers should avoid such offers because the substances might be harmful. Narcotics are illegal in Thailand. Pirated products, such as recordings of movies, music, and computer software, are common in Thailand. Organized crime syndicates are often behind trafficking in illegally reproduced goods. Visitors are legally prohibited from returning to the United States with pirated goods.

Calling home

There are 7 million land-based telephones and 40.8 million cell phones in Thailand. There are 973,941 Internet hosts.

Diplomatic contact in the United States

Ambassador Don Pramudwinai

1024 Wisconsin Avenue NW, Suite 401, Washington, DC 20007

Phone: (202) 944-3600 • Fax (202) 944-3611

Diplomatic contact from the United States

Ambassador Eric G. John

Embassy: 120-122 Wireless Road, Bangkok 10330

APO AP 96546

Phone: (66) (2) 205-4000 • Fax (66) (2) 254-2990, 205-4131

Consulate(s) general: Chiang Mai

Indonesia

Overview of geography, climate, and population

Indonesia is an archipelago of islands in Southeastern Asia, between the Indian Ocean and the Pacific Ocean. It slightly less than three times the size of Texas. Indonesia is made up of mostly coastal lowlands. Larger islands have interior mountains. The climate is tropical, hot, and humid and is more moderate in the highlands. The population is approximately 240 million.

Religion, ethnicity, and language in a nutshell

Languages include Bahasa Indonesia (the official language) as well as English, Dutch, and local dialects. Javanese make up 40.6 percent of the population, Sundanese 15 percent, Madurese 3.3 percent, Minangkabau 2.7 percent, Betawi 2.4 percent, Bugis 2.4 percent, Banten 2 percent, Banjar 1.7 percent, and other or unspecified 29.9 percent. Approximately 86.1 percent of residents are Muslim, 5.7 percent are Protestant, 3 percent are Roman Catholic, 1.8 percent are Hindu, and 3.4 percent are other or unspecified.

Brief political history and today's government

The Republic of Indonesia's capital city is Jakarta. It is made up on 30 provinces, two special regions, and one special capital city district. Indonesia declared independence from the Netherlands on August 17, 1945. In August 2005, the Netherlands announced it recognized the de facto Indonesian independence on the date in 1945.

Indonesia's President Susilo Bambang Yudhoyono has been in office since October 20, 2004 and is both chief of state and the head of the government. The government consists of a legislative and judicial branch.

Economic snapshot

Indonesia has weathered the global financial crisis relatively smoothly because of its heavy reliance on domestic consumption as the driver of economic growth. Although the economy slowed significantly in 2007 and 2008, the economy expand at 4 percent in the first half of 2009, and Indonesia outperformed its regional neighbors and joined China and India as the only G20 members posting growth during the crisis. TH country's major agriculture products include rice, cassava (tapioca), peanuts, rubber, cocoa, coffee, palm oil, copra; poultry, beef, pork, and eggs, and its major industries are petroleum and natural gas, textiles, apparel, footwear, mining, cement, chemical fertilizers, plywood, rubber, food, and tourism.

Peace Corps programs

- Education
- English education

Health

Bacterial diarrhea, hepatitis A and E, chikungunya, dengue fever, malaria, and typhoid fever are among the diseases and illnesses volunteers should be aware of in Indonesia.

Note: Highly pathogenic H5N1 avian influenza has been identified in this country; it poses a negligible risk with extremely rare cases possible among U.S. citizens who have close contact with birds.

The general level of sanitation and health care in Indonesia is far below U.S. standards. Some routine medical care is safely available in all major cities, although most expatriates leave the country for serious medical procedures. Psychological and psychiatric medical and counseling services are limited throughout Indonesia. Serious medical problems requiring hospitalization and/or medical evacuation to locations with acceptable medical care, such as Singapore, Australia, or the United States, can cost thousands of dollars. Doctors and hospitals often expect immediate cash payments or sizable deposits for health services.

Indonesian ambulance attendants lack paramedical training equivalent to U.S. standards. U.S. citizens staying in Indonesia for extended periods, especially those who have known health problems, are advised to investigate private ambulance services in their area and to provide family and close contacts with the direct telephone number(s) of the service they prefer.

Malaria, dengue, avian and swine influenza, and other tropical and contagious diseases are prevalent throughout Indonesia. In 2005, polio reemerged in Western Java. Avian influenza (H5N1) is endemic among poultry in Indonesia, and outbreaks in poultry have been reported in the majority of Indonesia's provinces.

Safety

Indonesian police and security forces take active measures against both ongoing threats posed by terrorist cells, including Jemaah Islamiyah (JI), a U.S. government-designated terrorist organization that carried out several bombings at various times from 2002 to 2009, and outbreaks of violence elsewhere. While Indonesia's counterterrorism efforts have been ongoing and partly successful, violent elements have demonstrated a willingness and ability to carry out deadly attacks with little or no warning. Most recently, in November 2009, unknown assailants shot at foreigners in Banda Aceh, North Sumatra, an area that was devastated by the 2004 tsunami and the scene of a long-running separatist conflict that ended in 2005. The gunfire wounded a European development worker. A house occupied by U.S. citizen teachers was targeted and hit by gunfire, but there were no U.S. citizen casualties. In July 2009, attacks by armed assailants in Papua resulted in several deaths, including security personnel and one Australian national. Also, in July, suspected JI elements bombed two Western hotels in Jakarta, killing nine Indonesians and foreigners and injuring over 50, including six U.S. citizens. U.S. citizens in Indonesia must be physically and mentally prepared to cope with future attacks even as they go about their normal daily routines.

Extremists may target both official and private interests, including hotels, clubs, and shopping centers. While it may be difficult to modify one's behavior to counter risks in a country in which U.S. citizens and other Westerners must congregate to live and work are well-known and few in number, it is also extremely necessary. In their work and daily living activities, and while traveling, U.S. citizens should be vigilant and prudent at all times. We urge U.S. citizens to monitor local news reports, vary their routes and times, and maintain a low profile. U.S. citizens must consider the security and safety preparedness of hotels, residences, restaurants, and entertainment or recreation venues that they frequent.

Crime can be a problem in some major metropolitan areas in Indonesia. Crimes of opportunity such as pickpocketing and theft occur throughout the country. The embassy recommends that official employees use reputable taxis only, such as Silver Bird or Blue Bird, which are found in a queue at major hotels or shopping centers, arranged by calling ahead or hailing them on the street. The embassy also advises official employees arriving at Jakarta's Soekarno-Hatta Airport to use only Silver Bird or Blue Bird taxis or arrange transport through their hotel. Airport touts should not be used. Criminals in Jakarta regularly rob customers in vehicles that have been painted to look like taxis from reputable companies; booking taxis by telephone directly from the company is the best way to avoid falling victim to this crime. Some airports, including those in Yogyakarta, Surabaya, Bali, and Lombok, offer competitive, reliable, prepaid taxi services.

Calling home

Domestic communication service is fair, and international service is good. Coverage provided by existing network has been expanded by use of over 200,000 telephone kiosks, many located in remote areas; mobile cellular subscribership is growing rapidly. There are 865,309 Internet hosts.

Diplomatic contact in the United States

Ambassador Sudjadnan Parnohadiningrat
2020 Massachusetts Avenue NW, Washington, DC 20036
Phone: (202) 775-5200 • Fax (202) 775-5365

Diplomatic contact from the United States

Ambassador Cameron R. Hume
Embassy: Jalan 1 Medan Merdeka Selatan 4-5, Jakarta 10110
Unit 8129, Box 1, FPO AP 96520
Phone: (62) (21) 3435-9000 • Fax (62) (21) 3435-9922
Consulate(s) general: Surabaya

The Caribbean

Antigua and Barbuda

Overview of geography, climate, and population

The islands are located southeast of Puerto Rico in the Caribbean. The climate is tropical maritime. The terrain consists primarily of lowlands, but there are also some volcanoes. There are 85,632 residents.

Religion, ethnicity, and language in a nutshell

A little more than 26 percent of the population belong to the Anglican Church, approximately 12 percent are Seventh-day Adventist, about 10 percent are Pentecostal, about 10 percent are Moravian, approximately 10 percent are Roman Catholic, about 8 percent are Methodist, approximately 5 percent are Baptist, about 5 percent belong to the Church of God, about 5 percent belong to another Christian denomination, and 8 percent follow another faith. Ninety-one percent of the population is black, about 4 percent is of mixed lineage, 2 percent are white, and 3 percent have another heritage. English is the official language, and several regional dialects are in use.

Brief political history and today's government

The earliest known residents were the Siboney people who settled the islands more than 2,000 years before the Christian era. Columbus arrived in 1493. The Spanish and French controlled the islands before they became British colonies in the late 1600s. Slavery was abolished in 1834, and Antigua and Barbuda joined the Commonwealth in the 1980s.

Economic snapshot

Tourism is the backbone of the economy. Construction is also an important sector. Agriculture and manufacturing such items as crafts, blankets, and electronics are other significant parts of the economy. Economic reforms are underway, but the national debt is still more than the gross domestic product.

Peace Corps programs

- IT
- Disaster readiness
- Disaster relief
- AIDS prevention

Health

There are many qualified doctors in Antigua and Barbuda, but medical facilities are limited to one public hospital and two private clinics. They do not meet U.S. standards. The principal medical facility on Antigua is Holberton Hospital, on Hospital Road, St. John's. There is no hyperbaric chamber; divers requiring treatment for decompression illness must be evacuated from the island to either Saba or Guadeloupe. Serious medical problems requiring hospitalization and/or medical evacuation to the United States can cost thousands of dollars. Doctors and hospitals often expect immediate cash payment for health services.

Safety

Violent crime does occur, including at hotels and main tourist venues, and visitors should take precautions to ensure their safety. In 2008 and 2009, three tourists were murdered in Antigua — a British couple on their honeymoon and an Australian yacht captain. Armed robbery and street crime also occur, and valuables left unattended on beaches, in rental cars, or in hotel rooms are vulnerable to theft. Visitors to Antigua and Barbuda are advised to be alert and maintain the same level of personal security used when visiting major U.S. cities.

Be especially vigilant when taking taxis in Antigua and Barbuda. Make certain that the taxi driver is licensed and is a member of the official taxi association. Unlicensed taxi operators have been known to extort money from passengers, despite having agreed to a fare beforehand. This can sometimes amount to double or triple the agreed-upon fare.

Calling home

There are 40,000 land-based telephones and 102,000 cell phones. There are 2,133 Internet hosts.

Diplomatic contact in the United States

Ambassador Deborah Mae Lovell
3216 New Mexico Avenue NW, Washington, DC 20016
Phone: (202) 362-5122 • Fax (202) 362-5225

Diplomatic contact from the United States

The United States does not have an embassy in Antigua and Barbuda.

Dominica

Overview of geography, climate, and population

Dominica is in the Caribbean between Puerto Rico and Trinidad and Tobago. The climate is tropical and rainy. The terrain features volcanic mountains. Dominica has a population of 72,660.

Religion, ethnicity, and language in a nutshell

Eighty-seven percent of the population are black, 9 percent are of mixed ancestry, about 3 percent are Carib Amerindian, nearly 1 percent are white, and nearly 1 percent have another heritage.

Nearly 62 percent are Roman Catholic, 6 percent are Seventh-day Adventist, about 6 percent are Pentecostal, approximately 4 percent are Baptist, about 4 percent are Methodist, a little more than 1 percent belong to the Church of God, and slightly more than 1 percent are Jehovah's Witnesses. Nearly 8 percent belong to other Christian denominations, slightly more than 1 percent are Rastafarians, nearly 2 percent follow other religions, and slightly more than 6 percent do not adhere to any faith. English is the official language, but French patois is also spoken.

Brief political history and today's government

Formerly under French rule, Dominica became a British colony in 1805. Dominica became independent in 1978. The few thousand Caribs on the island are the only indigenous people in the Eastern Caribbean. Dominica has a parliamentary democracy. The president is Nicholas Liverpool, and the prime minister is Roosevelt Skerrit. The legislature consists of the House of Assembly, with a judiciary that includes the Court of Appeal and the High Court, which make up the Eastern Caribbean Supreme Court.

Economic snapshot

Agriculture is central to the economy, with bananas figuring prominently. The tourism sector is growing due to government efforts. De-regulation and privatization efforts have led to economic growth during the 2000s. The government seeks to attract offshore investment and develop a geothermal energy market.

Peace Corps programs

- IT
- Disaster readiness
- Disaster relief
- AIDS prevention

Health

Medical care is limited. The major hospital is Princess Margaret Hospital. In addition, there is one other hospital in Dominica and several clinics. There is an operational hyperbaric chamber at the main hospital. The private hospital and clinics will take emergency cases. There is limited ambulance service on most of the island, and a sea rescue service is now available at the north end of the island. Serious medical problems requiring hospitalization and/or medical evacuation to the United States can cost thousands of dollars. Doctors and hospitals often expect immediate cash payment for health services.

Safety

Petty street crime occurs in Dominica. Valuables left unattended, especially on beaches, are vulnerable to theft.

Calling home

There are 21,000 land-based telephones and 41,800 cell phones. There are 257 Internet hosts.

Diplomatic contact

Ambassador (vacant): Charge d'Affaires Judith Ann Rolle
3216 New Mexico Avenue NW, Washington, DC 20016
Phone: (202) 364-6781 • Fax (202) 364-6791

Diplomatic contact from the United States

The United States does not have an embassy in Dominica.

Dominican Republic

Overview of geography, climate, and population

The Dominican Republic is a little more than two times as large as New Hampshire. The climate is tropical maritime with a fairly consistent temperature year-round. The terrain includes highlands and valleys. The population is 9.6 million.

Religion, ethnicity, and language in a nutshell

Residents speak Spanish. About 73 percent of residents are of mixed lineage, 16 percent are white, and 11 percent are black. About 50 percent of residents are mestizo, approximately 25 percent are Creole, a little more than 10 percent are Maya, slightly more than 6 percent are Garifuna, and nearly 10 percent are of other ancestry. About 95 percent of Dominicans are Roman Catholic, and the remaining 5 percent practice another religion.

Brief political history and today's government

Christopher Columbus was the first European to visit Hispaniola, the island the Dominican Republic now shares with Haiti. The Dominican Republic became independent of Spain in 1865. After a period of dictatorship, the country has held democratic elections since the 1960s. The president is Leonel Fernandez Reyna. The National Congress includes the Senate, with 32 publicly elected members, and the House of Representatives, with 178 publicly elected members. The legal system is derived from French law.

Economic snapshot

The gross domestic product has increased steadily since 2005, but unemployment is high. A robust tourism sector has no more jobs in the service industry than in agriculture. Nickel, sugar, coffee, and tobacco are essential exports. Trade with the United States as well as remittances from Dominican expatriates are important to the country's economy. Inflation has declined significantly, due in part to a loan from the International Monetary Fund. The most affluent 10 percent of Dominicans receive nearly half of the country's gross national product. The nation is a party to the Central America-Dominican Republic Free Trade Agreement, which seeks to increase international investment and exports and offset competition from textile manufacturers in even less affluent areas.

Peace Corps programs

- Disaster relief
- Disaster readiness
- Education

Health

Bacterial diarrhea, hepatitis A, dengue fever, malaria, leptospirosis, and typhoid fever are among the diseases and illnesses volunteers should be aware of in the Dominican Republic.

While adequate medical facilities can be found in large cities, particularly in private hospitals, the quality of care can vary greatly outside major population centers. There is an emergency 911 service within Santo Domingo, but its reliability is questionable. Outside the capital, emergency services range from extremely limited to nonexistent. Blood supplies at both public and private hospitals are often limited, and not all facilities have blood on hand, even for emergencies.

Many medical facilities throughout the country do not have staff members who speak or understand English. A private nationwide ambulance service, ProMed, operates in Santo Domingo, Santiago, Puerto Plata, and La Romana. ProMed expects full payment at the time of transport.

Dengue is endemic to the Dominican Republic. To reduce the risk of contracting dengue, visitor should wear clothing that exposes as little skin as possible and apply a repellent containing the insecticide DEET (concentration 30 to 35 percent) or Picaridin (concentration 20 percent or greater for tropical travelers). Because of the increased risk of dengue fever and the ongoing risk of malaria in the Dominican Republic, practicing preventative measures is recommended.

There are occasional reports of cases of malaria in areas frequented by U.S. and European tourists, including La Altagracia Province, the easternmost province in which many beach resorts are located. Malaria risk is significantly higher for travelers who go on some of the excursions to the countryside offered by many resorts.

Be aware that sexually transmitted diseases are common in the Dominican Republic. Take appropriate precautions to help stop the spread of sexually transmitted diseases. Condoms are effective against HIV/AIDS when used correctly each time one has sex. Abstinence and monogamy with a partner who has tested negative for HIV/AIDS are other proven ways to avoid contracting the disease.

Safety

American citizens should be aware that foreign tourists are often considered attractive targets for criminal activity and should maintain a low profile to avoid becoming victims of violence or crime. In dealing with local police, U.S. citizens should be aware that the standard of professionalism might vary. Police attempts to solicit bribes have been reported, as have incidents of police using excessive force.

Protests, demonstrations, and general strikes occur periodically. Previous political demonstrations have sometimes turned violent, with participants rioting and erecting roadblocks, and police sometimes using deadly force in response. Political demonstrations do not generally occur in areas frequented by tourists and are generally not targeted at foreigners. However, it is advisable to exercise caution when traveling throughout the country. Street crowds should be avoided. In urban areas, travel should be conducted on main routes whenever possible. Power outages occur frequently throughout the Dominican Republic, and travelers should remain alert during blackout periods, as crime rates often increase during these outages.

Crime continues to be a problem throughout the Dominican Republic. Street crime and petty theft involving U.S. tourists does occur, and precautions should be taken to avoid becoming a target. While pickpocketing and mugging are the most common crimes against tourists, reports of violence against both foreigners and locals are growing. Valuables left unattended in parked automobiles, on beaches, and in other public places are vulnerable to theft, and reports of car theft have increased.

The dangers present in the Dominican Republic are similar to those of many major U.S. cities. Criminals can be dangerous — many have weapons and are likely to use them if they meet resistance. Visitors walking the streets should always be aware of their surroundings. Be wary of strangers, especially those who seek you out at celebrations or nightspots. Travel with a partner or in a group if possible.

Drivers should exercise extreme caution when driving at night and use major highways when possible. In 2006, the U.S. Embassy received reports of Americans and others who were victims of vehicular-armed robberies in the northern provinces of the Dominican Republic. At least three of the reports indicate the victims were intercepted during the morning hours, when there was little other traffic, while driving on rural highways connecting Santiago and Puerto Plata.

Although kidnappings are not common in the Dominican Republic, in 2007, two American citizens were kidnapped and held for ransom, in separate instances.

Calling home

The Dominican Republic has 897,000 land-based telephones and 4.6 million cell phones. There are 81, 218 Internet hosts.

Diplomatic contact in the United States

Ambassador Roberto Saladin
1715 22nd Street NW, Washington, DC 20008
Phone: (202) 332-6280 • Fax (202) 265-8057

Diplomatic contact from the United States

Ambassador P. Robert Fannin
Embassy: Corner of Calle Cesar Nicolas Penson and Calle Leopoldo Navarro, Santo Domingo
Unit 5500, APO AA 34041-5500
Phone: (1) (809) 221-2171 • Fax (1) (809) 686-7437

Grenada

Overview of geography, climate, and population

Grenada is between the Caribbean Sea and the Atlantic Ocean. The island of 90,739 is about double the size of Washington, D.C. The climate is tropical and the terrain is mountainous.

Religion, ethnicity, and language in a nutshell

Fifty-three percent of Grenadians are Roman Catholic, about 14 percent are Anglican, and approximately 33 percent belong to non-Anglican protestant denominations. Eighty-two percent of residents are black, 13 percent are a mix of black and European, and 5 percent are a combination of European and East Indian. An undefined percentage of Grenadians are of Arawak/ Carib Amerindian. English is the official language; French patois is also spoken.

Brief political history and today's government

At the time of European contact, residents of what is now Grenada were Carib Indians. France took over Grenada in the 1600s and forced enslaved Africans to work sugar plantations there. The island came under British control in the late 1700s. Grenada became independent in 1974. The United States and other Caribbean nations invaded Grenada in 1983 to overthrow a militant communist regime.

Economic snapshot

Tourism is essential to the economy. Building, manufacturing, and offshore finance also figure prominently. Recovering from Hurricane Ivan in 2004 and Hurricane Emily in 2005 has put the island in significant debt.

Peace Corps programs

- Community development
- Health

Health

Medical care is limited. U.S. citizens requiring medical treatment may contact the U.S. Embassy in St. George's for a list of local doctors, dentists, pharmacies, and hospitals. Serious medical problems requiring hospitalization and/or medical evacuation to the U.S. can cost thousands of dollars. Doctors and hospitals often expect immediate cash payment for health services. Pharmacies are usually well-stocked, and prescription medicine is available. They periodically suffer shortages when deliveries from abroad are delayed though most pharmacies will check with others in the area to see if they can get what is needed. Travelers are advised to bring with them sufficient prescription medicine for the length of their stay. Grenada chlorinates its water, making it generally safe to drink. However, during especially heavy rains, quality control can slip, particularly in the city of St. George's. It is recommended that visitors to Grenada request bottled water, which is widely available and relatively inexpensive. Ambulance service is available, but response times vary greatly.

Malaria is not found in Grenada, but there are low levels of dengue fever. The government periodically fogs public areas in an attempt to reduce the mosquito population.

Safety
Many parts of Grenada have no sidewalks and few streetlights, forcing pedestrians to walk in the road. Visitors should take care if walking along the road after dark and wear light, reflective clothing.

Crime in Grenada is mostly opportunistic. Tourists have been the victims of robbery, especially in isolated areas, and thieves frequently steal credit cards, jewelry, cameras, U.S. passports, and money. Muggings, purse snatchings, and other robberies may occur in areas near hotels, beaches, and restaurants, particularly after dark. Recently, the St. George's main market square and the Grand Anse area known as Wall Street have experienced decreases in crime because the vendors have been working as a team and now have employed security in the area.

Visitors should exercise appropriate caution when walking after dark or when using the local bus system or taxis hired on the road. It is advisable to hire taxis to and from restaurants and to ask whether the driver is a member of the Grenada Taxi Association (GTA). Members of the GTA are required to pass additional driving tests and receive training from the Grenada Tourism Board. They are generally reliable and knowledgeable about the country and its attractions.

Calling Home
Grenada has 27,700 land telephone lines and 46,200 cell phones. There are seven Internet hosts.

Diplomatic contact in the United States
Ambassador Gillian M.S. Bristol
1701 New Hampshire Avenue NW, Washington, DC 20009
Phone: (202) 265-2561 • Fax (202) 265-2468

Diplomatic contact from the United States

The U.S. Ambassador to Barbados is accredited to Grenada
Embassy: Lance-aux-Epines Stretch, Saint George's
P. O. Box 54, Saint George's
Phone: (1) (473) 444-1173, 444-1174, 444-1175, 444-1176,
and 444-1177 • Fax (1) (473) 444-4820

Jamaica

Overview of geography, climate, and population

Jamaica is a little smaller than Connecticut. It is partly tropical and partly temperate. The terrain is primarily mountainous, with plains along the coasts. The population is about 2.8 million.

Religion, ethnicity, and language in a nutshell

Jamaicans speak English and English patois. About 91 percent of the population is black, a little more than 6 percent is of mixed race, and nearly 3 percent are of other heritage.

About 11 percent of Jamaicans are Seventh-day Adventist, approximately 10 percent are Pentecostal, a little more than 8 percent are part of the Church of God, a bit more than 7 percent are Baptist, slightly more than 6 percent are part of New Testament Church of God, about 5 percent are members of Church of God in Jamaica, about 4 percent attend Church of God Prophecy, nearly 4 percent are Anglican, and approximately 8 percent belong to another Protestant denomination. Approximately 3 percent of the population is Roman Catholic, 14.2 percent of Jamaicans are of an unspecified faith, and a little more than 20 percent follow no religion.

Brief political history and today's government

In 1494, Christopher Columbus was the first European to visit Jamaica, which was inhabited by the aboriginal Taino. The Spanish began to live in Jamaica in the 1500s. Jamaica came under British control at the end of the 1500s. Enslaved Africans provided the labor to support an agrarian economy in which cocoa, coffee, and sugar figured prominently. Abolition came in the 1830s. Jamaica became independent in 1962. The queen is Elizabeth II; her representative is Governor General Kenneth Hall. The prime minister is Bruce Golding. The parliament includes the Senate, which has 21 appointed members, and the House of Representatives, which has 60 popularly elected members. The legal system is derived from common law with a British influence. The judiciary consists of the Supreme Court and Court of Appeal.

Economic snapshot

The service sector is essential to Jamaica's economy. Tourism, remittances from Jamaicans working abroad, and exports of bauxite are important to Jamaica's international economic relations. Interest rates and unemployment are currently high, and the country has a large trade deficit. The debt to gross domestic product ratio is 135 percent.

Peace Corps programs

- Environment
- Education
- Youth development
- Health

Health

Medical care is more limited than in the United States. Comprehensive emergency medical services are located only in Kingston and Montego Bay, and smaller public hospitals are located in each parish. Emergency medical and ambulance services, and the availability of prescription drugs, are limited in outlying parishes. Ambulance service is limited both in the quality of emergency care and in the availability of vehicles in remote parts of the country. Serious medical problems requiring hospitalization and/or medical evacuation to the United States can cost thousands of dollars or more. Doctors and hospitals in Jamaica often require cash payment prior to providing services.

Sefety

Violence and shootings occur regularly in certain areas of Kingston and Montego Bay. Visitors are advised to avoid traveling into high-threat areas including, but not limited to, Mountain View, Trench Town, Tivoli Gardens, Cassava Piece, and Arnett Gardens in Kingston, and Flankers, Canterbury, Norwood, Rose Heights, Clavers Street, and Hart Street in Montego Bay. Sudden demonstrations can occur, during which demonstrators often construct roadblocks or otherwise block streets.

Crime, including violent crime, is a serious problem in Jamaica, particularly in Kingston and Montego Bay. While the vast majority of crimes occur in impoverished areas, the violence is not confined. The primary criminal concern for tourists is becoming a victim of theft. In several cases, armed robberies of Americans have turned violent when the victims resisted handing over valuables. Crime is exacerbated by the fact that police are understaffed and ineffective. Additionally, there have been frequent allegations of police corruption Tourists should take all necessary precautions, always pay extra attention to their surroundings when traveling, and keep windows up and doors locked while in a vehicle. Travelers should avoid walking alone, exercise special care after dark, and always avoid areas known for high crime rates.

In 2009, the Embassy received several reports of sexual assaults against American citizens, including two cases of alleged sexual assaults at tourist resorts. Americans should maintain careful watchfulness, avoid secluded places or situations, go out in groups, and watch out for each other.

Calling home

Jamaica has 319,000 land-based telephones and 2.8 million cell phones. There are 1.2 million Internet hosts in Jamaica.

Diplomatic contact in the United States

Ambassador Anthony Johnson
1520 New Hampshire Avenue NW, Washington, DC 20036
Phone: (202) 452-0660 • Fax (202) 452-0081

Diplomatic contact from the United States

Ambassador Brenda LaGrange Johnson
Embassy: 142 Old Hope Road, Kingston 6
P.O. Box 541, Kingston 5
Phone: (1) (876) 702-6000 • Fax (1) (876) 702-6001

St. Kitts and Nevis

Overview of geography, climate, and population

St. Kitts and Nevis are Caribbean islands a little larger than Washington, D.C. The climate is tropical and breezy. The wet season lasts from May through November. The terrain includes mountains and volcanoes. About 40,000 people live in St. Kitts and Nevis.

Religion, ethnicity, and language in a nutshell

Residents are Roman Catholic, Anglican, and other Protestant faiths. Kittians and Nevisians are black, British, Portuguese, and Lebanese. Residents speak English.

Brief political history and today's government

The British began to live in the islands in the early 1600s. The islands joined Anguilla to form an autonomous state in 1967. Anguilla separated in 1971, and St. Kitts and Nevis became independent in 1983.

Peace Corps programs

- IT
- Disaster readiness
- Disaster relief
- AIDS prevention

Health

Medical care is limited. The main hospitals are Joseph N. France General Hospital on St. Kitts and Alexandria Hospital on Nevis. St. Kitts has two additional hospitals, and both islands have several health clinics. Neither island has a hyperbaric chamber. Divers suffering from decompression illness are transported to the island of Saba, in the Netherlands Antilles. Serious medical problems requiring hospitalization and/or medical evacuation to the United States can cost thousands of dollars. Doctors and hospitals expect immediate cash payment for health services.

Safety

St. Kitts and Nevis experienced an increase in violent crime in 2008. Also, petty street crime and burglary continue to occur. Visitors and residents should take common-sense precautions. Avoid carrying large amounts of cash, and use hotel safety deposit facilities to safeguard valuables and travel documents. Do not leave valuables unattended on the beach or in cars. Walking alone at night is strongly discouraged.

Calling home

St. Kitts and Nevis have good interisland and international connections. There are 53 Internet hosts.

Diplomatic contact in the United States

Ambassador Dr. Izben Cordinal Williams
3216 New Mexico Avenue NW, Washington, DC 20016
Phone: (202) 686-2636 • Fax (202) 686-5740

Diplomatic contact from the United States

The United States does not have an embassy in St. Kitts and Nevis.

St. Lucia

Overview of geography, climate, and population

St. Lucia is a Caribbean island of 160,267 inhabitants, which is nearly four times the size of Washington, D.C. It has a tropical climate with a dry season from January through April and a rainy season from May through August. The terrain includes mountains, volcanoes, and valleys.

Religion, ethnicity, and language in a nutshell

About 68 percent of St. Lucians are Roman Catholic, approximately 9 percent are Seventh-day Adventist, about 6 percent are Pentecostal, slightly more than 2 percent are Rastafarian, 2 percent are Anglican, 2 percent are Evangelical, and slightly more than 5 percent belong to other Christian denominations. A little more than 2 percent of residents adhere to other or unspecified faiths. About 5 percent of St. Lucians are non-religious.

Nearly 83 percent of St. Lucians are black, and about 12 percent are of mixed lineage. About 2 percent are East Indian, and slightly more than 3 percent follow an unspecified faith. English is the official language; French patois is also spoken.

Brief political history and today's government

France and Great Britain alternated as rulers of St. Lucia in the 1600s and 1700s. Great Britain took possession of the island in the early 1800s. It became independent in 1979..

St. Lucia is a parliamentary democracy. Queen Elizabeth is the monarch; her representative is Governor General Dame Pearlette Louisy. The parliament includes the 11-member Senate and the 17-member House of Representatives. Senators are appointed and Representatives are elected. The island's judiciary is part of the Eastern Caribbean Supreme Court. The legal system stems from British common law.

Economic snapshot

Foreign investors are essential to the economy. Tourism and offshore finance figure prominently. The economy is relatively stable. However, debt is high, and unemployment is a problem.

Peace Corps programs

- IT
- Disaster relief
- Disaster readiness
- AIDS prevention

Health

Medical care is limited. There are two public hospitals and one private hospital in St. Lucia, none of which provide the same level of care found in an American hospital. The main hospital is Victoria Hospital. St. Jude's Hospital in Vieux Fort was destroyed by fire on September 9, 2009. A temporary facility is currently operating out of George Odlum Stadium in Vieux Fort, but lacks any operating room capacity, has no overnight stays, and is generally limited in the amount of care that can be provided. A new hyperbaric chamber capable of treating six patients is now located at Tapion Hospital. The chamber is undergoing the accreditation process by DAN (Divers Alert Network) but is fully operational. Serious medical problems requiring hospitalization and/or medical evacuation to the United States can cost thousands of dollars. Doctors and hospitals often expect immediate cash payment for health services.

Sefety

Crime, including armed robbery, does occur and is rising in St. Lucia. Violent crime is often connected to narcotics trafficking. Petty crime also occurs, with tourists being targeted often. Efforts by the St. Lucian authorities to improve public safety on the island are ongoing. Visitors should inquire about their hotel's security arrangements before making reservations. Valuables left unattended on beaches and in rental cars are vulnerable to theft. Visitors should use caution, especially at night and in less frequented areas.

Calling home

St. Lucia has 51,100 land-based telephones and 105,700 cell phones. There are 15 Internet hosts.

Diplomatic contact in the United States

Ambassador Michael Louis

3216 New Mexico Avenue NW, Washington, DC 20016

Phone: (202) 364-6792 through 6795 • Fax (202) 364-6723

Diplomatic contact from the United States

The United States does not have an embassy in St. Lucia.

St. Vincent and the Grenadines

Overview of geography, climate, and population

St. Vincent and the Grenadines are islands north of Trinidad and Tobago. The climate is tropical with a wet season from May through November. The terrain includes volcanoes and mountains. The population is about 104,574.

Religion, ethnicity, and language in a nutshell

About 47 percent of St. Vincentians are Anglican, approximately 30 percent of residents are Methodist, about 13 percent are Roman Catholic, and about 12 percent follow other faiths.

About 66 percent of residents are black, nearly 20 percent are of mixed race, 6 percent are East Indian, 4 percent are of European heritage, 2 percent are Carib Amerinidan, and 3 percent are of other descent. Residents speak English and French patois.

Brief political history and today's government

France and Great Britain vied for control of the islands in the 1700s. British rule began in the late 1700s. The islands became independent in 1979.

Economic snapshot

The economy depends largely on tourism, agriculture, and construction. Economic growth is steady, but the national debt is equivalent to one-quarter of the government's income.

Peace Corps programs

- IT
- Disaster relief
- Disaster readiness
- AIDS prevention

Health

Medical facilities are limited. The main hospital is Milton Cato Memorial Hospital. There is a hospital in the capital, Kingstown, but serious medical problems usually require evacuation to another island or to the United States. There is no hyperbaric chamber; divers requiring treatment for decompression illness must be evacuated from the island. The closest hyperbaric chamber is located in Barbados. Serious medical problems requiring hospitalization and/or medical evacuation to the United States can cost thousands of dollars. Doctors and hospitals usually expect immediate cash payment for health services.

Safety

Petty street crime occurs in St. Vincent and the Grenadines. From time to time, property has been stolen from yachts anchored in the Grenadines. Valuables left unattended on beaches are vulnerable to theft. Persons interested in nature walks or hikes in the northern areas of St. Vincent should arrange in advance with a local tour operator for a guide; these areas are isolated, and police presence is limited.

Calling home

There are 22,600 land-based telephones and 87,600 cell phones. The islands have 97 Internet hosts.

Diplomatic contact in the United States

Ambassador La Celia A. Prince
3216 New Mexico Avenue NW, Washington, DC 20016
Phone: (202) 364-6730 • Fax (202) 364-6736

Diplomatic contact from the United States

The United States does not have an embassy in St. Vincent and the Grenadines.

Central America and Mexico

Belize

Overview of geography, climate, and population

Belize is a little smaller than Massachusetts. Its climate is tropical with a rainy season from May to November and a dry season from February to May. The terrain consists of swamps, plains, and small mountains. The population was 307,899 as of 2009 estimates.

Religion, ethnicity, and language in a nutshell

English is the official language, but only 4 percent of the population speak it. Spanish is the language of 46 percent of the population. Creole speakers make up about 32 percent of the population. Nearly 9 percent use Mayan dialects. About 3 percent of the population speak Garifuna. A little more than 3 percent speak German. Slightly more than 1 percent speak other languages.

About 50 percent of residents are mestizo, approximately 25 percent are Creole, a little more than 10 percent are Maya, slightly more than 6 percent are Garifuna, and nearly 10 percent are of other ancestry. About 50 percent of those who live in Belize are Roman Catholic, a little more than 7 percent are Pentecostal, and slightly more than 5 percent are Anglican. About 5 percent of Belizians are Seventh-day Adventists, 4 percent are Mennonite, approximately 3 percent are Methodist, a little more than 1 percent are Jehovah's Witnesses, and 14 percent practice another religion. Slightly more than 9 percent follow no faith.

Brief political history and today's government

The Mayans began to inhabit what is now Belize from 1500 years before to 300 years after the Christian era began. The Mayan civilization was prominent in the area until 1200 CE. Christopher Columbus was the first European to see the coast of what is now known as Belize. The British established towns in the area beginning in 1638. Britain claimed Belize, under the name Colony of British Honduras, in the mid-19th century. The country became known as Belize in 1973, after establishing self-rule in 1964. Belize became independent in 1981. Belize is a parliamentary democracy. Queen Elizabeth II is the chief of state. The prime minister is Dean Barrow. The legislature includes the National Assembly, which consists of the Senate and the House of Representatives. The governor general appoints the 12 members of the Senate, six in consultation with the prime minister, three at the suggestion of the head of the opposing party, and the rest on the advice of national religious, business, civic, and labor groups. Members of the House of Representatives are popularly elected.

The judiciary consists of the Supreme Court of Judicature and the Court of Appeal. The governor general appoints the chief justice of the Supreme Court of Judicature in consultation with the prime minister. The legal system is based on British law.

Economic snapshot

Most foreign money that enters Belize flows into the tourist industry. Important exports include commodities harvested from the ocean, fruits, sugar, bananas, and clothing. Beginning in the late 1990s and continuing through the present, the gross domestic product grew consistently. The country still has significant international debt and a large trade deficit. The government is seeking foreign aid to alleviate poverty.

Peace Corps programs

- Education
- Community development
- Youth development
- Environment

Health

HIV/AIDS, diarrhea, hepatitis A, hepatitis B, typhoid, rabies, dengue fever, leptospirosis, malaria, leishmaniasis, and Chagas disease are among the diseases and illnesses volunteers should be aware of in Belize.

Most cities offer basic health care. Trauma services and extensive procedures are inadequate inside and outside the capital. In the countryside, advanced care is often non-existent. Medical evacuation is often necessary in severe cases.

Malaria is a hazard everywhere except the capital. Volunteers should buy and take the anti-malarial medicine chloroquine before leaving the United States. Anti-malarial drugs sold in Belize are often of poor quality and potentially harmful.

Visitors should not accept treatment with the anti-malarial drug halofantrine, sold under the brand name Halfan, because it causes potentially fatal heart problems. Patients should not take halofantrine unless doctors have diagnosed them with malaria that could be lethal, and no other anti-malarial pharmaceuticals are obtainable.

Leptospirosis is a bacterial infection contracted through contact with water in which sick animals have urinated. Avoiding freshwater sports is the primary way to reduce the risk of catching leptospirosis.

Visitors can reduce their risk of contracting insect-borne diseases such as malaria, leishmaniasis, and dengue fever by using mosquito netting. Travelers can also protect themselves by applying insect repellent containing 30 percent to 50 percent DEET. Insect repellent that contains 7 percent to 15 percent picardin has not been proved effective. Permethrin can be used to treat clothing and mosquito netting but should not be applied to skin.

A widespread infection with dengue fever occurred in the spring of 2005.

Safety

Water taxis and other boats often lack adequate lifesaving equipment, carry too many passengers, and sail in storms. Diving can be dangerous because excursion leaders do not always match the difficulty of the dives with the ability of the participants. Volunteers who wish to dive or snorkel should review the licenses, references, and equipment of those operating the boats in which they would ride.

The safety standards of even licensed boat operators might not meet those of their counterparts in the United States. Terrorism is not a concern.

Belize and Guatemala dispute their border, but the conflict has not prevented visitors from freely crossing the frontier. People traveling near the border with Guatemala should take cellular phones or other means of communication, ensure that the vehicles they take are in good repair, and have plenty of gas.

Police service is inadequate due to lack of expertise and funding. Foreigners should report crimes to the tourist police and call the U.S. Embassy in Belmopan at (501) 822-4011.

The legal consequences of possessing or consuming illicit drugs are more draconian than in the United States. Owning drug paraphernalia can also end in problems with the law.

Violent crimes of which foreigners should be wary include robbery, rape, sexual harassment, and murder. Visitors should be especially careful at resorts as well as on highways and rivers. Pickpockets and purse snatchers become especially active during holidays and spring break. Belize City has the highest crime rate, but incidents happen across the country, including in such popular destinations as Placencia, Caye Caulker, and San Pedro. Visitors should walk with others and refrain from going out after dark, whether in the city or the countryside. Travelers should store jewelry and valuables rather than carrying or wearing them in public. Pedestrians should hold their bags close to their body and keep them closed. Wallets should remain in front pockets. Visitors should avoid displaying cash. Only taxis with green license plates are safe to ride. Foreigners should refuse to enter taxis with other passengers already in them and should not agree to let other people get into cabs with them.

Female U.S. citizens have reported numerous rapes recently. The perpetrator in at least one case was an acquaintance who offered the survivor a ride, which she accepted. Armed robbers committed other sexual assaults. In at least one case, the victim was raped so brutally that she died. In 2006, armed robbers attacked U.S. citizens in the Caracol and Mountain Pine Ridge areas. Well-known Mayan ruins have been common robbery scenes. To reduce the risk of being targeted by criminals, travelers should remain in groups and should remain in well-traveled areas. When touring archaeological sites, volunteers are most vulnerable when walking from one ruin to another. To reduce the risk of serious injury, visitors should immediately cooperate with armed criminals if accosted by them. Due in part to the smuggling of people and drugs, travelers are especially vulnerable to crime when driving or walking on remote roads after dark. Volunteers can reduce their risk of falling victim to crime by organizing their travel through well-established travel agencies or sightseeing companies. When traveling in Belize, visitors should remain with other people, drive in convoys, and keep to well-traveled thoroughfares. A trusted person who is not part of the trip should always know volunteers' travel plans. Due to security concerns, travelers should avoid discount hotels and remain in popular tourist spots rather than taking back roads.

Buying or selling illegally reproduced items could violate Belizeans' laws. The United States prohibits the importation of pirated goods.

Calling home

Belize has 33,900 land-based telephones and 118,300 cell phones. There are 1,942 Internet hosts.

Diplomatic contact in the United States

Ambassador Nestor Mendez
2535 Massachusetts Avenue NW, Washington, DC 20008
Phone: (202) 332-9636 • Fax (202) 332-6888

Diplomatic contact from the United States

Ambassador (vacant): Charge d'Affaires J.A. Diffily
Embassy: Floral Park Road, Belmopan City, Cayo District
P.O. Box 497, Belmopan City, Cayo District, Belize
Phone: (501) 822-4011 • Fax (501) 822-4012

Costa Rica

Overview of geography, climate, and population

Costa Rica is a little smaller than West Virginia. The country is tropical and subtropical, with a dry season from December to April and a rainy season from May to November. Higher elevations are cooler than lowlands. The terrain consists of plains, mountains, and volcanoes. The population is 4.2 million.

Religion, ethnicity, and language in a nutshell

Spanish is the official language, but Costa Ricans also speak English. Ninety-four percent of Costa Ricans are white (including mestizo). Approximately 3 percent are black, 1 percent are Amerindian, 1 percent are Chinese, and 1 percent are of other ethnicities. About 76 percent of Costa Ricans are Roman Catholic, approximately 14 percent are Evangelical, a little more than 1 percent are Jehovah's Witnesses. Nearly 1 percent are Protestant, 5 percent follow another faith, and about 3 percent do not have a religion.

Brief political history and today's government

European contact led to the demise of almost all the aboriginals who initially inhabited what is now Costa Rica. The Spanish claimed Costa Rica as a colony in the 16th century. The country became independent in 1821. In 1823, Costa Rica became part of the United Provinces of Central America, which fell apart in 1838. Costa Rica declared independence the same year. In 1899, the country had its first democratic elections. The transfer of power in Costa Rica was peaceful and democratic with two exceptions: Dictator Federico Tinoco controlled the country from 1917 through 1919, and a contested national election led to a civil war in 1948. The country has no armed forces after a 1948 constitution banned the military. Costa Rica is a democratic republic, and the president is Oscar Arias Sanchez. The legislature consists of the Legislative Assembly, which has 57 members who are publicly elected, and the judiciary includes the Supreme Court, with 22 judges elected by the Legislative Assembly.

Economic snapshot

Agriculture, tourism, and exports of electronics are pillars of the Costa Rican economy. About 20 percent of the population is below the poverty line. Foreign investment is common due to a lack of trade barriers and a well-educated populace. Inflation and debt remain problems. Costa Ricans approved the Central American Free Trade Agreement by referendum.

Peace Corps programs

- Youth development
- Community development
- Business

Health

HIV/AIDS, diarrhea, hepatitis A, hepatitis B, typhoid, dengue fever, rabies, malaria, diarrhea, leishmaniasis, and Chagas disease are among the diseases and illnesses volunteers should be aware of in Costa Rica.

San Jose offers satisfactory medical care, but regions outside the capital do not. Pharmacies are well-stocked.

Visitors should buy the anti-malarial medicine chloroquine before leaving the United States. Anti-malarial medicine sold in Costa Rica is often of poor quality, and possibly harmful. Malaria is a hazard in the provinces of Alajuela Limo'n Guanacaste, and Heredia.

Visitors should not accept treatment with the anti-malarial drug halofantrine, sold under the brand name Halfan, because it causes potentially fatal heart problems. Patients should not take halofantrine unless doctors have diagnosed them with malaria that could be lethal, and no other anti-malarial pharmaceuticals are obtainable.

Visitors can reduce their risk of contracting insect-borne diseases such as malaria, leishmaniasis, and dengue fever by using mosquito netting. Travelers can also protect themselves by applying insect repellent containing 30 to 50 percent DEET. Insect repellent that contains 7 to 15 percent picardin has not been proved effective. Permethrin can be used to treat clothing and mosquito netting but should not be applied to skin.

Safety

Terrorism is not a concern in Costa Rica. Strikes and other acts of civil disobedience occur periodically and can cause difficulty for visitors. At least eight U.S. citizens die of drowning annually because both coasts have dangerous currents and perilous drop-offs, even in shallow water. Volunteers who wish to take adventure tours should arrange them only with companies that are registered with the government and have permits. The Ministry of Health enforces safety regulations. Criminals frequently target foreigners, particularly for theft of valuables, cash, and passports. Visitors should avoid nightlife districts, abandoned buildings, and vacant lots, especially at night. Travelers should refrain from walking alone, displaying cash or valuables, and responding to harassing comments by strangers. Passports should remain securely stored, and volunteers should carry only photocopies of them.

Locked rental cars parked in areas frequented by tourists are often the targets of thieves seeking to steal valuables and important documents. Visitors should take only licensed cabs, which are red and display numbered yellow triangles. At the airport, licensed taxis are orange. The safety belts, door handles, locks, and meters of legitimate taxis should work. Bus passengers should keep their luggage in sight at all times, rather than storing them in baggage bins.

Pairs or clusters of thieves often work together. Sometimes one criminal will drop something in a crowd and steal from people who try to return the item. Criminals also frequently slash the tires of a parked rental car before following the driver and offering to help change the flat. When the driver accepts assistance, the thieves, who are sometimes armed, steal valuables from the car. To change flat tires, motorists should drive to a gas station or other public place.

Major attractions have substations of the tourist police. Buying and selling pirated items is possibly a violation of Costa Rican law. The United States prohibits bringing pirated goods into the country.

Calling home

There are about 1.4 million land telephone lines and 1.4 million cell phones in Costa Rica. There are 13,792 Internet hosts.

Diplomatic contact in the United States

Ambassador Luis Diego Escalante
2114 S Street NW, Washington, DC 20008
Phone: (202) 234-2945 • Fax (202) 265-4795

Diplomatic contact from the United States

Ambassador Peter Cianchette
Embassy: Calle 120 Avenida O, Pavas, San Jose
APO AA 34020
Phone: (506) 519-2000 • Fax (506) 519-2305

El Salvador

Overview of geography, climate, and population

El Salvador is nearly the size of Massachusetts. The country is tropical, with a rainy season that lasts from May through October and a dry season that lasts from November through April. The climate ranges from tropical to temperate. The terrain includes mountains and plateaus. There are about 7.1 million inhabitants.

Religion, ethnicity, and language in a nutshell

Roman Catholics account for 83 percent of the population. Seventeen percent of Salvadorans follow other faiths. Spanish and Nahua are spoken. Ninety percent of Salvadorans are mestizo, 9 percent are white, and 1 percent are Amerindian.

Brief political history and today's government

El Salvador is a republic. The legislature consists of the Legislative Assembly. The judicial branch includes the Supreme Court. A former Spanish colony, El Salvador became independent in the 1800s. The legal system stems from civil law, Roman law, and common law.

Economic snapshot

Remittances and exports are essential to the economy. El Salvador is a party to the Central American Free Trade Agreement. In 2001, the U.S. dollar became official currency.

Peace Corps programs

- Sanitation
- Disaster relief
- Business
- Youth development
- Water quality
- Education
- Agroforestry
- Health education
- AIDS prevention
- Environment

Health

HIV/AIDS, hepatitis A, hepatitis B, typhoid, diarrhea, dengue fever, leptospirosis, rabies, and malaria are among the diseases and illnesses volunteers should be aware of in El Salvador.

Visitors should take the anti-malarial drug chloroquine. Malaria is a concern in rural Santa Ana, Ahuachapan, and La Union. Hospitals fall far below standards common in the United States. Medical evacuation is often necessary. Health care bills must be paid immediately. Many medicines are not available.

Visitors can reduce their risk of contracting insect-borne diseases such as malaria, leishmaniasis, and dengue fever by using mosquito netting. Travelers can also protect themselves by applying insect repellent containing 30 to 50 percent DEET. Insect repellent that contains 7 percent to 15 percent picardin has not been proved effective. Permethrin can be used to treat clothing and mosquito netting but should not be applied to skin.

Visitors should not accept treatment with the anti-malarial drug halofantrine, sold under the brand name Halfan, because it causes potentially fatal heart problems. Patients should not take halofantrine unless doctors have diagnosed them with malaria that could be lethal, and no other anti-malarial pharmaceuticals are obtainable.

Visitors should avoid tap water and ice cubes made with it.

Safety

Murder is prevalent, and the rate is rising significantly each year. Rape and other violent crimes occur.

Land mines are a hazard to hikers, so travelers should hire guides before trekking in the wilderness.

Visitors should be careful at banks and ATMs because criminals often target customers. Travelers should avoid mass transit. Instead, they should taxis from stands in front of major hotels.

Drivers should keep doors locked and windows closed. Motorists should remain on paved roads and should not venture outside cities after dark.

Calling Home

There are about 1 million land-based telephones and about 3.8 million cell phones in El Salvador. The country has about 12,500 Internet hosts.

Diplomatic contact in the United States

Ambassador (vacant): Charge d'Affaires Francisco Altschul Fuentes
1400 16th Street, Washington, DC 20036
Phone: (202) 265-9671 • Fax (202) 234-3763

Diplomatic contact from the United States

Ambassador (vacant): Charge d'Affaires Robert Blau

Embassy: Final Boulevard Santa Elena Sur, Antiguo Cuscatlan,
La Libertad, San Salvador
Unit 3450, APO AA 34023; 3450 San Salvador Place, Washington, DC
20521-3450
Phone: (503) 2501-2999 • Fax (503) 2501-2150

Guatemala

Overview of geography, climate, and population

Guatemala is a little smaller than Tennessee. The climate is tropical in the low country and cooler in the highlands. The terrain consists of mountains, plateaus, and plains. The population is 13.2 million.

Religion, ethnicity, and language in a nutshell

Sixty percent of Guatemalans speak Spanish; 40 percent use Amerindian languages, including Quiche, Cakchiquel, Kelchi, Mam, Garifuna, and Xinca.

About 60 percent of Guatemalans are Mestizo and European. Approximately 9 percent are of K'iche ancestry, a little more than 8 percent are Kaqchikel, about 8 percent are Mam, and slightly more than 6 percent are Q'eqchi. About 8 percent of the population trace their ancestry to other Mayan tribes. Non-Mayan aboriginal people comprise .2 percent of the population and .1 percent are of other ethnicities. Guatemalans are Roman Catholic, Protestant, and followers of indigenous faiths.

Brief political history and today's government

The Mayas inhabited what is now Guatemala before European contact. The Spanish claimed Guatemala as a colony in the 16th century, but Guatemala broke from Spain in the 1800s. Guatemala came under the control of the Mexican Empire immediately following independence. The country later joined a confederation known as the United Provinces of Central America. Military juntas and dictators held power in Guatemala from the middle of the 1800s to the 1980s, and Guerrilla fighters carried out a civil war, which lasted 36 years before a peace pact ended it in 1996. The establishment in 1987 of the Office of Human Rights Ombudsman, and the institution of legal reforms marked the administration of democratically elected president Vinicio Cerezo. Guatemala is a constitutional democratic republic. The president is Alvaro Colom Caballeros, and the legislature consists of the Congress of the Republic, which has 158 publicly elected members. The judiciary is made up of the Constitutional Court and the Supreme Court of Justice; the Constitutional Court includes five elected justices, and the Supreme Court of Justice includes 13 judges.

Economic snapshot

Agriculture is the backbone of Guatemala's economy, with coffee, sugar, and bananas figuring prominently. The 1996 end of the civil war improved the climate for foreign investment. Guatemala is a party to the Central American Free Trade Agreement, which has encouraged investment. Guatemalans living in the United States send home enough money to equal the value of two-thirds of exports.

Peace Corps programs

- Business
- Health
- Agriculture
- Environment

Health

HIV/AIDS, diarrhea, hepatitis A, hepatitis B, typhoid fever, dengue fever, malaria, leptospirosis, yellow fever, and rabies are among the diseases and illnesses volunteers should be aware of in Guatemala.

Anti-malarial medicines that protect visitors against strains of malaria prevalent in Guyana include atovaquone/proguanil, doxycycline, mefloquine, and primaquine, which should only be taken in special cases after G6PD screening. Chloroquine does not offer protection against the strains of malaria common in Guyana. Malaria is a concern in all areas of the countryside at elevations lower than 2,953 feet.

Visitors should not accept treatment with the anti-malarial drug halofantrine, sold under the brand name Halfan, because it causes potentially fatal heart problems. Patients should not take halofantrine unless doctors have diagnosed them with malaria that could be lethal, and no other anti-malarial pharmaceuticals are obtainable.

Visitors can reduce their risk of contracting insect-borne diseases such as malaria, leishmaniasis, and dengue fever by using mosquito netting. Travelers can also protect themselves by applying insect repellent containing 30 to 50 percent DEET. Insect repellent that contains 7 percent to 15 percent picardin has not been proved effective. Permethrin can be used to treat clothing and mosquito netting but should not be applied to skin.

Visitors should avoid tap water and ice cubes made with it.

Food from street stands is often unsafe to eat, as are unpasteurized dairy products. Travelers should ensure that any food they eat is cooked thoroughly.

Safety

Visitors should avoid crowds and rallies, for fear of violence. Major hotels and resorts lack emergency plans, adequate security, lifeguards, and first aid supplies.

Murder, burglary, kidnapping, and carjacking are hazards, particularly in commercial areas. Drivers should keep doors locked and windows closed. For fear of crime, travelers should avoid visiting or going through Buxton, which is a village on the road between Georgetown and New Amsterdam. Visitors should also avoid Agricola, a town on the East Bank highway. The public golf course in Lusignan, near Buxton, is not safe to use alone or at night.

Assailants have attacked travelers going to and from the Cheddi Jagan International Airport, so travelers should be cautious. Visitors are especially vulnerable to rape, armed assault, theft, purse snatching, and pickpocketing in Georgetown. Travelers are vulnerable to crime in the National Park and sections near the sea wall in Georgetown. Visitors are more likely to be targeted for crime in Georgetown after twilight. Taxis are the safest mode of transportation, though criminals have sometimes targeted passengers. Volunteers should avoid displaying valuables or cash because muggings sometimes happen during the day.

Calling home

There are about 1.3 million land telephone lines and 7.1 million cell phones in Guatemala. There are 40,927 Internet hosts.

Diplomatic contact in the United States

Ambassador Francisco Villagran de Leon
2220 R Street NW, Washington, DC 20008
Phone: (202) 745-4952 • Fax (202) 745-1908

Diplomatic contact from the United States

Ambassador Stephen G. McFarland
Embassy: 7-01 Avenida Reforma, Zone 10, Guatemala City
APO AA 34024
Phone: (502) 2326-4000 • Fax (502) 2326-4654

Honduras

Overview of geography, climate, and population

Honduras is a little larger than Tennessee. Its climate is subtropical in the low country and temperate in the highlands. The terrain is primarily mountainous with some plains along the coasts. The population is 7.7 million.

Religion, ethnicity, and language in a nutshell

Hondurans speak Spanish and Amerindian dialects. Ninety percent of Hondurans are mestizo, 7 percent are Amerindian, 2 percent are black, and 1 percent are white. Roman Catholics account for 97 percent of Hondurans. The remaining 3 percent of the population are Protestant.

Brief political history and today's government

Mayans, Lencas, and others were the first people to populate what is now Honduras. The ancient societies of the area traded with their counterparts in what are now Mexico and Panama. Columbus claimed Honduras as a Spanish territory in 1502, and the country became independent in the early 19th century. Honduras fell under the control of the Mexican Empire immediately following independence from Spain. In 1823, the country became part of a confederation known as the United Provinces of Central America. The confederation dissolved in 1838. Landowners from the United States who held banana plantations were central to the Honduran economy from the closing years of the 1800s through the first several decades of the 20th century. Military juntas held power in the middle of the 20th century. Beginning in 1982, a democratically elected administration held office. Nicaraguan guerrillas opposing the Sandinistas took refuge in Honduras during the 1980s.

Honduras is a democratic constitutional republic. The president is Manuel Zelaya Rosales, and the legislature includes the National Congress, which has 128 members. Congressional seats are apportioned according to how many votes representatives' parties gained in presidential elections.

Economic snapshot

Honduras is the second most impoverished Central American nation. Unemployment is common, and the gap between rich and poor is exceptionally wide. Money that expatriates send home equals more than a quarter of the gross domestic product. Exports, including bananas and coffee, are essential to the Honduran economy. Honduras' economic health is tied to that of the United States, with which it trades the most.

Peace Corps programs

- AIDS prevention
- Sanitation and water quality
- Environmental conservation
- Business
- Urban development
- Youth development

Health

HIV/AIDS, diarrhea, hepatitis A, hepatitis B, typhoid fever, malaria, and rabies are among the diseases and illnesses volunteers should be aware of in Honduras.

Volunteers should buy the anti-malarial medicine chloroquine before leaving the United States. Anti-malarial drugs sold in Honduras are often of poor quality and possibly dangerous. Malaria is a hazard across Honduras at elevations lower than 3,281 feet, on Roata'n island and Bay Islands. Malaria is a hazard in areas surrounding Tegucigalpa and San Pedo Sula.

Visitors should not accept treatment with the anti-malarial drug halofantrine, sold under the brand name Halfan, because it causes potentially fatal heart problems. Patients should not take halofantrine unless doctors have diagnosed them with malaria that could be lethal, and no other anti-malarial pharmaceuticals are obtainable.

Visitors can reduce their risk of contracting insect-borne diseases such as malaria, leishmaniasis, and dengue fever by using mosquito netting. Travelers can also protect themselves by applying insect repellent containing 30 to 50 percent DEET. Insect repellent that contains 7 to 15 percent picardin has not been proved effective. Permethrin can be used to treat clothing and mosquito netting but should not be applied to skin.

Visitors should bring a stock of their own prescription medicines to last until the end of their service.

Across the country, health care facilities fall short of Western standards. Advanced medical care is limited except in Tegucigalpa and San Pedro Sula.

Vast stretches of Honduras lack a hospital at which common surgeries can be performed. Nowhere in the country can patients undergo complex surgery.

Large cities offer ambulances, but service is restricted. Outside of cities, ambulances are scarce or not available.

Scuba accidents are especially dangerous for those diving in the water near the Bay Islands because of the rudimentary medical care available. Roatan and Utila offer decompression chambers but lack facilities for extensive medical procedures.

Tap water is not potable. Visitors should drink bottled or purified water and avoid ice cubes. Foods to avoid for fear of disease include raw vegetables, fruit that does not have a peel still on it, uncooked or undercooked seafood, mayonnaise, icing, and dairy goods that have not been pasteurized. Food from street vendors is not safe to eat. Vegetables and fruits should be washed with detergent and water. Visitors should soak produce that is to be consumed raw, and not peeled, in a mixture of 1 tablespoon of bleach with a gallon of water for fifteen minutes. The produce should be rinsed with water that is safe for drinking and set out to air dry.

Air pollution poses a significant health risk, particularly for people with respiratory illnesses. Volunteers should carry enough properly labeled medicine to last until the end of their service.

Safety

Rallies are usually nonviolent, but visitors should avoid them in case they turn dangerous. Volunteers should keep abreast of the news to learn when demonstrations are planned. Visitors should not attempt to cross roadblocks that demonstrators make.

Most unexploded land mines are gone from the land near the border with Nicaragua, but some might remain. Violent crimes such as murder, rape, abduction, and assault are prevalent and U.S. citizens are often targets. Mass murder is common, and the country's homicide rate per capita is among the highest across the globe.

Pickpockets often strike international visitors at airports, so passports and other valuables should remain in inside pockets. Armed robbers on motorcycles or in cars target pedestrians, especially on sparsely traveled thoroughfares. Bandits force cars off the road to rob and assault the occupants. Tourist police have headquarters in Tela, Tegucigalpa, San Pedro Sula, La Ceiba, and Roatan.

Visitors should refrain from talking about their itineraries in public because several attacks against U.S. citizens seem to have been the result of advice from people who talked with the victims near arrival gates. Travelers should refrain from visiting Coxen Hole on Roatan Island at night. Visitors are especially vulnerable to crime on remote beaches. Drivers should carry cellular phones as well as keep doors locked and windows closed to reduce the risk of carjacking and kidnapping. Particularly dangerous roads include Limones to La Union, and Route 41 (also known as Olancho) through Salama to Esquipulas Del Norte and Saba.

Law enforcement and the judicial system function poorly due to inadequate training, corruption, under-staffing, and lack of funds.

To reduce the risk of potentially fatal injury, travelers should immediately comply with robbers and carjackers.

Visitors should avoid hitchhiking and leaving bars and clubs with people they do not know. Remaining in groups helps reduce the risk of becoming a crime victim. Travelers should avoid walking after dark. Solitary walks in the countryside, at historic sites, on beaches, or on trails are dangerous and should be avoided.

Visitors should not wear jewelry, display cash, or show credit cards unnecessarily. Valuables should remain stored securely when not in use.

Calling home

There are about 708,400 land-based telephones and 2.2 million cell phones in Honduras. There are 4,672 Internet hosts.

Diplomatic contact in the United States

Ambassador (vacant): Charge d'Affaires Eduardo Enrique Reina Garcia
3007 Tilden Street NW, Suite 4-M, Washington, DC 20008
Phone: (202) 966-7702 • Fax (202) 966-9751

Diplomatic contact from the United States

Ambassador Hugo Llorens
Embassy: Avenida La Paz, Apartado Postal No. 3453, Tegucigalpa
American Embassy, APO AA 34022, Tegucigalpa
Phone: (504) 236-9320, 238-5114 • Fax (504) 238-4357

Mexico

Overview of geography, climate, and population

Mexico is a little less than three times as big as Texas. The climate ranges from desert to tropical, and Mexico's terrain includes high mountains, plains, plateaus, and desert. The population is about 111 million.

Religion, ethnicity, and language in a nutshell

Mexicans speak Spanish, a number of Mayan languages, Nahuatl, and various indigenous tongues.

About 60 percent of Mexicans are mestizo, 30 percent are Amerindian, 9 percent are white, and 1 percent are of another ethnicity.

About 76 percent of Mexicans are Roman Catholic, a little more than 1 percent are Pentecostal, a little more than 1 percent are Jehovah's Witnesses, and approximately 4 percent belong to other Protestant denominations. Followers of unspecified or other faiths make up about 14 percent of the population, and 3 percent are non-religious.

Brief political history and today's government

Societies that populated Mexico before European contact include the Toltecs, Mayas, Olmecs, and Aztecs. European contact began when the Spanish arrived in the 16th century and claimed the country as a colony. Mexico became independent in the 1820s. The country's constitution, which dates to 1917, established a republic governed by the president. The legislature includes the National Congress, which consists of a Senate and chamber of deputies. The Senate has 128 members, 96 of whom are publicly elected, 32 of whom are chosen by their parties. The judiciary consists of the Supreme Court of Justice, justices of whom are presidential appointees chosen with Senate approval.

Economic snapshot

Mexico's robust capitalist economy relies on a combination of industry and agriculture. There is a wide gap between rich and poor. Mexico is a party to the North American Free Trade Agreement, which went into effect in 1994 and increased its trade with the United States and Canada. Current economic needs include improving infrastructure, revising labor policies, and encouraging private investment.

Peace Corps programs

- Environment
- Business
- Water quality
- Technological research and development

Health

HIV/AIDS, diarrhea, hepatitis A, hepatitis B, typhoid fever, dengue fever, leptospirosis, malaria, and rabies are among the diseases and illnesses volunteers should be aware of in Mexico.

Major urban centers often offer health care that is adequate by U.S. standards. Emergency medical teams are often sparse and under-trained. Medical facilities in the countryside are rudimentary, and the quality of care in resort communities is unpredictable.

Visitors should refrain from drinking tap water and using ice cubes. Volunteers should use bottled or purified water. Food and drinks from street vendors are of questionable quality and safety.

Water in the ocean off the coast of beach resorts is often too contaminated for swimming. High altitude can cause insomnia, headaches, fatigue, breathing problems, and dizziness. Air quality in Mexico City and Guadalajara is poor, particularly from December through May. Volunteers with respiratory health problems should exercise caution.

Malaria is a concern near the borders with Guatemala and Belize in Chiapas, Quintana Roo, and Tabasco. Undeveloped sections of Nayarit, Oaxaca, and Sinaloa also have mosquitoes that carry malaria. Parts of Durango, Sonora, and Chihuahua have malarial mosquitoes. Malaria is not a concern near the border with the United States or in resort towns near the Gulf and Pacific coasts.

Volunteers should buy the anti-malarial drug chloroquine before leaving the United States. Anti-malarial medicines sold in Mexico are of dubious quality and could be harmful.

Visitors should not accept treatment with the anti-malarial drug halofantrine, sold under the brand name Halfan, because it causes potentially fatal heart problems. Patients should not take halofantrine unless doctors have diagnosed them with malaria that could be lethal, and no other anti-malarial pharmaceuticals are obtainable.

Visitors can reduce their risk of contracting insect-borne diseases such as malaria, leishmaniasis, and dengue fever by using mosquito netting. Travelers can also protect themselves by applying insect repellent containing 30 to 50 percent DEET. Insect repellent that contains 7 to 15 percent picardin has not been proved effective. Permethrin can be used to treat clothing and mosquito netting but should not be applied to skin.

Safety

Political violence is a concern, especially in Oaxaca, Chiapas, and Guerrero.

Foreigners are not allowed to involve themselves in politics, at risk of being deported or detained. Visitors should avoid rallies for fear of unexpected violence.

Separatists and violent gangs are active in Chiapas; some gangs target immigrants.

Violent crime is prevalent, particularly in Mexico City, Tijuana, Ciudad Juarez, Nuevo Laredo, Monterrey, Acapulco, and Sinaloa state. Criminals often go free because of ineffective law enforcement and prosecution. Buying or selling illegally copied materials could be against the laws of the communities in which volunteers reside. The United States prohibits importation of pirated goods.

Travelers should securely store valuables and avoid wearing jewelry or evidently expensive attire. Visitors should refrain from displaying cash or credit cards unnecessarily. Pickpocketing and theft of handbags is common, especially on mass-transit vehicles. Volunteers who rent cars should ensure that the signs of rental agencies are not displayed outside the vehicles. Valuables, including passports, should never be left in rental cars, even if they are locked.

U.S. citizens should beware of using counterfeit money they receive as change.

Solitary pedestrians are vulnerable to becoming victims of rape, kidnapping, and robbery. Using ATMs is an especially risky activity, as robbers frequently force victims to withdraw money from their accounts. Volunteers should only use automated teller machines during the day inside businesses. Abductions for ransom occur regularly in major metropolitan areas; victims include less-than-affluent Mexicans and foreign visitors.

Attacks on highways are common across the country. Drivers should not travel after dark and should remain on toll roads, which are less dangerous than free thoroughfares. Motorists should keep doors locked and windows raised. In traffic jams, drivers should ensure that they leave enough room between their car and others that they can drive away in case of a criminal attack. Volunteers should not hitchhike or pick up those who do. Visitors should remain in groups when hiking in the countryside or when visiting beaches, archaeological sites, or trails.

The staffs of some bars, restaurants, and nightclubs drug the drinks of patrons to make it easier to commit crimes against them. Visitors using buses should choose only first-class coaches and ride them exclusively during the day on toll roads. Hijacking is still a risk on toll roads but happens less often than on free highways. Armed robbers sometimes attack all passengers on a bus. Bus rides from Acapulco to Ixtapa or Huatulco are especially risky.

Police and other officials sometimes harass and extort international visitors. Before cooperating with people claiming to work in law enforcement, visitors should write down the identification numbers of the supposed police officers' cars and badges, as well as their names. Bribery of public officials is illegal.

Criminals attempt to extort money from victims by calling them on the phone, pretending to be public officials trying to prevent someone from being kidnapped. Another ruse is to request money to help get the victim's relative released from detention.

Calling home
There are 19.8 million land-based telephones and 57 million cell phones in Mexico. There are 7.6 million Internet hosts.

Diplomatic contact in the United States
Ambassador Arturo Sarukhan Casamitjana
1911 Pennsylvania Avenue NW, Washington, DC 20006
Phone: (202) 728-1600 • Fax (202) 728-1698

Diplomatic contact from the United States
Ambassador Antonio O. Garza, Jr.
Embassy: Paseo de la Reforma 305, Colonia Cuauhtemoc, 06500 Mexico, Distrito Federal
P. O. Box 9000, Brownsville, TX 78520-9000
Phone: (52) (55) 5080-2000 • Fax: (52) (55) 5511-9980

Consulate(s) general: Ciudad Juarez, Guadalajara, Monterrey, and Tijuana

Consulate(s): Hermosillo, Matamoros, Merida, Nogales, and Nuevo Laredo

Nicaragua

Overview of geography, climate, and population

Nicaragua is a little smaller than New York State. The lowlands are tropical and the high country is cool. The terrain includes mountains, plains, and volcanoes. The population is 5.8 million.

Religion, ethnicity, and language in a nutshell

Nearly 98 percent of Nicaraguans speak Spanish, which is the official language. About 2 percent use the Miskito tongue, and nearly 1 percent speaks other languages. English is also spoken on the Atlantic seaboard. Sixty-nine percent of Nicaraguans are mestizo, 17 percent are white, 9 percent are black, and 5 percent are Amerindian.

About 73 percent of Nicaraguans are Roman Catholic, 15 percent are Evangelical, and about 2 percent are Moravian. Episcopalians make up .1 percent of the population; followers of other beliefs account for 2 percent of Nicaraguans. About 9 percent of those who live in Nicaragua are non-religious.

Brief political history and today's government

Indigenous occupants populated the area now known as Nicaragua at least since the 13th century. The Spanish began to live in the area in 1524 and established the communities Granada and Leon. Nicaragua broke away from Spain in 1821. The country was under the control of imperial Mexico after leaving Spain's control. Nicaragua later joined a coalition of Central American countries. In 1938, the nation gained full independence. Nicaragua has had a number of civil wars since becoming independent. William Walker, of the United States, became president in 1856 after participating in a Nicaraguan civil war. Jose Santos Zelaya came to power in 1893. The United States invaded Nicaragua and backed armed forces, which ousted Zelaya in 1909. The United States occupied Nicaragua from 1912 through 1933. Anastasio Somoza Garcia, an ally of the United States, came to power in 1936. The Sandinista National Liberation Front overthrew Somoza in 1979. The Sandinistas had been fighting to oust the president for more than a decade. The United States cut off financial assistance to Nicaragua in 1981 out of opposition to the Sandinista regime's socialist policies. Washington issued an embargo on Nicaragua in 1985 and supported anti-Sandinista guerrillas.

Violeta Barrios de Chamorro came to power in a 1990 election after the Sandinistas came to terms with the rebels. Arnoldo Aleman succeeded Chamorro in 1997.

Nicaragua is a republic, and the president is Daniel Ortega Saavedra. The legislature consists of the National Assembly, which has 92 seats. Ninety of the assembly members are chosen from party lists. One position on the National Assembly is reserved for the president who most recently left office, and another is kept for the presidential candidate who lost the most recent election.

The judiciary is made up of the Supreme Court. The National Assembly elects the 16 justices of the Supreme Court, and Nicaragua's legal system is based on civil law. The Supreme Court has the option to review the actions of the president.

Economic snapshot

Many Nicaraguans are underemployed, and growth in the gross domestic product is sluggish. International aid is an important source of revenue. Through the Heavily Indebted Poor Countries program, Nicaragua received about $4.5 billion in debt relief in 2004. Nicaragua has been a party to the Central America Free Trade Agreement, which has opened foreign markets for its agricultural and industrial products.

Peace Corps programs

- Health
- Environment
- English education
- Business
- Agriculture

Health

HIV/AIDS, diarrhea, hepatitis A, hepatitis B, typhoid fever, malaria, dengue fever, and rabies are among the diseases and illnesses volunteers should be aware of in Nicaragua.

Managua offers basic health care as do some towns and villages. Patients with serious conditions must usually go to the capital for treatment if it is available at all. Spanish proficiency is necessary to obtain medical care. Patients must usually pay hospital bills in cash, but private hospitals take credit cards.

Travelers should buy the anti-malarial medicine chloroquine before leaving the United States. Malaria is a hazard in the countryside and in the outlying areas around Managua.

Visitors should not accept treatment with the anti-malarial drug halofantrine, sold under the brand name Halfan, because it causes potentially fatal heart problems. Patients should not take halofantrine unless doctors have diagnosed them with malaria that could be lethal, and no other anti-malarial pharmaceuticals are obtainable.

Visitors can reduce their risk of contracting insect-borne diseases such as malaria, leishmaniasis, and dengue fever by using mosquito netting. Travelers can also protect themselves by applying insect repellent containing 30 to 50 percent DEET. Insect repellent that contains 7 to 15 percent picardin has not been proved effective. Permethrin can be used to treat clothing and mosquito netting but should not be applied to skin.

Volunteers should avoid drinking tap water and using ice cubes.

Travelers should bring their own prescription medicines as some pharmacies are not well stocked.

Safety

Law enforcement is unreliable except in large cities. Sections of the country along the Atlantic Coast have especially poor police service.

Highway robbers attack on the sparsely traveled roads of the north and the northwest. Motorists should stay on main roads and travel during the day.

Visitors should avoid demonstrations and crowds for fear of violence. Foreign boaters have been held against their will and been fined after they entered waters that are central to a border dispute between Nicaragua and Colombia. The disputed waters are east of the 82nd meridian to the 79th meridian. The conflict also involves the San Andres island chain.

Drug smugglers are active in the Caribbean and Pacific near the coasts. Drownings are common in the Pacific Coastal waters because of dangerous currents. Stingrays are also a concern. Lifeguards and life preservers are scarce; beaches lack warning signs.

Hikes on the volcanoes on Ometepe Island are more perilous than they appear, and hikers have died after getting lost in the area. Trekkers should carry ample food and water.

Domestic airlines do not employ safety and security measures common in the United States.

Land mines are a danger in the northern countryside. Violent crime is prevalent in Managua and other urban areas. Pickpockets and armed robbers target victims on buses, in transit stations, and in outdoor markets including the Huembes Market and the Mercado Oriental. Drive-by shootings, assaults, stabbings, and robberies occur often in the Ticabus section of Managua as well as in neighborhoods near large hotels, markets, and mass transit stations.

Walking places visitors at risk of crime, so they should take registered cabs instead. Registered taxis pick up fares at the airport and major hotels. Murder, rape, beating and stabbing of taxi passengers is common in Managua. Visitors can reduce their risk of becoming crime victims by using only cabs with red license plates that have clearly visible numbers. A legitimate cab will also display the car company's name and logo. Passengers should write down the names and license numbers of drivers. Travelers should tell taxi drivers not to pick up other fares and should determine the price of the ride before the cab moves.

Thieves sometimes steal jewelry and purses from occupants of cars stopped at lights, so valuables should remain concealed. Drivers should keep windows raised and doors locked.

To reduce the risk of injury or death, volunteers should immediately comply with robbers. Visitors should not wear jewelry, or display cash or bank cards unnecessarily.

Volunteers should avoid hitchhiking or leaving establishments with strangers. Staying in groups reduces the risk of crime.

Calling home

There are 247, 900 land-based telephones and 1.83 million cell phones in Nicaragua. There are 27,941 Internet hosts.

Diplomatic contact in the United States

Ambassador (vacant): Charges d'Affaires Alcides J. Montiel Barillas

1627 New Hampshire Avenue NW, Washington, DC 20009
Phone: (202) 939-6570, (202) 939-6573 • Fax (202) 939-6545

Diplomatic contact from the United States

Ambassador Robert J. Callahan

Embassy: Kilometer 5.5 Carretera Sur, Managua

American Embassy Managua, APO AA 34021

Phone: (505) 252-7100, 252-7888; 252-7634 (after hours) • Fax (505) 252-7304

Panama

Overview of geography, climate, and population

Panama borders the Caribbean Sea, the North Pacific Ocean, Colombia, and Costa Rica. The terrain includes mountains, plains, and hills. Panama's climate is characterized by heat and humidity, and the rainy season occurs from May to January; the dry season takes place from January to May. Panama is not quite as big as South Carolina, but there are 3.3 million residents.

Religion, ethnicity, and language in a nutshell

Spanish is the official language, and 14 percent of Panamanians speak English. Seventy percent of Panamanians are mestizo, and 14 percent are combined Amerindian and West Indian. About 85 percent of Panamanians are Roman Catholic; 15 percent are Protestant.

Brief political history and today's government

Those who inhabited what is now Panama before European contact were known as the Coclé and Cuevas people. The Spanish brought illness and war to the original residents in the 16th century. The first European navigator to arrive in Panama was Rodrigo de Bastidas, who came in the early 1500s looking for treasure. Columbus founded the first European town, called Darien, in Panama in 1502. In 1513, the Spanish discovered Panama's strategic value as a passage between the Pacific and Atlantic oceans and began using it as a route to transport the precious metals they were taking back to their country.

Imperial Spain ruled Panama between the 16th and 19th centuries.

The first try at building what later became the Panama Canal occurred in the late 19th century. The French businessman Ferdinand de Lesseps failed to build a waterway where the Panama Canal now stands. Panama became independent in

1903 and entered a pact with the United States, under which the states received the right to build the Panama Canal. The canal was finished in 1914.

Until 1968, the country was a constitutional monarchy; that year, the public elected a president. A military coup overthrew the president the same year and installed Brigadier General Omar Torrijos as ruler. General Mauel Noriega came to power in the early 1980s and held office in spite of a 1989 election that made one of his opponents president. In 1987, after an assault on the U.S. Embassy, Washington cut off civilian and military aid to the country. The United States invaded in 1989, in part to protect access to the Panama Canal. After the U.S. armed forces removed Noriega from power in 1989, the Electoral Tribunal put into office Guillermo Endara, who had won a civilian election in 1989. Ernesto Perez Balladares succeeded Endara through a democratic election in 1994. Panama is currently a constitutional democracy. The president is Martin Torrijos. The legislature includes the National Assembly, which has 78 publicly elected members, and the judiciary consists of the Supreme Court of Justice, which has nine appointed judges, who sit for ten years. Five superior courts and three appellate courts are also part of the judicial system. Civil law and judicial review of bills passed by the National Assembly are the foundations of the legal system.

Economic snapshot

The service industry produces 75 percent of the gross domestic product. Expansion of the Panama Canal, slated to be finished in 2014 should spur economic development and create jobs by increasing the number of ships that can use the waterway. The government seeks to attract more tourists and to participate in regional trade. Panama is not a party to the Central American Free Trade Agreement but has its own free trade deal with the United States.

Peace Corps programs

- Agroforestry
- Environmental education
- Agricultural education
- Community development
- Environmental conservation
- Business

Health

HIV/AIDS, diarrhea, hepatitis A, hepatitis B, yellow fever, dengue fever, malaria, leptospirosis, rabies, and typhoid fever are among the diseases and illnesses volunteers should be aware of in Panama.

The capital offers some health facilities that meet U.S. standards, but medical care is limited outside the city. Health care providers typically require cash payment in advance of treatment. Patients can sometimes use credit cards to pay for hospital bills, but not fees due to doctors.

Volunteers should take different anti-malarial medicines, depending on where in Panama they will be living. Chloroquine protects against the strain of malaria common in Bocas Del Toro. Atovaquone/proguanil, doxycycline, or mefloquine are the preferred medicines for people visiting Darie'n and San Blas. Primaquine should only be used in special cases after patients have undergone G6PD screening.

Malaria is not a concern in Panama City or in what was once the Canal Zone. The disease occurs in the countryside of the provinces of Boca Del Toro, Darie'n, and San Blas. Mosquitoes also carry malaria on the San Blas Islands.

Visitors should not accept treatment with the anti-malarial drug halofantrine, sold under the brand name Halfan, because it causes potentially fatal heart problems. Patients should not take halofantrine unless doctors have diagnosed them with malaria that could be lethal, and no other anti-malarial pharmaceuticals are obtainable.

Visitors can reduce their risk of contracting insect-borne diseases such as malaria, leishmaniasis, and dengue fever by using mosquito netting. Travelers can also protect themselves by applying insect repellent containing 30 to 50 percent DEET. Insect repellent that contains 7 to 15 percent picardin has not been proved effective. Permethrin can be used to treat clothing and mosquito netting but should not be applied to skin.

Safety

The U.S. Department of State advises visitors to avoid Darien Province, including Darien National Park, for fear of murderers and kidnappers who target international visitors. Militia members and drug smugglers are active near the border with Colombia.

Visitors should avoid demonstrations, which could unexpectedly turn violent. Some protesters are especially antagonistic toward U.S. citizens.

Drowning occurs annually on Pacific beaches. Visitors should not travel by boat near the southeastern coast of the San Blas Islands. Volunteers wishing to visit the

National Park on Coiba Island must get permits from the Ministry of Government and Justice, as well as the National Environment Authority.

Search and rescue operations available to boaters, but do not meet standards common in the United States.

Panama City and Colon have especially high crime rates. Visitors are especially vulnerable to crime in San Miguelito, Rio Abajo, El Chorillo, Ancon, Curundu, Veracruz Beach, Panama Viejo, and at the lookout above the Madden Dam. Rape, banditry, kidnapping, armed robbery, mugging, and handbag theft are among the crimes foreigners regularly experience. Visitors should be particularly cautious when using automated teller machines because criminals often target customers for abduction and robbery.

Calling home
Panama has 432,900 land-based telephones and 1.6 million cell phones. There are 7,078 Internet hosts.

Diplomatic contact in the United States
Ambassador Jaime Eduardo Aleman Healy
2862 McGill Terrace NW, Washington, DC 20008
Phone: (202) 483-1407 • Fax (202) 483-8416

Diplomatic contact from the United States
Ambassador Barbara J. Stephenson
Embassy: Edificio 783, Avenida Demetrio Basilio Lakas Panama, Apartado Postal 0816-02561, Zona 5, Panama City
American Embassy Panama, Unit 0945, APO AA 34002
Phone: (507) 207-7000 • Fax (507) 317-5568

Eastern Europe and Central Asia

Albania
Overview of geography, climate, and population
Albania is a country of 3.6 million about the size of Maryland. The climate is temperate to damp. Winters are chilly, overcast, and rainy. Summers are warm and dry. The country is prone to floods, droughts, earthquakes, and tsunamis.

Religion, ethnicity, and language in a nutshell

Seventy percent of Albanians are Muslim, 20 percent are part of the Albanian Orthodox church, and 10 percent adhere to Roman Catholicism. Ninety-five percent of the nation's residents are ethnically Albanian, 3 percent trace their ancestry to Greece, and the remaining 2 percent are of Vlach, Roma, Serb, Macedonian, and Bulgarian lineage. The official language is Albanian; other dialects spoken include Greek, Vlach, Romani, and Slavic.

Brief political history and today's government

Albania left the Ottoman Empire in 1912 and came under Italian control in 1939. Communists came to power in 1944. In the 1990s, Albania became a multi-party democracy. Albania's government is seeking to join NATO and the EU.

The legislature consists of the Assembly, which has 140 members. One-hundred Assembly members are directly elected by the public, and 40 seats are filled by proportional vote. The judiciary includes the Constitutional Court, Supreme Court, and district and appeals courts. The nation's legal system is one of civil law.

Economic snapshot

Albania is developing a free market economy and looking for opportunities for international investment.

Peace Corps programs

- Community development
- English education
- Health

Health

HIV/AIDS, hepatitis A, hepatitis B, typhoid, and rabies are among the diseases and illnesses volunteers should be aware of in Albania.

Visitors can rely only on the most basic of medical treatment. Hospitals and clinics cannot respond well to emergencies, conditions requiring extensive treatment, or problems for which patients would need surgery. The country has a shortage of specialists, pharmaceuticals, equipment and supplies. Visitors should carry their own medicines.

An unstable supply of electricity can lead to food spoilage at restaurants. When eating at restaurants, volunteers should ensure that chefs cook food completely to kill potentially harmful bacteria.

Safety

Organized crime and corruption are concerns throughout Albania. Travelers should avoid journeying to the northern areas of Shkoder, Malesi E Madhe, and Tropoje without secured vehicles and an escort. Police cannot always provide adequate protection.

To avoid conflicts with government officials, visitors should not photograph any military installations or areas that might be seen as sensitive to national security.

Travelers should avoid crowds for fear that they will unexpectedly become violent demonstrations.

Albanian criminals rarely target foreigners as victims because they fear the negative consequences of harming international visitors. Volunteers should attend to their safety as they would in any major city in the United States. Travelers should beware of early morning gunfights and other violence in bars in Tirana.

Carjacking is a concern, and victims should cooperate right away to minimize their risk of injury.

Pickpocketing as well as theft of passports and other valuables is prevalent, particularly after dark.

Calling home

There are ten land-based telephones and 60 cell phones for every 100 people. There are 852 Internet hosts.

Diplomatic contact in the United States

Ambassador Aleksander Sallabanda
2100 S Street NW, Washington, DC 20008
Phone: (202) 223-4942 • Fax (202) 628-7342

Diplomatic contact from the United States

Ambassador John L. Withers, II
Embassy: Rruga e Elbasanit, Labinoti #103, Tirana
US Department of State, 9510 Tirana Place, Dulles, VA 20189-9510
Phone: (355) (4) 2247285 • Fax (355) (4) 2232222

Armenia

Overview of geography, climate, and population

Armenia is a landlocked country a little smaller than Maryland, which has hot summers and cold winters. It borders Turkey. Armenia is partly mountainous; it is prone to droughts and earthquakes. The population is 2.9 million.

Religion, ethnicity, and language in a nutshell

About 95 percent of Armenians are of the Apostolic faith, about 4 percent belong to other sects of Christianity, a little more than 1 percent adhere to the Yezidi faith.

About 98 percent of the nation's residents are ethnically Armenian, about 1 percent are Yezidi, slightly less than 1 percent are Russian, and nearly half a percent are of another ancestry.

Approximately 98 percent of inhabitants speak Armenian, about 1 percent are Yezidi speakers, and a little less than 1 percent use the Russian tongue. Less than half a percent speak another language.

Brief political history and today's government

The legislature consists of the National Assembly with 131 members. Ninety members are elected by their parties, and 41 seats are filled by public election. The judiciary includes the Constitutional Court and an Appeals Court. The nation's legal system is based on civil law.

Economic snapshot

In 1994, the International Monetary Fund worked with the Armenian Government to liberalize the country's economy, which has resulted in decreased poverty, reduced inflation, more stable currency, and a growing private sector. The economy has moved from industry to agriculture. Armenia has been a member of the World Trade Organization since 2003.

Peace Corps programs

- Business
- Education
- Health
- Environment

Health

HIV/AIDS, hepatitis A, hepatitis B, typhoid, rabies, and malaria are among the diseases and illnesses volunteers should be aware of in Armenia.

Doctors are generally well-trained but often lack adequate facilities in which to practice. Prescription pharmaceuticals are often available but their effectiveness is not necessarily reliable.

Safety

Armed clashes at the Armenia-Azerbaijan border occur occasionally, so travelers should be especially careful when visiting this area. The borders with the Nakhichevan Autonomous Republic of Azerbaijan, Azerbaijan, and Turkey are closed and guarded by armed military members. Territory near the border contains land mines.

Visitors should avoid demonstrations because marchers might unexpectedly become violent, and the police might use force to dispel protesters. Earthquakes and landslides are hazards.

The condition of the Armenia Nuclear Power plant outside of Metsamor continues to create safety concerns. Radiation poisoning and chlorine gas spills are among the common industrial hazards in Armenia.

Criminals rarely target foreigners, and the violent crime rate is lower than that of most metropolitan areas of the United States. Theft and vehicle break-ins are prevalent. Visitors should refrain from walking or driving alone in Yerevan at night.

Calling home

The telecommunications system is fairly reliable in urban areas and less dependable in the countryside. There are about 594,000 land-based telephones and 318,000 cell phones. There are 8,270 Internet hosts.

Diplomatic contact in the United States

Ambassador Tatoul Markarian
2225 R Street NW, Washington, DC 20008
Phone: (202) 319-1976 • Fax (202) 319-2982

Diplomatic contact from the United States

Ambassador Marie L. Yovanovitch
Embassy: 1 American Ave., Yerevan 0082
American Embassy Yerevan, US Department of State, 7020 Yerevan Place, Washington, DC 20521-7020
Phone: (374) (10) 464-700 • Fax (374) (10) 464-742

Azerbaijan

Overview of geography, climate, and population

Azerbaijan is a country of 8.2 million that is not quite the size of Maine. The dry and semi-arid nation borders the Caspian Sea, Iran, and Russia.

Religion, ethnicity, and language in a nutshell

About 93 percent of the population practice Islam, approximately 3 percent are Russian Orthodox, and a little more than 2 percent practice Armenian Orthodoxy. About 90 percent speak Azerbaijani; a little more than 2 percent speak Lezgi. Russian is the native tongue of about 2 percent of the population. About 2 percent of Azerbaijanis speak Armenian; approximately 3 percent speak other languages. About 1 percent of the population communicates in unspecified tongues.

Brief political history and today's government

Azerbaijan became independent of the U.S.S.R. in 1991. It is involved in a long-standing territorial conflict with Armenia. Poverty has decreased, but government corruption is rampant.

Azerbaijan is a republic. The legislature consists of a 125-seat National Assembly, members of which are elected by the public. The Supreme Court comprises the judiciary. The legal system is derived from civil law.

Economic snapshot

Oil exports are on the rise, and foreign investors have strongly supported drilling for oil. Important trading partners include European countries and Turkey. The economy is becoming increasingly market-driven.

Peace Corps programs

- Environment
- Education
- Health
- Business development

Health

HIV/AIDS, hepatitis A, hepatitis B, typhoid, rabies, malaria, and avian flu are among the diseases and illnesses volunteers should be aware of in Azerbaijan.

A small number of medical facilities in Baku offer health care that meets Western standards. The sanitary conditions of clinics in other areas are poor. Disposable needles, vaccines, drugs, and other supplies are often scarce. Visitors should bring their own medicines.

Travelers should avoid visiting farms on which fowl are raised and markets at which birds are sold. Visitors should take care not to touch surfaces on which birds have defecated. Volunteers should ensure that poultry and eggs are cooked completely before eating.

Safety

Armenian military personnel occupy the Nagorno-Karabakh section and its environs near the Azerbaijan-Iran and Azerbaijan-Armenia borders. Travelers should avoid visiting the area due to the risk of gun fighting and land mines.

Volunteers of Armenian heritage should recognize that the government of Azerbaijan has stated that it will not be responsible for their safety while they are in the country.

Visitors should avoid rallies because they could unexpectedly turn violent. Azerbaijan has relatively little crime. Foreigners should avoid solitary walks after dark for fear of assault and non-violent crime.

Calling home

There are approximately 1.2 million land telephones and 3.3 million cell phones in Azerbaijan. There are about 15 land lines for every 100 people and 40 cell phones for every 100 people. There are about 3,000 Internet hosts.

Diplomatic contact in the United States

Ambassador Yashar Aliyev
2741 34th Street NW, Washington, DC 20008
Phone: (202) 337-3500 • Fax (202) 337-5911

Diplomatic contact from the United States

Ambassador (vacant)
Embassy: 83 Azadlig Prospecti, Baku AZ1007
American Embassy Baku, US Department of State, 7050 Baku Place, Washington, DC 20521-7050
Phone: (994) (12) 4980-335 through 337 • Fax (994) (12) 4656-671

Bulgaria

Overview of geography, climate, and population

Bulgaria is a mountainous country that borders the Black Sea and has a temperate climate. It is about the size of Tennessee. The population is about 7.2 million.

Religion, ethnicity, and language in a nutshell

About 83 percent of the population belong to the Bulgarian Orthodox church; approximately 12 percent follow Islam. Non-orthodox Christians account for about 1 percent of Bulgarians, and 4 percent of residents adhere to other religions. Approximately 85 percent of the population speak Bulgarian, and about 10 percent communicate in Turkish. Roma is the mother tongue of about 4 percent of the population; approximately 2 percent follow an unspecified religion. About 84 percent are of Bulgarian lineage, about 10 percent are Turks, about 5 percent are of Roma heritage, and 2 percent are of other ancestry.

Brief political history and today's government

In the 800s, Bulgarians and Slavs established the earliest country known as Bulgaria. In the 1300s, Bulgaria became part of the Ottoman Empire. It became a Soviet state in 1946, and Bulgaria gained independence from the U.S.S.R. in 1990. Bulgaria is a member of NATO and the European Union and is a parliamentary democracy. The president is Georgi Parvanov, and the prime minister is Sergei Stanishev. The legislature consists of the National Assembly, with 240 publicly elected members. The judiciary includes the Supreme Administrative Court, the Supreme Court of Cassation, Constitutional Court, and the Supreme Judicial Council.

Economic snapshot

Bulgaria's economy has grown steadily since the mid-1990s. Foreign investment is a pillar of the economy. Government-sponsored fiscal reforms are ongoing, but so are corruption and inflation.

Peace Corps programs

- Community development
- Youth development
- English education

Health

HIV/AIDS, typhoid, rabies, hepatitis A, and hepatitis B are among the diseases and illnesses that volunteers should be aware of in Bulgaria.

Doctors are well-trained, but most lack the facilities to run practices that meet Western standards. Physicians tend to work in poorly maintained clinics which lack equipment. First aid supplies are typically available. Prescription and over-the-counter pharmaceuticals are often available. Facilities offering specialized care are virtually non-existent, so patients might need to be evacuated to the United States at great expense.

Safety

Organized crime and credit card fraud are concerns. Perpetrators of fraud can copy credit cards and steal ATM cards from bank machines after preventing the owners from retrieving them. Members of organized crime rings typically drive new SUVs, travel in groups, and patronize posh clubs, restaurants, and hotels.

Pickpockets and purse-snatchers target foreigners, particularly those who appear wealthy. Theft often occurs in crowded areas. Perpetrators of scams frequently target passengers on mass transit vehicles. Travelers should refuse offers of assistance while using cash machines and avoid disclosing their personal identification numbers to anyone.

Visitors should ask people who present themselves as government employees to provide identification.

Volunteers should refuse all food and drink offered by strangers, even if the items are in sealed containers. Food and drink could contain drugs that criminals use to make it easier to assault or steal from victims.

When patronizing bars and nightclubs, visitors should keep track of how much they are being charged for beverages. Staff of some establishments have charged thousands of dollars for drinks and threatened patrons with violence if they refused to pay.

Cab drivers sometimes cheat foreigners, most often on rides beginning at the Sofia Airport and the Central Train Station. Travelers can reduce their risk of being overcharged by taking metered cabs in which lists of rates are shown. The government does not regulate taxi fares, so drivers may charge whatever price they choose. Drivers of cabs in which price lists are shown are required to charge the fares displayed. The Sofia Airport arrivals section has a taxi booth at which visitors can arrange to hire metered taxis. The Central Train Station offers fewer metered taxis, so travelers should ask about rates before riding if there is no metered cab available. Passengers should be certain they have all their luggage and personal items before leaving cabs.

Theft of items from luggage checked at the Sofia Airport is common, so travelers should avoid packing valuables.

Vehicle theft is a concern, and police rarely recover stolen cars. Thieves are especially likely to steal new European sedans and vehicles with four-wheel drives.

Criminals often break car windows to steal valuables. Residential burglaries are common, so volunteers should have window grates, strong locks, steel doors, and alarms installed.

Visitors should avoid making online credit card purchases using sites with which they are not familiar. Scam artists commit credit card fraud via Web sites that advertise non-existent businesses.

Calling home
There are about 2.4 million land telephones and 8.3 million cell phones in Bulgaria. The country has about 300,000 Internet hosts.

Diplomatic contact in the United States
Ambassador Elena B. Poptodorova
1621 22nd Street NW, Washington, DC 20008
Phone: (202) 387-0174 • Fax (202) 234-7973

Diplomatic contact from the United States
Ambassador (vacant): Charge D'Affaires Susan Sutton
Embassy: 16 Kozyak Street, Sofia 1407
American Embassy Sofia, US Department of State, 5740 Sofia Place, Washington, DC 20521-5740
Phone: (359) (2) 937-5100 • Fax (359) (2) 937-5320

Georgia
Overview of geography, climate, and population
Georgia borders the Black Sea, Russia, and Turkey. Its terrain includes mountains and lowlands. The climate is Mediterranean, and the country of 4.6 million is approximately the size of South Carolina.

Religion, ethnicity, and language in a nutshell

About 84 percent of Georgians are Orthodox Christians, approximately 10 percent are Muslims, about 4 percent are Armenian-Gregorian, nearly 1 percent are Catholic, almost 1 percent follow another religion, and about 1 percent do not adhere to any faith. About 71 percent of the population speak the official Georgian language, nearly 10 percent speak Russian. Armenian is the native tongue of 7 percent of the population. Six percent speak Azeri; 7 percent speak another language.

Brief political history and today's government

The Romans controlled what is now Georgia in the early centuries of the Christian era. Georgians took over the region in the 1000s and ruled for 200 years. The area was under dispute by the Ottomans and the Persians before it became part of the Russian Empire in the 1800s. Georgia was self-governing from 1918 to 1921. It became part of the Soviet Union and re-gained independence in 1991. Georgia contains the Russian-backed separatist regions of Abkhazia and South Ossetia.

Georgia is a republic. The president is Mikheil Saakashvili, and the Prime Minister is Vladimir Gurgenidze. The legislature consists of the parliament, which has 250 members. Parliamentary positions are allocated according to population. The judiciary includes the Supreme Court, the Constitutional Court, and other lower courts. The legal system is based on civil law.

Economic snapshot

Foreign investment is key to Georgia's significant annual economic growth. Agriculture, mining, and industry are central to the economy. The International Monetary Fund and the World Bank loan money to Georgia. Construction, banking, and mining are growing industries. The economy is becoming increasingly privatized, and the government is working to reduce corruption and collect unpaid taxes. Agriculture and the service sector are essential parts of the economy.

Peace Corps programs

- Education
- Development of non-governmental organizations

Health

HIV/AIDS, hepatitis A, hepatitis B, rabies, malaria, typhoid, and diarrhea are among the diseases and illnesses volunteers should be aware of in Georgia.

Health care is rudimentary, and basic medical supplies are extremely scarce. Patients frequently must pay cash before receiving treatment.

Safety

Independence fighters control the regions of South Ossetia, in the north-central section, and Abkhazia in the northwest. The Georgian military sometimes clashes with the separatists, so volunteers should avoid the areas.

The Georgia-Russia border is closed even to those who have visas from either or both countries.

The Georgian military has occasionally battled Chechen rebels, terrorists, and fugitives from justice who hide in the Pankisi Gorge. Visitors should refrain from visiting the Pankisi Gorge. Volunteers should be particularly careful during journeys through the northern mountains near the border with Russia, particularly in Dagestan and Chechnya.

Hate crimes against those whose religious practice differ from that of the majority sometimes occur. Jehovah's Witnesses, Assembly of God adherents, Baptists, and Pentecostals have been among the targets. Assailants have severely beaten believers, burned their literature, and destroyed their property. The leader of the attackers was imprisoned in 2005, but adherents should still be wary of hate crimes.

Criminals frequently target foreigners for such incidents as burglary, carjacking, car theft, and armed robbery because international visitors are wealthier than those who live in Georgia. Minor theft, pickpocketing, and purse snatching are typical. Many criminals use illegal guns and other arms.

International travelers are especially vulnerable to crime in the capital. Assaults and robberies occur at high rates in neighborhoods of Tbilisi popular with foreign visitors. Minor thoroughfares in the Vake and Vera sections of the city are especially dangerous. The Saburtalo section of the capital as well as Rustaveli and Chavchavadze avenues are also particularly hazardous. Volunteers should avoid being alone at night.

Thieves often strike on the subway and public minivans in Tbilisi. Robberies occur regularly on above-ground trains. Visitors should thus take cabs or private cars from reputable companies.

Foreigners in and near the capital are especially at risk of being abducted and held for ransom. Kidnappers could also strike anywhere across the nation.

Crime is especially prevalent in Abkhazia and South Ossetia because police service is limited. Visitors are also particularly vulnerable to crime in upper Svanetia, Samtskhe-Javakheti, the border between Georgia and Russia and the Abkhazia frontier. Visitors who choose to travel in these high-crime areas should take with them an escort who was born in the country and knows the region.

Police respond well to emergencies but often do not investigate adequately.

To reduce the risk of becoming victims of crime, volunteers should avoid going to and from work by the same route every day. Travelers should also refrain from running errands or going to work on a predictable schedule. Visitors should not wear jewelry or display cash. Walking with others on well-traveled roads is advisable. When traveling in Georgia, volunteers should restrict their trips to the daytime and leave a travel plan and relevant phone numbers with a trusted acquaintance.

If attacked, visitors should reduce their risk of injury by complying immediately.

Calling home
There are 544,000 land-based telephones and 2.4 million cell phones. In the cities, there are approximately 20 telephones per 100 Georgians. In the countryside, there are four phones for every 100 residents. There are about 30,000 Internet hosts in Georgia.

Diplomatic contact in the United States
Ambassador Batu Kutelia
2209 Massachusetts Avenue NW, Washington, DC 20008
Phone: (202) 387-2390 • Fax (202) 393-4537

Diplomatic contact from the United States
Ambassador John F. Tefft
Embassy: 11 George Balanchine Street, T'bilisi 0131
7060 T'bilisi Place, Washington, DC 20521-7060
Phone: (995) (32) 27-70-00 • Fax (995) (32) 53-23-10

Macedonia

Overview of geography, climate, and population

Macedonia is a landlocked nation about the size of Vermont. Its summers and falls are warm with little rainfall. Winters are cold and snowy. The population is 2 million.

Religion, ethnicity, and language in a nutshell

65 percent of Macedonians are Macedonian Orthodox, 33 percent follow Islam, and less than 1 percent are non-Orthodox Christian. Nearly 2 percent of the population follow other faiths. Sixty-seven percent of the population speak Macedonian, 25 percent speak Albanian, 4 percent communicate in Turkish, 2 percent speak Roma, a little more than 1 percent speak Serbian, and 2 percent of the population speak other languages. About 65 percent of the population are of Macedonian descent, 25 percent are of Albanian ancestry, and 4 percent are Turkish. Nearly 3 percent of Macedonians are Roma, about 2 percent are Serbian, and approximately 2 percent are of another heritage.

Brief political history and today's government

The country seceded from Yugoslavia in 1991. Albanians in the country staged an uprising in 2001, citing discrimination as their motive. A peace agreement provided expanded rights for Albanians. Macedonia is a parliamentary democracy. The president is Branko Crevenkovski, and the prime minister is Nikola Gruevski. The legislature consists of the 120-member assembly, and the judiciary includes the Supreme Court, the Constitutional Court, and the Republican Judicial Council. The legal system stems from civil law; the judiciary is responsible for reviewing laws passed by the assembly.

Economic snapshot

The economy began to grow steadily in the mid-1990s and continued to do so until civil strife erupted in 2001. Economic stability and growth have returned to the country. Inflation is low, but official estimates place unemployment at about 35 percent.

Peace Corps programs

- Education
- Community development

Health

HIV/AIDS, hepatitis A, hepatitis B, rabies, typhoid, and diarrhea are among the diseases and illnesses volunteers should be aware of in Macedonia.

Doctors are generally well-trained. Some private medical facilities in the capital have adequate equipment. Basic supplies are obtainable, but patients often cannot get specialized care.

Safety

Visitors should avoid rallies, roadblocks, and strikes for fear of violence. Macedonia's crime rate is lower than that of the United States. Criminals rarely target foreigners but pickpockets and thieves often strike in tourist areas. Visitors should hide valuables, particularly electronic goods, rather than leaving them visible in parked cars. Volunteers should lock the windows and doors of their homes when they leave.

Periodic fights between organized crime rings are a concern. Visitors rarely have problems with crime while using automatic teller machines.

Calling home

There are 490,900 land telephones and 1.4 million cell phones in Macedonia. There are 6,001 Internet hosts.

Diplomatic contact in the United States

Ambassador Zoran Jolevski
2129 Wyoming Avenue NW, Washington, DC 20008
Phone: (202) 667-0501 • Fax (202) 667-2131

Diplomatic contact from the United States

Ambassador Philip T. Reeker
Embassy: Bul. Ilindenska bb, 1000 Skopje
American Embassy Skopje, US Department of State, 7120 Skopje Place, Washington, DC 20521-7120 (pouch)
Phone: (389) 2 311-6180 • Fax (389) 2 311-7103

Moldova

Overview of geography, climate, and population

Moldova is a country of 4.3 million that is about the size of Maryland. The landlocked nation has relatively mild winters, and the terrain is mostly steppe.

Religion, ethnicity, and language in a nutshell

Ninety-eight percent of Moldovans are Eastern Orthodox, nearly 2 percent are Jewish, and half a percent are Baptist or another religion. Nearly 79 percent of residents are of Moldovan/Romanian extraction. About 8 percent are Ukrainian. Nearly 6 percent are Russian, a little more than 4 percent are Gagauz, 2 percent are Bulgarian, and a little more than 1 percent trace their ancestry to other groups. Moldovan is the official language. Russian and Gagauz are also spoken.

Brief political history and today's government

Moldova was part of Romania before it became part of the U.S.S.R. after World War II. The country gained its sovereignty in 1991. Russian troops remain in the country to help separatists in the Transnistria area.

Economic snapshot

The country is one of Europe's poorest. The economy is primarily agrarian, with produce figuring prominently along with wine and tobacco. Moldova relies on Russia for its energy supply. The European Union's newly favorable trading relationship with Russia should stimulate Moldova's economy.

Peace Corps programs

- English education
- Agriculture
- Environmental education
- Agribusiness

Health

HIV/AIDS, tuberculosis hepatitis A, hepatitis B, and hepatitis C are among the diseases and illnesses volunteers should be aware of in Moldova.

Medical facilities are inadequate. For extensive procedures, volunteers should be evacuated to Western Europe. Ambulances are available for emergencies. Medicines are in short supply, so volunteers should bring their own prescription and over-the-counter pharmaceuticals. Drugs do not have English labels, and counterfeit medicines are common.

Safety

Criminals do not specifically target Westerners, but visitors should be as cautious as they would be in any major city in the United States. Burglary and theft are common. Criminals have sometimes used devices to record ATM card numbers and stolen money from travelers' bank account. Visitors should carry their passports whenever they go out because officials frequently ask for identification.

Theft on trains and buses is common. Theft of mailed packages and letters is also a concern.

Separatists control the Transnistria region and operate road checkpoints, so travelers should be careful when they visit or pass through the area. Visitors should avoid photographing buildings, military equipment, checkpoints, or security forces in Transnistria.

Discrimination and harassment sometimes affect U.S. citizens of African, Arab, or Asian descent.

Moldovan criminals and accomplices sometimes pose as potential romantic partners and contact U.S. citizens via the Internet. The Moldovans persuade the unsuspecting Americans to send thousands of dollars before severing ties. In some cases, the U.S. citizens go to Moldova to meet the people with whom they have been communicating, only to find themselves victims of extortion or imprisonment.

Calling home
There are 1 million land-based telephones and 1.3 million cell phones in Moldova. There are 112,026 Internet hosts.

Diplomatic contact in the United States
Ambassador Nicolae Chirtoaca
2101 S Street NW, Washington, DC 20008
Phone: (202) 667-1130 • Fax (202) 667-1204

Diplomatic contact from the United States
Ambassador Asif Chaudhry
Embassy: 103 Mateevici Street, Chisinau MD-2009
Phone: (373) (22) 40-8300 • Fax (373) (22) 23-3044

Romania
Overview of geography, climate, and population
Romania is a country of 22 million that borders the Black Sea, Ukraine, and Bulgaria. It is not quite as large as Oregon. The climate is temperate. Winters have a lot of precipitation, and summers are sunny with some storms. Geographic features include the Transylvanian Basin, the Plain of Moldavia, the Carpathian Mountains, the Walachian Plain, and the Transylvanian Alps.

Religion, ethnicity, and language in a nutshell

Ninety percent of the population are Romanian. Not quite 7 percent are Hungarian; nearly 3 percent are Roma. Less than 1 percent are Ukrainian, less than 1 percent are German, less than 1 percent are Russian, less than 1 percent are Turkish, and less than 1 percent trace their heritage otherwise. A little less than 87 percent of Romanians follow Eastern Orthodoxy, nearly 8 percent are Protestant, almost 5 percent are Roman Catholic, and less than 1 percent adhere to other or unspecified religions. Ninety-one percent of the population speak the official Romanian language. Nearly 7 percent speak Hungarian, a little more than 1 percent speak Romany, and slightly more than 1 percent speak another tongue.

Brief political history and today's government

After Wallachia and Moldavia became independent of the Ottoman Empire in 1856, they later joined to form Romania. Romania fought alongside the Allies in World War I, and Transylvania became part of Romania in 1940. The country fought on the Axis side in World War II. Romania came under Soviet control after the war ended, and Nicolae Ceausescu ruled repressively from the 1960s until he was executed in the late 1980s. Communists stopped holding office in Romania in 1996. Romania has been part of NATO since 2004, and the country became a member of the European Union in 2007.

Economic snapshot

Romania's economy has grown steadily in the past few years. A middle class is starting to form, but many residents remain impoverished. Inflation, weak currency, and the increasing price of energy are among the country's economic problems.

Peace Corps programs

- Community development
- Environmental education
- English education
- Environmental management
- Institutional development

Health

Typhoid, rabies, hepatitis A, hepatitis B, diarrhea, tick-borne encephalitis, and HIV/AIDS are among the diseases and illnesses volunteers should be aware of in Romania. Health care generally falls below Western standards. Basic supplies are scarce but are sometimes available in large cities. Some clinics in the capital provide health care that meets Western expectations of quality.

Safety

Visitors should avoid rallies for fear of violence. Violent crime is relatively rare, but tourists sometimes are victims of robbery and mugging. Gangs of pickpockets and thieves target victims on mass transit vehicles and in stations. Assaults and thefts occur frequently on night trains. Thieves have sometimes targeted passengers in closed cars. Volunteers should beware of impostors who pretend to be plainclothes officers, show badges, and ask for passports and wallets, which they steal. To reduce the risk of fraud, visitors should use cash rather than credit cards. Some shopkeepers have used customers' credit card numbers to make unauthorized purchases. Identity thieves sometimes steal information used to automatically withdraw cash so travelers should check for signs of tampering before using ATMs. Volunteers should choose ATMs in banks rather than outdoor cash machines.

Some Romanian criminals and accomplices pretend to be looking for romantic partners and contact U.S. citizens via Internet. Once the U.S. residents go to Romania to meet the people with whom they have been communicating, they find themselves victims of extortion. Visitors should also beware of the packs of stray dogs that sometimes roam Bucharest.

Stringent rules govern the importing and exporting of guns, antiques, and pharmaceuticals. Volunteers must declare sums in excess of 10,000 Euros. Earthquakes occur periodically in Romania.

Calling home

There are 4.2 million land-based telephones and 17.4 million cell phones in Romania. There are 1.4 million Internet hosts.

Diplomatic contact in the United States

Ambassador Adrian Cosmin Vierita
1607 23rd Street NW, Washington, DC 20008
Phone: (202) 332-4846, 4848, 4851, 4852 • Fax (202) 232-4748

Diplomatic contact from the United States

Ambassador Mark Gitenstein
Embassy: Strada Tudor Arghezi 7-9, Bucharest
American Embassy Bucharest, US Department of State, 5260 Bucharest Place, Washington, DC 20521-5260 (pouch)
Phone: (40) (21) 200-3300 • Fax (40) (21) 200-3442

Ukraine

Overview of geography, climate, and population

Ukraine borders the Black Sea, Poland Romania, Russia, and Moldova. The climate is temperate continental in most areas. The climate is Mediterranean along the southern coast. Winters range from cool to cold and summers vary from warm to hot. The terrain consists of steppes, plateaus, and mountains. There are nearly 46 million people in Ukraine.

Religion, ethnicity, and language in a nutshell

Slightly more than half of Ukrainians are members of the Ukrainian Orthodox, Kyiv Patriarchate. About a quarter of the population belong to the Ukrainian Orthodox Moscow Patriarchate. About 8 percent are Ukrainian Greek Catholic. A little more than 7 percent are Ukrainian Autocephalous Orthodox. A little more than 2 percent are Roman Catholic, slightly more than 2 percent are Protestant, less than 1 percent are Jewish, and slightly more than 3 percent follow other faiths.

Brief political history and today's government

In the 1,000s and 1,100s, Ukraine was part of the strongest country in Europe. In the 1600s, Ukraine became the Cossack Hetmanate before becoming part of the Russian Empire in the 1700s. After the Russian Revolution, Ukraine became independent in 1917 and remained so until 1920 when the Soviets took over. Ukraine regained its independence with the dissolution of the U.S.S.R. Ukraine is a republic. Viktor Yushchenko is the president, and Yuliya Tymoshenko is the Prime Minister. The legislature consists of a Supreme Council with proportionally elected members.

Economic snapshot

Agriculture and industry are central to Ukraine's economy. In 2005, the government stimulated economic growth by reducing taxes. Ukraine's economy is currently strong and growing. Steel exports, as well as increasing salaries, are essential to continued growth.

Peace Corps programs

- Community economic development
- Youth development
- English education

Health

HIV/AIDS, avian flu, hepatitis A, hepatitis B, typhoid, rabies, and diarrhea are among the diseases and illnesses volunteers should be aware of in Ukraine.

Medical care is below Western standards. Some clinics can provide routine treatment. Health care providers have some basic supplies, but hospitals rely on people in patients' social networks to bring food, bandages, and pharmaceuticals. Visitors should bring their own medicines. Volunteers requiring extensive treatment will likely require evacuation by air to the United States or Europe.

Travelers should refrain from eating produce sold on the street as well as wild fruit, mushrooms, game, and fowl because they could contain excessive radiation left over from the 1986 accident at the Chernobyl nuclear plant.

If outdoor radiation exceeds safe limits, staff of the U.S. Embassy will warn citizens by e-mail and text message.

Safety

Visitors should avoid rallies for fear the gatherings might suddenly turn violent.

Neo-Nazis and "skinheads" commit hate crimes, such as assault and harassment, against people of religious minorities or non-European lineage in major tourist areas. Police present at crime scenes have reportedly not protected or aided victims.

Criminals target foreigners, who tend to be more affluent than Ukrainians. Pickpocketing, handbag theft, and robbery are common crimes. Patrons of bars, restaurants, and nightclubs should keep their drinks within sight at all times to avoid being drugged by criminals wishing to rob them. Visitors are vulnerable to assault in apartment building stairwells, elevators, and hallways. Armed burglary happens periodically.

Criminals sometimes drop wallets or packages of cash near victims and wait for the property to be returned. The perpetrators accuse the victims of stealing some of the money in the wallets or packages and demand restitution. If the victims refuse to pay, the perpetrators threaten to summon police or demand to count the money in the victims' wallets. If the victims produce their wallets, the perpetrators steal them and run away. In some cases two perpetrators, one of whom impersonates a police officer claiming to inspect the victim's wallet, work together.

Fraud involving credit and ATM cards is common. Visitors should pay cash except at well-known international businesses.

Burglary, car break-ins, car theft, and vandalism against vehicles are common. Volunteers should not wire money or buy anything via Internet unless they know the recipient of their payment.

U.S. citizens should beware of fraudulent online dating and matrimonial services that offer to match them with Ukrainians. Confidence schemers hide behind a non-existent agency that advertises assistance with finding a Ukrainian spouse, then requires several money transfers ostensibly to cover immigration fees.

Calling home

There are 12.3 million land-based telephones and 49 million cell phones in Ukraine. There are 234,349 Internet hosts.

Diplomatic contact in the United States

Ambassador Oleh V. Shamshur

3350 M Street NW, Washington, DC 20007

Phone: (202) 333-0606 • Fax (202) 333-0817

Diplomatic contact from the United States

Ambassador William B. Taylor, Jr.

Embassy: 10 Yurii Kotsiubynsky Street, 01901 Kyiv

5850 Kiev Place, Washington, DC 20521-5850

Phone: (380) (44) 490-4000 • Fax (380) (44) 490-4085

Kazakhstan

Overview of geography, climate, and population

Kazakhstan is a country of about 15 million, which is nearly four times as large as Texas. The climate is continental with arid and semiarid regions. The terrain includes mountains, plains, and deserts.

Religion, ethnicity, and language in a nutshell

Nearly 50 percent of the population follow Islam, approximately 44 percent are Russian Orthodox, 2 percent are Protestant, and 7 percent adhere to other faiths. About 53 percent are of Kazakh descent, 30 percent are Russian, approximately 4 percent are Ukrainian, about 2 percent are of Uzbek lineage, about 2 percent are of German heritage, 2 percent are Tatar, a little more than 1 percent are Uygur, and about 5 percent follow other faiths. Approximately 95 percent of residents speak Russian, the official language. About 65 percent speak Kazakh.

Brief political history and today's government

Nomads settled what is now Kazakhstan in the 1200s. Russia began to rule the region in the 1900s, and the Soviets took over in 1936. The country became independent in 1991.

Economic snapshot

Fossil fuels, minerals, and metals are central to the economy. Agriculture also figures prominently.

Peace Corps programs

- Education
- Community assistance

Health

HIV/AIDS, tuberculosis, hepatitis A, hepatitis B, typhoid, and rabies are among the diseases and illnesses volunteers should be aware of in Kazakhstan.

Health care is far below Western standards. Antibiotics, disposable needles, and anesthetics are scarce. Patients requiring intensive care are usually evacuated to Western Europe. Pharmaceuticals are in short supply, so volunteers should bring their own. Volunteers who will be working in institutions should be tested for tuberculosis before leaving the United States and again after they return. Visitors should follow their initial TB tests with annual screenings. Tuberculosis is airborne and carried in unpasteurized dairy products. Some strains of tuberculosis are drug resistant.

Safety

Terrorist organizations such as al-Qaeda, Islamic Jihad Union, the Islamic Movement of Uzbekistan, and the Eastern Turkistan Islamic Movement could target U.S. citizens in Kazakhstan.

Government security employees sometimes tap visitors' phones and fax machines as well as search their belongings. Travelers should absolutely avoid photographing any areas or people of military or security value to avoid conflict with government officials. Visitors should practice the same crime awareness they would in major metropolitan areas in the United States. Assault, robbery, handbag theft, and pickpocketing are among the typical crimes of which international visitors become victims. Robbers and pickpockets usually strike near international hotels, transit stations, and outdoor markets. Travelers should refrain from carrying more cash than they need while shopping. Police routinely ask visitors to present passports or certified copies. To protect themselves against document theft, visitors should carry certified copies of their passports rather than the passports themselves. The U.S. Embassy's consular section offers certified copies of passports at their offices in Astana and Almaty from 9 a.m. to 5 p.m. Monday through Friday.

Criminals impersonating police officers often demand the wallets of unwary foreigners. Visitors should ask for identification from anyone claiming to be a police officer. Travelers who encounter impostors claiming to be police officers should record their license plate numbers, badge numbers, if any, and name. Visitors should report the incident as well as the identifying information used by the false police officer to law enforcement and the U.S. Embassy.

In one commonly used ruse, a thief will pretend to be looking for a lost wallet and demand that victims prove they do not have the missing billfold by showing the insides of their pockets or purses. The thief will then steal valuables from the open handbags or pockets. Another trick involves one criminal claiming to have found a wallet and offering to split its contents with the victim. A second person approaches, claims to own the found wallet, and insists upon restitution for money the victim supposedly stole from the billfold.

At the Almaty International Airport, criminals impersonating airport staff usher unsuspecting international visitors into cars supposedly bound for hotels. Passengers find themselves far from town with a driver who demands an exorbitant gas fee for the return trip. Before arriving, volunteers should arrange transportation from the airport. Visitors and their drivers should agree ahead of time on how they will identify each other. Travelers should never leave the airport with anyone but their designated contacts, even if other people hold placards on which the visitors' names are printed.

Mugging is a common problem. Volunteers should walk only in groups or twosomes in well-traveled, brightly lit sections of town. Volunteers should exit nightspots if other patrons start brawling.

Corrupt officials regularly extort money from foreigners at the Almaty airport and other places. Dishonest customs employees, for example, have attempted to collect fines of up to $500 by falsely accusing international visitors of breaking laws. Officials sometimes order departing U.S. citizens to pay huge fines for no legitimate reason. Visitors should contact the U.S. Embassy or airport supervisors before paying any questionable fines.

Calling home
There are about 3 million land-based telephones and about 8 million cell phones. There are 33,000 Internet hosts.

Diplomatic contact in the United States
Ambassador Yerlan Idrisov
1401 16th Street NW, Washington, DC 20036
Phone: (202) 232-5488 • Fax (202) 232-5845

Diplomatic contact from the United States
Ambassador Richard E. Hoagland
Embassy: Ak Bulak 4, Str. 23-22, Building #3, Astana 010010
Phone: (7) (7172) 70-21-00 • Fax (7) (7172) 34-08-90

Kyrgyzstan Republic
Overview of geography, climate, and population
The country of 5.3 million is nearly the size of South Dakota. The terrain includes mountains, peaks, glaciers, and lakes.

Religion, ethnicity, and language in a nutshell
Three-quarters of the population is Muslim, 20 percent are Russian Orthodox, and 5 percent follow another faith. Nearly 65 percent of the population speak the official Kyrgyz language, nearly 14 percent communicate in Uzbek, about 13 percent use the official Russian language, and about 1 percent speak Dungun. Approximately 8 percent communicate in other tongues. About 65 percent of the population are of Kyrgyz descent, about 14 percent are of Uzbek lineage, about 13 percent are of Russian ancestry, about 1 percent are Dungan, 1 percent are Ukrainian, 1 percent are Uygur, and about 6 percent are of other lineage.

Brief political history and today's government

Kyrgyzstan is a republic. The legislature consists of a Supreme Council. The judiciary includes the Supreme Court and Constitutional Court. Russia took over Kyrgyzstan in 1876. The country overthrew the Russian empire in 1916. Kyrgyzstan became part of the U.S.S.R. in 1936 and gained independence in 1991.

Peace Corps programs

- Sustainable community development
- Education

Health

HIV/AIDS, tuberculosis, malaria, rabies, hepatitis A, hepatitis B, typhoid, and diarrhea are among the diseases and illnesses volunteers should be aware of in Kyrgyzstan.

Visitors should buy anti-malarial medicine, preferably chloroquine, before leaving the United States. Anti-malarial drugs sold in Central Asia often do not work and could be harmful. Travelers should refrain from using the common anti-malarial drug halofantrine, sold under the brand name Halfan, because it can cause heart problems and kill patients. Volunteers should only take halofantrine if it is the only remedy available after a doctor has diagnosed them with potentially fatal malaria. Visitors are most at risk of contracting malaria in Bishkek, Batken, Osh, Jalal-Abad, sections near the borders with Tajikistan and Uzbekistan, and the southern and western regions.

Safety

Foreigners are especially vulnerable to violence, including hostage takings, near the borders with Uzbekistan and Tajikistan and regions south and west of the capital.

In 2006, clashes between the Kyrgyz armed forces and troops believed to be religious fighters occurred at the border with Tajikistan and in the Batken area. Land mines are a danger in Batken Oblast and near the border with Tajikistan.

Terrorist organizations such as al-Qaeda, Islamic Jihad Union, the Islamic Movement of Uzbekistan, and the Eastern Turkistan Islamic Movement could target U.S. citizens in the Kyrgyz Republic.

For fear of unexpected violence, visitors should avoid protests. Although rallies can occur anywhere, they often happen near the Presidential Administration building and in the Alatoo Square in Bishkek, the capital. Violent criminals often target foreigners, who tend to have more money than most residents of Kyrgyzstan. Visitors should refrain from riding mass transit or walking at night. Travelers are especially vulnerable to attack in parks, hotels, bars, and anywhere foreigners congregate. Criminal gangs and extremely brutal muggers are prevalent throughout the country.

Criminals impersonate police officers to harass and extort money from victims. Travelers should insist on seeing the identification of anyone who claims to be a police officer and should refuse to cooperate in the absence of proper ID.

Calling home

The telecommunications infrastructure is being upgraded; loans from the European Bank for Reconstruction and Development (EBRD) are being used to install a digital network, digital radio-relay stations, and fiber-optic links. Fixed line penetration remains low and concentrated in urban areas; multiple mobile cellular service providers with growing coverage; mobile cellular subscribership exceeded 60 per 100 persons in 2008. There are 82,496 Internet hosts.

Diplomatic contact in the United States

Ambassador Zamira Sydykova
2360 Massachusetts Ave. NW, Washington, DC 20008
Phone: (202) 338-5141 • Fax (202) 386-7550

Diplomatic contact from the United States

Ambassador Tatiana C. Gfoeller
Embassy: 171 Prospect Mira, Bishkek 720016
Phone: (996) (312) 551-241, (517) 777-217 • Fax (996) (312) 551-264

Turkmenistan

Overview of geography, climate, and population

Turkmenistan is about the size of California. The climate is subtropical and arid. The terrain includes desert and mountains. About 4.8 million people live in Turkmenistan.

Religion, ethnicity, and language in a nutshell

Eighty-nine percent of Turkmen are Muslim, 9 percent follow Eastern Orthodoxy, and the religion of 2 percent is unknown. Eighty-five percent of residents are of Turkmen ancestry, 5 percent are Uzbek, 4 percent are Russian, and 6 percent trace their lineage to another ethnic group.

Seventy-two percent of residents speak Turkmen, 12 percent speak Russian, 9 percent communicate in Uzbek, and 7 percent speak other tongues.

Brief political history and today's government

The country now known as Turkmenistan was once part of Persia. It became part of Russia in the late 19th century and a republic of the U.S.S.R. in the 1920s.

Turkmenistan is a republic in which the president has most of the power. The legislature consists of the People's Council, which has 2,500 members, and a National Assembly of 50 members. Some members of the People's Council come to power by appointment, and others gain their seats in popular elections. The judiciary consists of the Supreme Court, which has presidentially appointed justices. The legal system is derived from civil and Islamic law.

Economic snapshot

Turkmenistan's economy relies on oasis-based agriculture, gas, and oil. The export sector has been growing. The government is seeking to increase foreign investment and tourism.

Peace Corps programs

- English education
- Health education

Health

HIV/AIDS, typhoid, rabies, hepatitis A, hepatitis B, malaria, tuberculosis, diphtheria, and tick-borne encephalitis are among the diseases and illnesses volunteers should be aware of in Turkmenistan.

Health care falls far short of Western standards. Severe conditions and emergencies require medical evacuation to Western Europe or North America. Hospitals often lack such supplies as disposable needles, antibiotics, and anesthetics. Medicine is scarce, so volunteers should bring their own. Visitors should buy anti-malarial medicine before leaving the United States. Volunteers should avoid using halofantrine, sold under the brand name Halfan, to treat malaria because it can cause fatal heart problems. Patients should only accept treatment with halofantrine if doctors have diagnosed them with potentially lethal malaria, and no other drugs are available. Medicines sold in Turkmenistan are sometimes unsafe.

Safety

Due to security concerns, foreigners are forbidden to travel near the borders with Iran, Uzbekistan, and Afghanistan without special government permission. International visitors also need a special government permit to enter the region of Dashoguz, as well as sections along the coast of the Caspian Sea, for fear of violence.

Volunteers should be prepared to present their passports, visas, registration forms from the State Service for the Registration of Foreigners, and migration cards at the request of police officers who routinely perform identity checks. Visitors should ask for identification before cooperating with those who claim to be police officers.

International travelers are subject to government surveillance, including tapping of phones and fax lines in hotels. Government officials may also legally search visitors' belongings. Volunteers should ask official permission to photograph buildings and any other subjects that could be of military or security importance.

Assault, murder, and rape are among the crimes regularly committed against international visitors.

Foreigners are vulnerable to minor crimes in crowded public places, so they should avoid displaying cash and be especially careful with their passports and valuables in such areas. Criminals often target foreigners. Visitors should stay in groups when walking after dark and should remain on well-traveled streets. Taxis are often unsafe, so travelers should use car services offered through hotels or travel agencies.

Drug use and prostitution are illegal but common. Sex workers sometimes steal from their customers. The police typically detain on suspicion of soliciting prostitutes foreign men leaving nightspots with female Turkmenistanis. It is a violation of U.S. federal law to hire a sex worker younger than 18 years regardless of the country in which the encounter takes place.

Volunteers should hire a driver to transport them at night because police officers frequently conduct fraudulent identity checks to solicit bribes from foreigners who walk, take taxis, or use public transit after dark.

Calling home

There are 495,000 land telephone lines and 216,900 cell phones. The country has 97 Internet hosts.

Diplomatic contact in the United States

Ambassador Meret Bairamovich Orazow

2207 Massachusetts Avenue NW, Washington, DC 20008

Phone: (202) 588-1500 • Fax (202) 588-0697

Diplomatic contact from the United States

Ambassador (vacant): Charge d'Affaires Richard M. Miles

Embassy: No. 9 1984 Street (formerly Pushkin Street), Ashgabat, Turkmenistan 744000

7070 Ashgabat Place, Washington, DC 20521-7070

Phone: (993) (12) 35-00-45 • Fax (993) (12) 39-26-14

North Africa and the Middle East

Jordan

Overview of geography, climate, and population

Jordan is not quite as large as Indiana. It tends to be dry, but the western section of the country gets rain from November through April. The terrain includes highlands and arid plateaus. Major geographic features include the Great Rift Valley and the Jordan River. The population of Jordan is about 6.3 million.

Religion, ethnicity, and language in a nutshell

About 92 percent of Jordanians are Sunni Muslim, and 6 percent belong to Christian sects, including Greek Orthodox, Greek and Roman Catholic, Syrian Orthodox, Coptic Orthodox, Armenian Orthodox, and Protestant. Two percent of Jordanians follow other religions such as Shi'a Muslim and Druze.

Approximately 98 percent of Jordanians are of Arabic lineage, 1 percent are Circassian, and 1 percent are Armenian. Arabic is the official language, and English is widely used.

Brief political history and today's government

About 2,000 years before the dawn of the common era, Semitic Amorites began to inhabit the area now known as Jordan. Rulers of the region who followed the Amorites include Hittites, Egyptians, Israelites, Assyrians, Babylonians, Persians, Greeks, Romans, Arab Muslims, Catholic Crusaders, Mameluks, and Ottoman Turks. The League of Nations gave to England the region including countries that are now called Jordan, Jerusalem, Gaza, the West Bank, and Israel. Jordan became independent as the Hashemite Kingdom of Transjordan in 1957.

The 1949 peace treaties, which ended the Arab-Israeli War, put the West Bank under the rule of Jordan. Jordan gave up its right to rule the West Bank in 1988 and six years later entered a pact with Israel, which gave Jordan control over some sacred Islamic sites. The number of Palestinian refugees in Jordan grew after the war in 1967. Jordan fought alongside Syria in the 1973 war between Arabs and Israelis, and Jordan agreed to a peace pact with Israel in 1994.

Jordan is a constitutional monarchy. The king is Abdallah II and the prime minister is Nader al-Dahabi. The legislature consists of the National Assembly, which includes the Senate and the Chamber of Deputies. The king appoints the 55 senators. The Chamber of Deputies has 110 members who are publicly elected. Six members of the Chamber of Deputies must be women.

The judiciary includes the Court of Cassation and the Supreme Court. The legal system stems from French law and Islamic codes. A High Tribunal reviews laws passed by the legislature.

Economic snapshot

Many Jordanians are impoverished and unemployed. Inflation is a problem. Under a free trade agreement, the country can sell goods to the United States without tariffs. Jordan reduced its ratio of debt to gross domestic product considerably in 2006. The government seeks to increase economic self-sufficiency, lure international investors, and decrease unemployment.

Peace Corps programs

- Education
- Youth development

Health

HIV/AIDS, hepatitis A, hepatitis B, typhoid fever, rabies, diarrhea, leshmaniasis, West Nile virus, measles, and avian flu are among the diseases and illnesses volunteers should be aware of in Jordan.

Travelers should refrain from petting animals they do not know for fear of contracting rabies.

Wearing shoes helps prevent infections by fungi and parasites, as does washing and drying feet regularly.

Visitors can reduce their risk of contracting insect-borne diseases such as West Nile virus by using mosquito netting. Travelers can also protect themselves by applying insect repellent containing 30 to 50 percent DEET. Insect repellent that contains 7 to 15 percent picardin has not been proved effective. Permethrin can be used to treat clothing and mosquito netting but should not be applied to skin.

Safety

Local terrorist groups as well as al-Qaida target U.S. interests in Jordan, including international hotels. Suicide bombers strike civilian targets.

Hotels, restaurants, bars, nightclubs, transit centers, houses of worship, malls, and schools are potential terrorist targets. Visitors should vary their travel routines. Travelers should immediately report any suspicious objects to the police.

Violent criminals sometimes target U.S. citizens due to passions related to the conflict between Israel and Palestine and to the war in Iraq. Visitors should avoid demonstrations, such as those that often occur near mosques on Fridays.

The Jordan-Iraq border is dangerous because of war. The rate of violent crime is low. Pickpockets target visitors in crowds, so travelers should be particularly vigilant in well-traveled areas.

Purse snatchers in cars sometimes steal handbags from pedestrians, often injuring them by dragging. Visitors should hide their bags and keep a safe distance from the street.

Thieves sometimes target victims at automated teller machines, so travelers should be especially aware of their surroundings when using them. Rape, sexual harassment, and stalking against Western women occur. Female volunteers should avoid solitary travel, revealing clothes, and nighttime visits to places they do not know.

Calling home

Jordan has 614,000 land-based telephones and 4.3 million cell phones. There are 2,500 Internet hosts.

Diplomatic contact in the United States

Ambassador Zeid Ra'ad Zeid al-Hussein, Prince
3504 International Drive NW, Washington, DC 20008
Phone: (202) 966-2664 • Fax (202) 966-3110

Diplomatic contact from the United States

Ambassador Robert S. Beecroft

Embassy: Abdoun, Amman

P.O. Box 354, Amman 11118 Jordan; Unit 70200, Box 5, DPO AE 09892-0200

Phone: (962) (6) 590-6000 • Fax (962) (6) 592-0121

Morocco

Overview of geography, climate, and population

Morocco is a little bigger than California. The climate is mostly Mediterranean. The terrain includes mountains, plateaus, valleys, and plains. The population is 34.8 million.

Religion, ethnicity, and language in a nutshell

Arabic is the official language. Moroccans also speak dialects of Berber. Government, business, and international affairs are frequently conducted in French.

Ninety-nine percent of Moroccans are of Arab-Berber descent, and 0.7 percent is of other ethnicities. Jews comprise 0.2 percent of the population of Morocco.

About 99 percent of Moroccans are Muslim, approximately 1 percent are Christian, and 0.2 percent are Jewish.

Brief political history and today's government

Morocco was under the control of Phoenicians, Romans, Visigoths, and Vandals one after another before the Arabs took over in the 600s CE. The Alaouite royal family currently rules Morocco, which has been in power since the 1600s. The Portuguese began ruling the Atlantic coast of Morocco in the 1400s. Spain took control of the northern section of the country in the late 19th century. France claimed central Morocco as a protectorate in 1912. Spain made the northern and southern sections of Morocco a protectorate the same year. Morocco gained independence in 1956. Morocco is a constitutional monarchy, and the King is Mohamed VI and the Prime Minister is El Fassi.

The legislative branch includes a Parliament, which consists of a Chamber of Counselors and a Chamber of Representatives. The Chamber of Counselors has 270 members, which are chosen by labor organizations, professional groups, and local councils. The Chamber of Representatives has 325 members, 30 of which are elected from lists of female candidates. The judiciary includes the Supreme Court, justices of which are chosen by the Supreme Council of the Judiciary under the oversight of the king.

Economic snapshot

About 20 percent of Moroccans are unemployed. A drought in 2007 made for sluggish economic growth by hampering farm productivity and forcing Morocco to pay steep prices for foreign grains. The government began the National Initiative for Human Development in 2005 to try to improve urban housing, alleviate poverty and reduce unemployment. Rabat seeks to lure foreign investors by implementing economic reforms. Morocco is a party to an Association Agreement with the European Union and a Free Trade Agreement with the United States. The government is working to expand the tourism and textile industries to create jobs and narrow the divide between the affluent and impoverished.

Peace Corps programs

- Environment
- Business
- Health
- Youth development

Health

Adequate medical care is available in Morocco's largest cities, particularly in Rabat and Casablanca, although not all facilities meet high-quality standards. Specialized care or treatment may not be available. Medical facilities are adequate for non-emergency matters, particularly in the urban areas, but most medical staff will have limited or no English skills. Most ordinary prescription and over-the-counter medicines are widely available. However, specialized prescriptions may be difficult to fill, and availability of all medicines in rural areas is unreliable. Emergency and specialized care outside the major cities is far below U.S. standards, and in many instances may not be available at all. Travelers planning to drive in the mountains and other remote areas may wish to carry a medical kit and a Moroccan phone card for emergencies.

In the event of vehicle accidents involving injuries, immediate ambulance service usually is not available.

Safety

In March and April 2007, a series of terrorist bombings occurred in Casablanca, two of which simultaneously occurred outside the U.S. Consulate General and the private American Language Center. In 2003, a series of similar attacks in Casablanca targeted hotels and restaurants. The potential for terrorist violence against American interests and citizens remains high in Morocco. Moroccan authorities continue to disrupt groups seeking to attack U.S.- or Western-affiliated and Moroccan government targets, arresting numerous individuals associated with international terrorist groups. With indications that such groups still seek to carry out attacks in Morocco, it is important for American citizens to be keenly aware of their surroundings and adhere to prudent security practices, such as avoiding predictable travel patterns and maintaining a low profile. Establishments that are readily identifiable with the United States are potential targets for attacks. These may include facilities where U.S. citizens and other foreigners congregate, including clubs, restaurants, places of worship, schools, hotels, movie theaters, and other public areas. Such targets may also include establishments where activities occur that may offend religious sensitivities, such as casinos or places where alcoholic beverages are sold or consumed.

Demonstrations occur frequently in Morocco and usually center on local domestic issues. During periods of heightened regional tension, large demonstrations may take place in the major cities. All demonstrations require a government permit, but on occasion spontaneous unauthorized demonstrations occur, which have greater potential for violence. In addition, different unions or groups may organize strikes to protest an emerging issue or government policy. Travelers should be cognizant of the current levels of tension in Morocco and stay informed of regional issues that could resonate in Morocco and create an anti-American response. Avoid demonstrations if at all possible. If caught in a demonstration, remain calm and move away immediately when provided the opportunity.

The Western Sahara, with a population of approximately 350,000, was long the site of armed conflict between government forces and the POLISARIO Front, which continues to seek independence for the territory. A cease-fire has been fully in effect since 1991 in the U.N.-administered area. There are thousands of unexploded mines in the Western Sahara and in areas of Mauritania adjacent to the Western Saharan border. Exploding mines are occasionally reported, and they have caused death and injury. Travel to the Western Sahara remains restricted; persons planning to travel to the region should obtain information on clearance requirements from the Moroccan Embassy.

Crime in Morocco is a serious concern, particularly in the major cities and tourist areas. Aggressive panhandling, pickpocketing, purse-snatching, theft from occupied vehicles stopped in traffic, and harassment of women are the most frequently reported crimes. Criminals have used weapons, primarily knives, during some street robberies and burglaries. These have occurred at any time of day and night, not only in isolated places or areas less frequented by visitors, but in crowded areas as well. It is always best to have a travel companion and utilize taxis from point to point, particularly at night and when moving about unfamiliar areas. Residential break-ins also occur and have on occasion turned violent, but most criminals look for opportunities based on stealth rather than confrontation.

Women walking alone in certain areas of cities and rural areas are particularly vulnerable to harassment from men. Women are advised to travel with a companion or in a group when possible and to ignore any harassment. Responding to verbal harassment can escalate the situation. The best course of action is generally not to respond or make eye contact with the harasser.

Joggers should be mindful of traffic and remain in more heavily populated areas. It is always best to have a companion and avoid isolated areas or jogging at night. Taxis in Morocco are generally crime-free, although city buses are not considered safe. Trains are generally safe, but theft, regardless of the time of day, sometimes occurs. Avoid carrying large sums of cash, and be alert when using ATMs.

Calling home

There are 1.2 million land-based telephones and 16 million cell phones in Morocco. There are 137,187 Internet hosts.

Diplomatic contact in the United States

Ambassador Aziz Mekouar
1601 21st Street NW, Washington, DC 20009
Phone: (202) 462-7979 • Fax (202) 265-0161

Diplomatic contact from the United States

Ambassador Samuel L. Kaplan
Embassy: 2 Avenue de Mohamed El Fassi, Rabat
PSC 74, Box 021, APO AE 09718
Phone: (212) (37) 76 22 65 • Fax (212) (37) 76 56 61
Consulate(s) general: Casablanca

Pacific Islands

Fiji

Overview of geography, climate, and population

Fiji is an archipelago between Hawaii and New Zealand. The island chain is not quite as large as New Jersey. The climate is tropical and the terrain is mountainous. There are about 944,720 residents.

Religion, ethnicity, and language in a nutshell

About 54 percent of the population are Fijian. Approximately 38 percent of residents are Indian, and 8 percent are of other ancestry. English and Fijian are the official languages. Residents also speak Hindustani. Methodists make up about 35 percent of the population. Hindus account for about 34 percent of residents; approximately 7 percent are Muslim. A little more than 7 percent of Fijians are Roman Catholic, about 4 percent belong to the Assembly of God, and approximately 3 percent are Seventh-day Adventist. About 6 percent of Fijians follow an unspecified faith.

Brief political history and today's government

People have inhabited the islands now called Fiji for at least 3,500 years. Missionaries and merchants came from Europe in the early 1800s. The aboriginals who lived in the archipelago had a series of wars in the early 19th century, after which the primary chief turned the islands over to England in 1874.

Fiji fought in the Solomon Islands during World War II on the side of the Allies. The country was also home to U.S. military bases. Fiji gained independence in 1970. The Alliance Party of Ratu Sir Kamisese Mara was central to politics in Fiji after the country became independent. Voters democratically elected Timoci Bavadra to be prime minister in 1987, but a military coup d'etat overthrew him after a few weeks and established a republican government. The first president of the republic was Ratu Sir Penaia Ganilau, who was appointed in 1987.

Economic snapshot

Remittances from expatriates, sugar exports, and tourism account for most of the flow of foreign money into Fiji. The European Union gives the nation's sugar preferential trade status. Service sector jobs have declined because a coup d'etat in 2006 harmed the tourist industry. The country's account deficit was about a quarter of the gross domestic product in 2006. The European Union has frozen aid until the post-coup government plans elections.

Peace Corps programs
- Environment
- Youth development
- Health

Health

HIV/AIDS, hepatitis A, hepatitis B, typhoid fever, and diarrhea are among the diseases and illnesses that volunteers should be aware of in Fiji.

Visitors should bring their own prescription medicines in original containers because pharmacies are not consistently well-stocked.

Visitors should avoid tap water and ice cubes made with it.

Food from street stands is often unsafe to eat, as are unpasteurized dairy products. Travelers should ensure that any food they eat is cooked thoroughly.

Facilities are available for routine health care. Emergency services are extremely restricted. Limited emergency services are available at hospitals in the capital and in Lautoka. Patients with serious conditions must often be evacuated to the United States, Australia, or New Zealand. Medical professionals require patients to pay cash at the time of service.

Safety

Visitors should avoid demonstrations and crowds for fear of violence. Travelers are especially vulnerable in areas of Suva in which military exercises are occurring.

The crime rate is especially high in cities. Visitors should secure their valuables and should refrain from telling strangers details about their itinerary or lodging. Travelers should avoid solitary walks in remote places or after dark. Taxi passengers should not allow drivers to pick up other fares and should not take cabs with other people riding in them. Earthquakes and cyclones are hazards in Fiji.

Calling home

There are 112,500 land-based telephones and 205,000 cell phones in Fiji. There are 12,137 Internet hosts in Fiji.

Diplomatic contact in the United States

Ambassador Winston Thompson

2000 M Street, NW, Suite 710, Washington, DC 20036

Phone: (202) 466-8320 • Fax (202) 466-8325

Diplomatic contact from the United States

Ambassador C. Steven McGann

Embassy: 31 Loftus Street, Suva

P. O. Box 218, Suva

Phone: (679) 331-4466 • Fax (679) 330-0081

Micronesia

Overview of geography, climate, and population

The Federated States of Micronesia are four times the size of Washington, D.C. The climate is tropical and rainy, particularly in the east. Typhoons occur occasionally. The islands have mountains, coastal plains, desert, and plateaus. The country has 107, 434 people.

Religion, ethnicity, and language in a nutshell

English is the official language. Micronesians also speak Trukese, Pohnpeian, Yapese, Kosrean, Ulithian, Woleaian, Nukuoro, and Kapingamarangi. About 50 percent of Micronesians are Roman Catholic; nearly 50 percent are Protestant. The remaining 3 percent follow other faiths. Approximately 50 percent of the population are Chuukese, about 25 percent are Pohnpeian, around 6 percent are Kosraean, a little more than 5 percent are of Yapese lineage, about 5 percent are descendants of those who inhabit the Yap outer islands, approximately 2 percent are Asian, about 2 percent are Polynesian, about 6 percent are of other ethnicities, and 1 percent are of unknown ancestry.

Brief political history and today's government

Those from whom modern Micronesians are descended began to inhabit the Caroline Islands more than 4,000 years ago. A loosely connected network of chieftains governed the islands before giving way to an empire before European contact. Portuguese and Spanish navigators arrived in the 1500s. The Spanish ruled until ceding sovereignty to Germany in 1899. The Japanese acquired Micronesia under the Treaty of Versailles. The United States took control of Micronesia in the late 1940s when the archipelago was under the umbrella of the United Nations

Trust Territory of the Pacific Islands. The Federated States of Micronesia evolved out of the U.N. Trust Territory of the Pacific Islands in 1979. Micronesia became independent in 1986.

The Federated States of Micronesia have a constitutional government, which is part of a Compact of Free Association with the United States. The country is made up of four states, each of which has a separate constitution, governor, and legislative branch. The President is Emmanuel Mori. The legislative branch includes a Congress of 14 members. One Congressional representative is elected from each of the four states, and ten are elected to serve their respective districts. The judiciary consists of the Supreme Court. The legal system is based on policies that existed when the country was part of the Trust Territory, common law, Micronesian customs, municipal codes, and legislative acts.

Economic snapshot

Fishing and agriculture form the backbone of Micronesia's economy. The country has limited natural resources, isolation has hobbled the establishment of a tourist industry, and private sector growth is slow. Micronesia is a party to a Compact of Free Association under which the United States has agreed to provide yearly financial assistance through 2023. Under the compact, the United States must also contribute to a trust fund from which Micronesia can draw after 2023.

Peace Corps programs

- Youth and community development
- Natural resources conservation

Health

Hepatitis A, hepatitis B, typhoid fever, diarrhea, and dengue fever are among the diseases and illnesses volunteers should be aware of in Micronesia.

Each of the four major islands has a hospital, and there are several clinics. Supplies and pharmaceuticals are sometimes lacking.

Medical evacuation services do not always arrive promptly.

Visitors should bring their own prescription medicines in original containers.

Visitors should avoid tap water and ice cubes made with it.

Food from street stands is often unsafe to eat, as are unpasteurized dairy products. Travelers should ensure that any food they eat is cooked thoroughly.

Safety
Micronesia has a low crime rate. Theft, harassment, and minor assaults are the most common crimes committed against foreigners.

Bathing suits commonly worn in the United States are more revealing than Micronesian clothing, so visitors wearing them are sometimes subjected to harassment.

Calling home
There are 12,400 land-based telephones and 14,100 cell phones in Micronesia. There are 632 Internet hosts.

Diplomatic contact in the United States
Currently Ambassador Yosiwo George
1725 N Street NW, Washington, DC 20036
Phone: (202) 223-4383 • Fax (202) 223-4391

Diplomatic contact from the United States
Ambassador Miriam K. Hughes
Embassy: 101 Upper Pics Road, Kolonia
P. O. Box 1286, Kolonia, Pohnpei, 96941
Phone: (691) 320-2187 • Fax (691) 320-2186

Palau
Overview of geography, climate, and population
Palau is a little more than two and a half times the size of Washington, D.C. The climate is tropical with a rainy season occurring from May to November. The main island has mountains, while the others are made of coral. The population is about 20,796.

Religion, ethnicity, and language in a nutshell
About 70 percent of residents are Palauan, and approximately 15 percent are Filipino. About 5 percent are Chinese; around 2 percent trace their lineage to somewhere else in Asia; about 2 percent are white; 1.4 percent are Carolinian; about 1 percent are Micronesian; and 3.2 percent are of another lineage.

About 42 percent of residents are Roman Catholic. Approximately 23 percent of inhabitants are Protestant; about 9 percent are Modekngei. Seventh-day Adventists account for around 5 percent of the population. Jehovah's Witnesses comprise .9 percent of those who live in Palau. Latter-day Saints make up .6 percent of the population; about 3 percent belong to other religions, and approximately 16 percent are of an unspecified faith or follow no religion.

Official languages include, Japanese, Angaur, Palauan, Sonsoralese, Tobi, and English. About 65 percent of the population speak Palauan. Approximately 14 percent of the population speaks Filipino, 10 percent are English speakers, and about 6 percent speak Chinese. Approximately 2 percent of those who live in Palau are Carolinian speakers, nearly 2 percent speak Japanese, a little more than 2 percent speak other Asian languages, and nearly 2 percent speak other non-Asian languages.

Brief political history and today's government

People have inhabited Palau for at least 4,000 years. The British established commercial contact with Palau in the 17th century. The Spanish took control of Palau in the 1800s. After Spain lost the Spanish-American War, Germany bought Palau in 1899. Japan took over the islands in 1914. Palau became part of the Trust Territory of the Pacific Islands, which was ruled by the United States and the United Nations beginning in 1947. In 1979, four members of the Trust Territory joined in a federation. Palau gained independence in 1994.

Palau has a constitutional government, which is part of a Compact of Free Association with the United States. The president is Tommy Esang Remengesau, Jr. The legislature consists of the National Congress, which includes the Senate and House of Delegates. The Senate has nine publicly elected members chosen based on population. The House of Delegates has 16 publicly elected members. The judiciary is made up of the Supreme Court, the Court of Common Pleas, and the Land Court. The legal system stems from codes that existed when the country was a part of the Trust Territory of the Pacific Islands, customary law, common law, municipal ordinances, and legislative acts.

Economic snapshot

Tourism, non-commercial farming, and fishing are essential to Palau's economy. The country is a party to the Compact of Free Association under which the United States contributes yearly financial assistance and Palau provides bases for the armed forces. Foreign investment in infrastructure and growth of the tourism industry are key to the nation's economic future.

Peace Corps programs
- Youth and Community Development
- Natural resources conservation

Health
Hepatitis A, hepatitis B, typhoid fever, and dengue fever are among the diseases and illnesses volunteers should be aware of in Palau.

Visitors should avoid tap water and ice cubes made with it.

Medical facilities provide routine care but vary in quality and quantity. Severe conditions could require medical evacuation to the United States.

Food from street stands is often unsafe to eat, as are unpasteurized dairy products. Travelers should ensure that any food they eat is cooked thoroughly.

Travelers should bring their own prescription medicines, and make sure to keep them in their original containers.

Safety
The crime rate is low, but foreigners should secure their valuables and remain aware of their surroundings.

Calling home
Palau has 6,700 land-based telephones and 1,000 cell phones. There is one Internet host.

Diplomatic contact in the United States
Ambassador Hersey Kyota
1701 Pennsylvania Avenue NW, Suite 300, Washington, DC 20006
Phone: (202) 452-6814 • Fax: (202) 452-6281

Diplomatic contact from the United States
Charge d'Affaires Mark Bezner
Embassy: Koror (no street address)
P. O. Box 6028, Republic of Palau 96940
Phone: (680) 488-2920, 2990 • Fax: (680) 488-2911

Samoa

Overview of geography, climate, and population

Samoa is a little smaller than Rhode Island. The climate is tropical with a rainy season from November to April and a dry season from May to October. Samoa has two large islands and many smaller ones. The terrain includes plains and volcanic mountains. The population is 219,998.

Religion, ethnicity, and language in a nutshell

About 93 percent are Samoan, 7 percent are Euronesians, and .4 percent are of European origin.

About 35 percent of Samoans are Congregationalists; 20 percent of the population are Roman Catholic. About 15 percent are Methodist; Latter-day Saints account for 13 percent of Samoans. Members of the Assembly of God church make up about 7 percent of the population; about 4 percent of residents are Seventh-day Adventist. About 1 percent of Samoans are members of Worship Centre; other Christians account for about 5 percent of the population. Two percent of Samoans are of another faith and .1 percent follow an unspecified faith. Residents speak Samoan and English.

Brief political history and today's government

People began inhabiting Samoa more than two millennia ago. Europeans arrived in the 18th century. Merchants and missionaries arrived from Britain in the 19th century. The United States claimed some of the islands in 1904, and they are now called American Samoa. New Zealand took control of the rest of the islands in 1914, and these became known as Western Samoa. Western Samoa became independent in 1962.

Samoa is a parliamentary democracy. The Chief of State is Tuiatua Tupua Tamasese Efi and the Prime Minister is Sailele Malielegaoi Tuila'epa. The legislature consists of the Legislative Assembly, which has 49 members. District-based electors choose 47 of the assembly members. Electors not associated with particular districts select two assembly members. The judiciary includes a Court of Appeal, Supreme Court, District Court, and a Land and Titles Court. The legal system is derived from British common law and Samoan customs. The judiciary reviews laws passed by the assembly.

Economic snapshot

Foreign aid, remittances from expatriates, farming, and fishing are pillars of the Samoan economy. Copra, coconut cream, and coconut oil are major exports. The tourist industry is growing. The government seeks to lure investors and increase growth in the finance industry. Some strong points of the Samoan economy include low inflation and a manageable debt burden.

Peace Corps programs

- Education
- Village-based development
- IT

Health

Hepatitis A, hepatitis B, typhoid fever, diarrhea, and dengue fever are among the diseases and illnesses volunteers should be aware of in Samoa.

Routine care is up to Western standards, but facilities are scarce. In cases of severe illness or injury, visitors must be medically evacuated, possibly to the United States.

Dental care is generally lacking, but emergency dentists are available in Pago Pago, American Samoa.

Decompression chambers are not available, so scuba divers requiring them are usually evacuated to Suva, Fiji, or New Zealand.

Visitors should avoid tap water and ice cubes made with it.

Food from street stands is often unsafe to eat, as are unpasteurized dairy products. Travelers should ensure that any food they eat is cooked thoroughly.

Patients must immediately pay cash for medical care.

Safety

Visitors should avoid stray dogs for fear of attack. Ferries are often crowded to an unsafe degree. Visitors should remain in the passenger sections of ferries and avoid the areas in which cars are transported.

Travelers should keep a safe distance from blowholes and avoid standing between them and the ocean to avoid drowning.

Volunteers who wish to dive or snorkel in lagoons should ask tour guides for information on changing tides and other hazards.

Travelers should lock the doors to their homes at night and should secure their valuables. Burglary, robbery, and petty theft are the most common crimes. Rape also occurs, though rarely. Police service is unreliable outside Apia.

Calling home
Samoa has 19,500 land-based telephones and 24,000 cell phones. There are 10,156 Internet hosts.

Diplomatic contact in the United States
Ambassador Aliioaiga Feturi Elisaia
800 Second Avenue, Suite 400D, New York, NY 10017
Phone: (212) 599-6196, 6197 • Fax (212) 599-0797

Diplomatic contact from the United States
U.S. Ambassador to New Zealand is accredited to Samoa
Embassy: Accident Corporation Building, 5th Floor, Matafele, Apia
P. O. Box 3430, Matafele, Apia
Phone: (685) 21436/21631/21452/22696 • Fax (685) 22030

Tonga

Overview of geography, climate, and population
Tonga is about four times as big as Washington, D.C. The climate is tropical with trade winds. The warm season runs from December to May and the cool season lasts from May to December. The population is 120,898.

Religion, ethnicity, and language in a nutshell
Tongans are Christians, mostly Free Wesleyans. Residents include Polynesians and Europeans. Residents speak Tongan and English.

Brief political history and today's government
The islands of Tonga have been inhabited since 500 B.C. Some historians think that the original Tongans were settlers from the archipelago now called Samoa.

European contact with the islands began when explorers from Holland first saw them in 1616. Captain James Cook came to Tonga in the 1770s. Missionaries from Britain began coming to the island chain in 1747 and persuaded the heir to the throne to become a Christian. After converting, the king, George Tupou I, formed the first known confederation of the islands, and Christianity spread. The king set up a British-influenced parliament. Beginning in 1862, he allowed all men to rent for a very low price about 8 acres in addition to nearly an acre on which to build a house. The British made Tonga a protectorate at the turn of the 20th century.

The United States and New Zealand based troops on the main island of Tongatapu during the World War II. Tongans fought alongside New Zealanders in the Solomon Islands. Tonga gained independence in 1970. Tonga is a constitutional monarchy. The king is George Tupou V, and the Prime Minister is Feleti Sevele. The legislature consists of the Legislative Assembly, which has 32 members, including 14 ministers; nine nobles are chosen by members of the aristocracy, and nine are publicly elected. The judiciary includes the Supreme Court and the Court of Appeal. The king appoints justices to the Supreme Court. The Privy Council chooses and approves justices of the Court of Appeal.

Economic snapshot

Yams, squash, vanilla beans, and fish constitute more than 60 percent of exports. Tonga has a significant trade deficit and imports many edible commodities from New Zealand. Remittances from expatriates and foreign assistance are key elements of Tonga's economy. The Tongan government seeks to spur growth in private industry and lure investors. The government is allocating more of the national budget for health and education. Economic problems include inflation, and unemployment.

Peace Corps programs

- Education
- Business

Health

Hepatitis A, hepatitis B, typhoid, rabies, and diarrhea are among the diseases and illnesses volunteers should be aware of in Tonga.

Visitors should avoid tap water and ice cubes made with it.

Food from street stands is often unsafe to eat, as are unpasteurized dairy products. Travelers should ensure that any food they eat is cooked thoroughly.

Safety

Visitors should avoid demonstrations, which occur frequently and are sometimes violent.

Emergency numbers include 911, which serves the same purpose as in the United States; 922, which connects callers to the police; and 933, which connects callers to a hospital.

The crime rate is low. Theft is the most common crime, so visitors should secure their valuables. Violent crime is quite rare but does happen.

Calling home

There are 13,700 land-based telephones and 29,900 cell phones in Tonga. There are 18,653 Internet hosts.

Diplomatic contact in the United States

Ambassador Fekitamoeloa Utoikamanu
250 East 51st Street, New York, NY 10022
Phone: (917) 369-1025 • Fax (917) 369-1024

Diplomatic contact from the United States

The United States does not have an embassy in Tonga; the ambassador to Fiji is accredited to Tonga.

Vanuatu

Overview of geography, climate, and population

Vanuatu is a little bigger than Connecticut. The climate is tropical with trade winds from May to October and rain from November to April. Cyclones sometimes occur between December and April. The terrain includes mountains and plains. The population is 218,519.

Religion, ethnicity, and language in a nutshell

More than 98 percent of inhabitants are Ni-vanuatu, and 1.5 percent are of other ethnicities.

Approximately 31 percent of inhabitants are Presbyterians; about 13 percent are Anglican. About 13 percent of residents are Roman Catholic; approximately 11 percent are Seventh-day Adventist. Christians of other denominations account for 14 percent of the population; 6 percent hold indigenous beliefs. Ten percent of those who live in Vanuatu adhere to other religions, 1 percent do not practice a religion, and a little more than 1 percent follow an unspecified faith.

Inhabitants speak more than 100 local languages; about 73 percent speak Bislama, about 23 percent speak English, about 1 percent speak French, 0.3 percent speak other languages, and 0.7 use unspecified tongues.

Brief political history and today's government

People have inhabited the Vanuatu islands for at least 4,000 years. Historians believe that the first residents spoke Austronesian languages. The Portuguese adventurer Pedro Fernandez De Quiros arrived in 1606 and was the first European to discover the archipelago when he landed on the island Espiritu Santo. French explorer Louis Antoine de Bougainville came to what is now Vanuatu in 1768, and British navigator Captain Cook arrived in 1774 and called the island chain the New Hebrides. In the mid-19th century, more than 50 percent of the men who lived in the New Hebrides became indentured workers in Samoa, New Caledonia, Fiji, and Australia. Christian missionaries as well as farmers who wished to grow cotton came from Australia and were followed by the French in the 1880s. France and Britain shared control of the archipelago beginning at the turn of the 20th century but would not allow the Aboriginals to become citizens. Vanuatu became an independent parliamentary republic in 1980. The president of Vanuatu is Kalkot Matas Kelekele. The Prime Minister is Ham Lini. The legislature consists of the parliament, which has 52 popularly elected members. The judicial branch includes the Supreme Court. The president is responsible for appointing three Supreme Court justices favored by the judicial service commission and the chief justice based partly on the views of the prime minister and leader of the non-dominant political party. The legal system is based on British and French law.

Economic snapshot

Small farms employ more than 60 percent of residents. The financial sector, the tourist industry, and fishing are essential to the country's economy. The government has sought to increase tourism by investing in air and cruise ship service as well as building resorts. Vanuatu's government also intends to expand the animal husbandry industry. Foreign assistance comes mainly from Australia and New Zealand.

Peace Corps programs

- Education
- Agriculture
- Community health
- Business
- Environment

Health

Hepatitis A, hepatitis B, typhoid fever, and malaria are all threats in this area.

Health care is limited. More reliable medical facilities are available in Australia and New Zealand.

Hyperbaric chambers for scuba divers are available in Luganville and Port Vila. Some patients with diving injuries are evacuated to Australia or New Zealand.

Medical professionals require patients to pay cash at the time of service.

Emergency services are also available. Pharmacies are often poorly stocked, so volunteers should bring their own prescription medicines.

Effective anti-malarial medicines include atovaquone/proguanil, doxycyline, and mefloquine. Patients should use primaquine exclusively in special cases after they have undergone G6 PD screening. Chloroquine will not protect travelers against the strains of malaria prevalent in Vanuatu. Malaria is a concern across the country.

Visitors should purchase anti-malarial drugs before leaving the United States.

Visitors should not accept treatment with the anti-malarial drug halofantrine, sold under the brand name Halfan, because it causes potentially fatal heart problems. Patients should not take halofantrine unless doctors have diagnosed them with malaria that could be lethal, and no other anti-malarial pharmaceuticals are obtainable.

Visitors can reduce their risk of contracting insect-borne diseases such as malaria, leishmaniasis, and dengue fever by using mosquito netting. Travelers can also protect themselves by applying insect repellent containing 30 to 50 percent DEET. Insect repellent that contains 7 to 15 percent picardin has not been proved effective. Permethrin can be used to treat clothing and mosquito netting but should not be applied to skin.

Safety

Visitors should avoid demonstrations, which occur infrequently. To reduce the risk of being raped or harassed, female travelers should stay in groups or pairs.

The rate of burglaries has increased recently. The rate of violent crime is extremely low. Earthquakes, volcanic eruptions, tropical storms, and cyclones are hazards. The cyclone season runs from November through April. For information on earthquakes and volcanic eruptions, travelers can call the Department of Geology and Mines at 22423.

Calling home

There are 7,000 land-based telephones and 12.7 cell phones in Vanuatu. There are 1,010 Internet hosts.

Diplomatic contact in the United States

Vanuatu does not have an embassy in the United States. It does, however, have a Permanent Mission to the UN.

Diplomatic contact from the United States

The United States does not have an embassy in Vanuatu; the ambassador to Papua New Guinea is accredited to Vanuatu.

South America

Bolivia

Overview of geography, climate, and population

Bolivia is a landlocked country nearly three times as large as Montana. Altitude largely determines the climate, which ranges from tropical to cold and dry. The Andes dominate the terrain, which also includes plateaus, hills and low country. There are about 9.7 million people in Bolivia.

Religion, ethnicity, and language in a nutshell

Thirty percent of Bolivians are Quechua. Thirty percent of inhabitants are mestizo; Aymara make up 25 percent of the population. Fifteen percent of the population are white.

Approximately 95 percent of Bolivians are Roman Catholic. About 5 percent are Evangelical Methodist.

Official languages include Spanish, Quechua, and Aymara.

Brief political history and today's government

The area that is now Bolivia has been home to a civilization for at least 2,000 years. The land was under the control of the Aymaras and the Incas. Spain took over the area in the 16th century and named it Upper Peru, according to the *Kingfisher Reference Atlas*. Bolivia became independent in 1825 and took its name from the soldier Simon Bolivar. Approximately 200 coups d'etat have occurred in Bolivia since it broke from Spain. A civilian administration came to power in the early 1980s. The public elected Juan Evo Morales, a socialist, president in 2005; he remains in power. Bolivia is a republic. The legislature consists of the National Congress, which includes the Chamber of Senators and the Chamber of Deputies. The Chamber of Senators has 27 members who are chosen from party lists. The Chamber of Deputies has 130 members, 70 of which are popularly elected by district constituents, 60 of which are chosen from party lists. The judiciary consists of the Supreme Court, district courts, provincial courts, local courts, a constitutional tribunal, and national electoral court. The National Congress appoints justices to the Supreme Court as well as magistrates to the Constitutional Tribunal. The president, congress, Supreme Court, and the party, which gets the most votes, are responsible for filling the national electoral court.

Economic snapshot

During the last decade of the 20th century, the economy grew, the number of Bolivians living below the poverty line decreased and investment increased. Energy companies that used to be privately held began to come under state control during the 1990s. The first year in many that Bolivia had a budget surplus was 2006. High inflation is a key problem.

Peace Corps programs

- Agriculture
- Environmental education
- Water and sanitation
- Natural resource management
- Youth development
- Business

Health

HIV/AIDS, diarrhea, hepatitis A, hepatitis B, typhoid fever, dengue fever, malaria, yellow fever, rabies, leptospirosis, and altitude sickness are among the diseases and illnesses that volunteers should be aware of in Bolivia.

Food borne illnesses are common due to poor sanitation and lack of personal hygiene on the part of restaurant workers.

Even visitors in good health are at risk of death from altitude sickness.

Health care in urban areas is usually adequate for routine care but the quality of medicine is not predictable. Emergency care is lacking. Pharmacies are generally well stocked with non-prescription medicines.

Dengue fever is a concern in the eastern part of the country, even in the city of Santa Cruz.

Visitors should take the anti-malarial medicines atovaquone/proguaril, doxycycline, or mefloquine.

Chloroquine will not protect travelers against the strains of malaria prevalent in Bolivia. Malaria is a concern in sections of the Beni, Chuquisaca, La Paz, Pando, Santa Cruz, and Tarija departments at elevations lower than 8,202 feet. Malaria is not a hazard in the city of La Paz.

Visitors can reduce their risk of contracting insect-borne diseases such as malaria, leishmaniasis, and dengue fever by using mosquito netting. Travelers can also protect themselves by applying insect repellent containing 30 to 50 percent DEET. Insect repellent that contains 7 to 15 percent picardin has not been proved effective. Permethrin can be used to treat clothing and mosquito netting but should not be applied to skin.

Visitors should not accept treatment with the anti-malarial drug halofantrine, sold under the brand name Halfan, because it causes potentially fatal heart problems. Patients should not take halofantrine unless doctors have diagnosed them with malaria that could be lethal, and no other anti-malarial pharmaceuticals are obtainable.

Visitors should bring their own prescription medicines and keep them in their original containers.

Visitors should avoid tap water and ice cubes made with it.

Food from street stands is often unsafe to eat, as are unpasteurized dairy products. Travelers should ensure that any food they eat is cooked thoroughly.

Safety

To report a police emergency, visitors should call 911. To report a fire, call 119.

Demonstrations can hinder transportation and become violent, so visitors should avoid them. Visitors should not try to get through roadblocks constructed by protesters.

Rallies are particularly likely to occur when the government is changing. Travelers should beware of pickpocketing, assaults that occur after they have taken money out of automated teller machines, theft of valuables from parked cars, and purse snatching. Crime is particularly prevalent at bus terminals and on buses. Carjacking, sometimes accompanied by murder, is also a hazard.

Visitors are especially vulnerable to violent crime on the Coronilla Hill in Cochabamba, so the police advise travelers to avoid the area. Kidnappers and robbers have struck bus passengers traveling from Copacabana to La Paz. The driver of the night bus stops the coach before it reaches its destination, often near the General Cemetery. Passengers leave the bus and get into a taxi waiting nearby, where criminals blindfold them and steal their valuables and ATM cards. Thieves have released the victims after taking cash out of their bank accounts. Volunteers should buy tickets at the Copacabana bus station and refuse to purchase them from unofficial vendors. Travelers should ride the bus only by day.

Visitors should beware of impostors who pretend to be police officers and take foreigners to false police stations to be robbed. If supposed police officers attempt to detain foreigners, the travelers should immediately request to see the arrest warrant and to contact the United States consulate in La Paz, Cochabamba, or Santa Cruz.

Criminals sometimes introduce to victims an accomplice who poses as an international visitor. The supposed visitor develops trust with the victims, then asks for help or suggests traveling together. Victims eventually find themselves in a false police station or an unidentifiable building in which they are detained until they turn over their personal identification numbers or bank cards. Some travelers have been murdered after such a scam. Theft of visitors' bags is common, particularly in La Paz and Altiplano. Thieves also smear something unpleasant on the bags of their intended victims, offer to help remove it as a means of distracting the victims, then steal the satchels and run.

Rapists have attacked women hiking in the Yungas Valley near Coroico, so trekkers should remain in large groups. Women have accused a tour guide in the Rurrenabaque, Beni region, of drugging and raping them. Visitors should refuse any medicine or other substances offered by strangers.

Calling home

There are 646,300 land-based telephones and 2.4 million cell phones. There are 24,363 Internet hosts.

Diplomatic contact in the United States

Ambassador (vacant): Charge d'Affaires Erika Angela Duenas Loayza
3014 Massachusetts Avenue NW, Washington, DC 20008
Phone: (202) 483-4410 • Fax (202) 328-3712
Note: As of September 2008, the U.S. has expelled the Bolivian ambassador to the U.S.

Diplomatic contact from the United States

Ambassador (vacant): Charge d'Affaires John Creamer
Embassy: Avenida Arce 2780, Casilla 425, La Paz
P. O. Box 425, La Paz; APO AA 34032
Phone: (591) (2) 216-8000 • Fax (591) (2) 216-8111
Note: As of September 2008, the Bolivian government has expelled the U.S. Ambassador to Bolivia.

Ecuador

Overview of geography, climate, and population

Ecuador has 14.5 million residents. It borders the Pacific Ocean, Colombia, and Peru. The country is not quite as large as Nevada. The climate is tropical in some regions and chilly in others. The terrain includes plains, highlands, and jungle.

Religion, ethnicity, and language in a nutshell

About 65 percent of Ecuadorans are mestizo, approximately 25 percent are Amerindian, 7 percent are Spanish, and 3 percent are black. Ninety-five percent of the population is Catholic, and 5 percent follows other faiths. Spanish is the official language; many Amerindian languages, particularly Quechua, are also spoken.

Brief political history and today's government

The area now known as Ecuador was under Inca control from at least the 15th century to 1533, when the Spanish invaded. In 1563, Quito, which is now the capital, became a hub of Spanish governmental activity. Quito was incorporated into the Viceroyalty of New Granada in 1717. Quito, Venezuela, and what is now Colombia joined to become Gran Colombia after gaining independence from European powers in the early 19th century. Quito declared independence from the federation in 1830 and started calling itself the Republic of the Equator. In the early 20th century, Ecuador's borders shrunk when it lost land in several regional wars. The country went to war with Peru from 1995 to 1999 over a border dispute. The nation has had democratically elected presidents since the late 20th century.

Ecuador is a republic. The president is Rafael Correa Delgado. The legislature consists of the National Congress, which has 100 members elected from party lists. The judiciary includes the Supreme Court, sitting judges of which are responsible for choosing new justices. The legal system is based on civil law.

Economic snapshot

Petroleum is central to the economy. After a fiscal disaster in 2000, the government made the U.S. dollar an accepted currency. The dollar, as well as growth in the export sector, helped the economy return to normal. In the early 2000s, the annual economic growth rate was steady. The Palacio administration confiscated Occidental Petroleum's holdings in 2006 and heavily taxed foreign petroleum firms. The United States broke off free trade talks with Ecuador in response. The current Correa administration has increased the taxes international oil companies have to pay. Investment declined, and economic growth became sluggish.

Peace Corps programs

- Youth development
- Health •
- Environmental conservation
- Agriculture

Health

HIV/AIDS, diarrhea, hepatitis A, hepatitis B, typhoid fever, dengue fever, malaria, yellow fever, rabies, and leptospirosis are among the diseases and illnesses volunteers should be aware of in Ecuador.

Medical care is adequate in large cities. In smaller communities, health care facilities are generally less than adequate. Ambulances are extremely scarce. The Galapagos Islands do not have emergency services for patients requiring surgery or treatment for heart problems. Visitors should avoid people who describe themselves as pharmacists because they are generally poorly trained.

Altitude sickness is a concern, and hyperbaric chambers are scarce. Malaria, dengue fever, and yellow fever are hazards at elevations below 4,500 feet.

Yellow fever is a risk in the Morona-Santiago, Napo, Orellana, Pastaza, Sucumbios, and Zamora-Chinchipe provinces. Yellow fever is also prevalent in all sections of the eastern Andes Mountains except the cities of Quito and Guayaquil. Yellow fever is not a concern on the Galapagos Islands.

Visitors should take the anti-malarial medicines atovaquone/proguaril, doxycycline, or mefloquine.

Chloroquine will not protect travelers against the strains of malaria prevalent in Ecuador.

Malaria is not a risk in Quito, Guayaquil, tourist areas in the central highlands and the Galapagos Islands.

Visitors can reduce their risk of contracting insect-borne diseases such as malaria, leishmaniasis, and dengue fever by using mosquito netting. Travelers can also protect themselves by applying insect repellent containing 30 to 50 percent DEET. Insect repellent that contains 7 to 15 percent picardin has not been proved effective. Permethrin can be used to treat clothing and mosquito netting but should not be applied to skin.

Visitors should not accept treatment with the anti-malarial drug halofantrine, sold under the brand name Halfan, because it causes potentially fatal heart problems. Patients should not take halofantrine unless doctors have diagnosed them with malaria that could be lethal, and no other anti-malarial pharmaceuticals are obtainable.

Visitors should bring their own prescription medicines in original containers.

Visitors should avoid tap water and ice cubes made with it.

Food from street stands is often unsafe to eat, as are unpasteurized dairy products. Travelers should ensure that any food they eat is cooked thoroughly.

Safety

Terrorism, kidnapping, murder, organized crime, drug smuggling, and weapons trafficking are concerns in the areas of Sucumbios, Orellana, Carchi, and northern Esmeraldas.

Visitors should avoid demonstrations for fear of violence. Terrorists have sometimes planted small bombs at government buildings and international businesses.

Visitors should carry their identification and proof of citizenship all the time.

Warning signs are not posted on beaches, in spite of the existence of dangerous currents. Lifeguards are not always on duty. The rate of violent and non-violent crime is high. Rapists target victims even in groups and crowded areas. Carjacking, shooting, and kidnapping are concerns but are relatively uncommon. Visitors should refrain from wearing jewelry, and walking in remote areas, especially after dark. Armed robbery of tourists in Otavalo, Manta, and Cuenca, as well as on trails and beaches, is common. Pickpockets target victims in airports, mass transit stations, restaurants, markets, and well-traveled streets. Drivers should keep windows raised and doors locked. Motorists should hide valuables.

Volunteers should not hike to the top of Pichincha for fear of rape and other types of assault. Attackers have targeted victims in groups of up to eight people.

Rapists sometimes use sedatives to facilitate committing attacks. Visitors should refuse strangers' offers to buy them drinks and should keep their beverages in sight all the time.

Calling home
There are 1.8 million land-based telephones and 8.4 million cell phones. There are 28,420 Internet hosts.

Diplomatic contact in the United States
Ambassador Luis Benigno Gallegos Chiriboga
2535 15th Street NW, Washington, DC 20009
Phone: (202) 234-7200 • Fax (202) 667-3482

Diplomatic contact from the United States
Ambassador Heather Hodges
Embassy: Avenida Avigiras E12-170 y Avenida Eloy Alfaro, Quito
Avenida Guayacanes N52-205 y Avenida Avigiras
Phone: (593) (2) 398-5000 • Fax (593) (2) 398-5100
Consulate(s) general: Guayaquil

Guyana

Overview of geography, climate, and population

Guyana borders the Atlantic Ocean, Venezuela, and Suriname. The climate is tropical with a rainy season from May to August, and another from November to January. The population is 772,298. The terrain includes highlands, plains, and savanna.

Religion, ethnicity, and language in a nutshell

Fifty percent of residents are East Indian, 36 percent are black, 7 percent are Amerindian, and 7 percent are white, Chinese, and mixed. About half the population of Guyana is Christian, 35 percent are Hindu, 10 percent are Muslim, and the remaining 5 percent follow other faiths. Residents speak English, Amerindian dialects, Creole, Caribbean Hindustani, and Urdu.

Brief political history and today's government

The Dutch claimed Guyana as a colony in the 1600s, and the British took control of the country in 1815. Guyana became independent in 1966 and has been governed by socialist-leaning administrations since then. Cheddi Jagan became president in a public election in 1992. Jagan's wife, Janet, succeeded him after he died in 1997. In 1999, Bharrat Jagdeo took office after Janet Jagan stepped down, citing illness. Voters put Jagdeo back in office in 2001 and 2006.

Guyana is a republic. The legislature includes a National Assembly, which has 65 publicly elected members. Two secretaries who are presidential appointees and do not have votes are also members of the National Assembly.

Economic snapshot

Growth in farming- and mining-spurred economic development, a business-friendly climate, and low inflation. Foreign investment and remittances from expatriates are important sources of revenue. Poor infrastructure and an untrained workforce are ongoing economic problems. The Inter-American Development Bank canceled enough of the country's debt to equal about 40 percent of the gross domestic product. Transferring bauxite mines from public to private hands should strengthen the industry, although revenue from mining exports has declined in recent years.

Peace Corps programs

- Health
- Community development
- Education

Health

HIV/AIDS, diarrhea, hepatitis A, hepatitis B, typhoid fever, dengue fever, malaria, leptospirosis, yellow fever, and rabies are among the diseases and illnesses volunteers should be aware of in Guyana.

Anti-malarial medicines that protect visitors against strains of malaria prevalent in Guyana include atovaquone/proguanil, doxycycline, mefloquine, and primaquine, which should only be taken in special cases after G6PD screening. Chloroquine does not offer protection against the strains of malaria common in Guyana. Malaria is a concern in all areas of the countryside at elevations lower than 2,953 feet.

Visitors should not accept treatment with the anti-malarial drug halofantrine, sold under the brand name Halfan, because it causes potentially fatal heart problems. Patients should not take halofantrine unless doctors have diagnosed them with malaria that could be lethal, and no other anti-malarial pharmaceuticals are obtainable.

Visitors can reduce their risk of contracting insect-borne diseases such as malaria, leishmaniasis, and dengue fever by using mosquito netting. Travelers can also protect themselves by applying insect repellent containing 30 to 50 percent DEET. Insect repellent that contains 7 to 15 percent picardin has not been proved effective. Permethrin can be used to treat clothing and mosquito netting but should not be applied to skin.

Visitors should avoid tap water and ice cubes made with it.

Food from street stands is often unsafe to eat, as are unpasteurized dairy products. Travelers should ensure that any food they eat is cooked thoroughly.

Safety

Visitors should avoid crowds and rallies, for fear of violence. Major hotels and resorts lack emergency plans, adequate security, lifeguards, and first aid supplies.

Murder, burglary, kidnapping, and carjacking are hazards, particularly in commercial areas. Drivers should keep doors locked and windows closed. For fear of crime, travelers should avoid visiting or going through Buxton, which is a village on the road between Georgetown and New Amsterdam. Visitors should also avoid Agricola, a town on the East Bank highway. The public golf course in Lusignan, near Buxton, is not safe to use alone or at night.

Assailants have attacked travelers going to and from the Cheddi Jagan International Airport, so travelers should be cautious. Visitors are especially vulnerable to rape, armed assault, theft, purse snatching, and pickpocketing in Georgetown. Travelers are vulnerable to crime in the National Park and sections near the sea wall in Georgetown. Visitors are more likely to be targeted for crime in Georgetown after twilight. Taxis are the safest mode of transportation, though criminals have sometimes targeted passengers. Volunteers should avoid displaying valuables or cash because muggings sometimes happen during the day.

Calling home

Guyana has about 110,000 land-based telephones and 281,000 cell phones. There are 3,000 Internet hosts.

Diplomatic contact in the United States

Ambassador Bayney Karran
2490 Tracy Place NW, Washington, DC 20008
Phone: (202) 265-6900 • Fax (202) 232-1297

Diplomatic contact from the United States

Ambassador John Melvin Jones
Embassy: U.S. Embassy, 100 Young and Duke Streets, Kingston, Georgetown
P. O. Box 10507, Georgetown; US Embassy, 3170 Georgetown Place, Washington DC 20521-3170
Phone: (592) 225-4900, 225-4901, 225-4902, 225-4903, 225-4904, 225-4905, 225-4906, 225-4906, 225-4907, 225-4908, and 225-4909
Fax (592) 225-8497

Paraguay

Overview of geography, climate, and population

Paraguay is nearly as big as California. The climate is subtropical to temperate with heavy rain in the east. The west is semiarid. Paraguay's terrain includes plains, marsh, forest, and scrub. The population is 6.9 million.

Religion, ethnicity, and language in a nutshell

Ninety-five percent of the population is mestizo. Five percent of the population is of other ethnicities.

Nearly 90 percent of those who live in Paraguay are Roman Catholic, and a little more than 6 percent are Protestant. Other sects of Christianity account for approximately 1 percent of the population; nearly 2 percent of residents follow other faiths or adhere to unspecified religions. One percent of the population does not hold religious beliefs. Spanish and Guarani are the official languages.

Brief political history and today's government

The Spanish ruled Paraguay beginning in the 16th century, and the country became independent in 1818. The nation suffered a devastating war with Uruguay, Brazil, and Argentina from 1865-1870 in which the borders shrank considerably, and at least 60 percent of the men died. Fifty years of fiscal doldrums followed the war. Paraguay captured land from Bolivia in the Chaco War of 1932-1935. A military dictator named Alfredo Stroessner ruled from 1954 to 1989. Democratic elections have occurred since Stroessner left power.

Paraguay is a constitutional republic. The president is Nicanor Duarte Frutos. The legislature consists of a Congress made up of a Chamber of Senators and a Chamber of Deputies. The Chamber of Senators has 45 publicly elected members. The Chamber of Deputies has 80 publicly elected members. The judiciary includes the Supreme Court of Justice, which includes nine justices nominated by the Council of Magistrates. The legal system is derived from Roman, Argentine, and French law. The Supreme Court is responsible for reviewing bills passed in the legislature.

Economic snapshot

Paraguay's economic statistics are somewhat uncertain because of the importance of informal economic enterprises, such as street-based vending stands and businesses that re-sell imports to other countries in the region. Subsistence agriculture is also essential to the country's economy. Per-person buying power has stayed the same since 1980. Political instability, government corruption and limited infra-structure contribute to Paraguay's lack of economic development until 2003. Expanding international commodities markets led to steady growth between 2003 and 2007.

Peace Corps programs

- Agriculture
- Business
- Elementary education
- Health
- Youth development

- Beekeeping
- Municipal development
- Environmental education
- Sanitation
- Agroforestry

Health

HIV/AIDS, diarrhea, hepatitis A, hepatitis B, typhoid fever, dengue fever, malaria, yellow fever, and rabies are among the diseases and illnesses volunteers should be aware of in Paraguay.

Only the capital offers adequate medical care, medicine, and supplies. Travelers should take the anti-malarial medicine chloroquine. Malaria is a concern in the departments of Alto Parana, Caaguazu, and Canendiyu.

Visitors can reduce their risk of contracting insect-borne diseases such as malaria, leishmaniasis, and dengue fever by using mosquito netting.

Travelers can also protect themselves by applying insect repellent containing 30 to 50 percent DEET. Insect repellent that contains 7 to 15 percent picardin has not been proved effective. Permethrin can be used to treat clothing and mosquito netting but should not be applied to skin.

Visitors should not accept treatment with the anti-malarial drug halofantrine, sold under the brand name Halfan, because it causes potentially fatal heart problems. Patients should not take halofantrine unless doctors have diagnosed them with malaria that could be lethal, and no other anti-malarial pharmaceuticals are obtainable.

Visitors should avoid tap water and ice cubes made with it.

Food from street stands is often unsafe to eat, as are unpasteurized dairy products. Travelers should ensure that any food they eat is cooked thoroughly.

Safety

The section of Paraguay near the borders with Paraguay, Brazil, and Argentina is unsafe due to the activities of militias. Drug trafficking occurs in the Department of Amambay.

Kidnappers have targeted wealthy victims in the Alto Parana department. Visitors should avoid protests, roadblocks, and crowds for fear of violence. Rape, kidnapping, armed robbery, carjacking, and assault are among the crimes that affect foreigners.

Visitors should hide valuables and beware of pickpockets on public buses. Travelers should refuse to buy tickets from unofficial vendors at the Asuncion bus station because they sometimes sell tickets for runs that do not exist.

Calling home

Paraguay has 331,100 land-based telephones and 3.2 million cell phones. There are 12,497 Internet hosts.

Diplomatic contact in the United States

Ambassador James Spalding Hellmers
2400 Massachusetts Avenue NW, Washington, DC 20008
Phone: (202) 483-6960 through 6962 • Fax (202) 234-4508

Diplomatic contact from the United States

Ambassador Liliana Ayalde
Embassy: 1776 Avenida Mariscal Lopez, Casilla Postal 402, Asuncion
Unit 4711, APO AA 34036-0001
Phone: (595) (21) 213-715 • Fax (595) (21) 228-603

Peru

Overview of geography, climate, and population

The climate in the Andes ranges from temperate to frigid. At sea level, the climate ranges from tropical in the east to desert in the west. The terrain includes the Andes, jungle, and plains. The population is 29.5 million.

Religion, ethnicity, and language in a nutshell

Forty-five percent of the population are Amerindian; 37 percent of Peruvians are mestizo, 15 percent are white, and 3 percent are black, Chinese, Japanese, and other.

About 81 percent of Peruvians are Roman Catholic; about 1 percent is Seventh-day Adventist. Christians of other sects account for 0.7 percent of the population; 0.6 percent of Peruvians follow other faiths. About 16 percent of those who live in Peru follow an unspecified religion or are not religious.

Spanish and Quechua are the official languages. Aymara and many Amazonian languages are also spoken.

Brief political history and today's government

Andean civilizations existed in Peru beginning about 10,000 years ago. The society of the Incas, the best known of the ancient Andean civilizations, fell to the Spanish in 1533. Peru became independent in the early 19th century. The 20th century has included some military regimes and some civilian governments. Alberto Fujimori became president in 1990 and worked to spur economic growth and quell an insurgency that had developed in the previous decade. Fujimori left office in 2000, and a transitional government took over until 2001 when Alejandro Toledo became president. Alan Garcia became president in 2006 on a platform of moderate budgeting and addressing societal problems. Alan Garcia Perez is the president of Peru, which is a constitutional republic. The legislative branch consists of the Congress of the Republic of Peru. The Congress has 120 publicly elected members. The judiciary includes the Supreme Court of Justice, judges of which are selected by the National Council of the Judiciary.

Economic snapshot

Mineral mining and fishing are essential to the Peruvian economy. Poor infrastructure impedes investment and trade. Peru's economy grew steadily from 2002 through 2006 and significantly in 2007 because of high international prices for minerals and metals. The exchange rate remained consistent, and inflation was low. Exports of farm goods, minerals, and fabrics are expected to drive future growth.

Peace Corps programs

- Business
- Community health

- Youth development
- Environmental awareness

Health

HIV/AIDS, diarrhea, hepatitis A, typhoid fever, dengue fever, malaria, Oroya fever, and yellow fever are among the diseases and illnesses volunteers should be aware of in Peru.

Malaria is a concern in the areas of Alto Paraná, Caaguazú, and Canendiyú.

Visitors should not accept treatment with the anti-malarial drug halofantrine, sold under the brand name Halfan, because it causes potentially fatal heart problems. Patients should not take halofantrine unless doctors have diagnosed them with malaria that could be lethal, and no other anti-malarial pharmaceuticals are obtainable.

Visitors can reduce their risk of contracting insect-borne diseases such as malaria, leishmaniasis, and dengue fever by using mosquito netting. Travelers can also protect themselves by applying insect repellent containing 30 to 50 percent DEET. Insect repellent that contains 7 to 15 percent picardin has not been proved effective. Permethrin can be used to treat clothing and mosquito netting but should not be applied to skin.

Visitors should avoid tap water and ice cubes made with it.

Food from street stands is often unsafe to eat, as are unpasteurized dairy products. Travelers should ensure that any food they eat is cooked thoroughly.

Safety

Terrorists that have targeted U.S. interests are a concern in the provinces of Ayacucho, Huancavelica, Huanuco, Junin, and San Martin. Terrorism occurs primarily in the countryside. Land mines are a danger near the border with Ecuador. Violence and drug trafficking are dangers near the border with Colombia. Volunteers should generally avoid traveling outside cities at night for fear of crime. Bus travel on the Pan-American Highway is safer than driving. Trekkers wishing to use the Inca Trail should hike with a guide who is leading a group. Volunteers should register with the staff of national parks. Climbers have died on Huayna Picchu, near Machu Picchu. Medical services on Machu Picchu are rudimentary.

Hikers have died of falls, and rescue services are inadequate. Dangerous currents are a hazard in the Pacific and in rivers. Crocodiles, snakes, and caimans are hazards associated with swimming in lakes and rivers. Volunteers should ask locals for recommendations of where to swim. Visitors swimming in lakes and rivers or entering the jungle should carry waterproof identification cards listing emergency contacts and should leave their itineraries with the authorities and with friends.

Kidnappers often use ATM machines to drain the bank accounts of victims. Carjacking, armed robbery, and assault occur frequently in Lima and other major metropolitan areas. Victims should reduce their risk of serious injury by complying immediately with criminals.

Thieves often break the windows of stopped cars on the major highways near the Jorge Chavez International Airport in Lima to steal visible valuables. Such theft can occur anywhere. Visitors should call taxis by phone instead of hailing them. Taxi drivers have committed crimes against passengers. Travelers should beware of theft of passports and luggage at the airport. Volunteers should not take cabs for hire outside the airport, but should arrange for taxis at counters inside. Drivers of some taxis outside the airport significantly overcharge passengers or take them to unsafe areas. Petty theft is most common in crowds, particularly near tourist attractions and international hotels in Lima. Minor crimes are also a concern in other cities. Visitors should travel in groups escorted by tour guides. Unofficial change bureaus should be avoided, as their proprietors often deal in counterfeit currency.

Travelers should not carry purses, wear jewelry, or use credit cards. Visitors should carry copies of their passports rather than the documents themselves.

Calling home
Peru has 2.3 million land-based telephones and 8.5 million cell phones. There are 270,193 Internet hosts.

Diplomatic contact in the United States
Ambassador Luis Valdivieso Montano
1700 Massachusetts Avenue NW, Washington, DC 20036
Phone: (202) 659-8124 • Fax (202) 659-8124

Diplomatic contact from the United States
Ambassador P. Michael McKinley

Embassy: Avenida La Encalada, Cuadra 17s/n, Surco, Lima 33

P. O. Box 1995, Lima 1; American Embassy (Lima), APO AA 34031-5000

Phone: (51) (1) 434-3000 • Fax (51) (1) 618-2397

Suriname

Overview of geography, climate, and population

The climate is tropical with trade winds. The terrain includes hills, swamps, and plains. The population is 481,267.

Religion, ethnicity, and language in a nutshell

Thirty-seven percent of residents are Hindustani, 31 percent are Creole, 15 percent are Javanese, 10 percent are of African lineage, 2 percent are Amerindian, 2 percent are Chinese, 1 percent is white, and 2 percent are of other heritage.

About 30 percent of residents are Hindu; about 26 percent of inhabitants are Protestant, mostly Moravian. Nearly 23 percent of Surinamese are Catholic; about 20 percent follow Islam, and 5 percent practice indigenous faiths.

Dutch is the official language, but English is quite common.

Brief political history and today's government

Suriname is a constitutional democracy. The president is Runaldo Ronald Venetiaan. The legislative branch consists of the National Assembly, which has 51 publicly elected members. The judiciary includes cantonal courts and a court of justice, on which judges sit for life. Holland claimed Suriname in 1667, but Spanish explorers and British colonists entered the country in the 1500s and 1600s. Suriname gained independence in 1975. In 1980, a military government took power and established socialism. In 1987, democratic voting took place, and a civilian government took office. A military coup ended the civilian government's reign in 1990. In 1991, civilian power was restored and is still in effect.

Economic snapshot

Mining is the backbone of Suriname's economy, with the bulk of exports consisting of gold, oil, and alumina. Inflation control and development of mines are essential to economic growth in the near future. Mid-range economic development depends on The European Development Fund. The Netherlands and Belgium have contributed foreign aid to support Suriname's mining industry. The state oil company is exploring for new offshore wells.

Peace Corps programs

- Hygiene education
- Water quality
- Economic development
- Sanitation
- Education

Health

HIV/AIDS, diarrhea, hepatitis A, hepatitis B, typhoid fever, dengue fever, mayaro virus, malaria, leptospirosis, yellow fever, and rabies are among the diseases and illnesses volunteers should be aware of in Suriname.

Travelers should take the anti-malarial medicines atovaquone/proguanil, doxycycline, mefloquine, and primaquine in special instances after G6PD screening.

Malaria is a concern everywhere except in Paramaribo and coastal areas of Nickerie, Coronie, Saramacca, Wanica, Commewijne, and Marowijne at latitudes north of 5 degrees north.

Visitors can reduce their risk of contracting insect-borne diseases such as malaria, leishmaniasis, and dengue fever by using mosquito netting. Travelers can also protect themselves by applying insect repellent containing 30 to 50 percent DEET. Insect repellent that contains 7 to 15 percent picardin has not been proved effective. Permethrin can be used to treat clothing and mosquito netting but should not be applied to skin.

Visitors should not accept treatment with the anti-malarial drug halofantrine, sold under the brand name Halfan, because it causes potentially fatal heart problems. Patients should not take halofantrine unless doctors have diagnosed them with malaria that could be lethal, and no other anti-malarial pharmaceuticals are obtainable.

Visitors should avoid tap water and ice cubes made with it.

Safety

Travelers should refrain from joining crowds to avoid unexpected violence that could occur during seemingly peaceful demonstrations. Visitors should note that inadequate transportation and communication infrastructure can prevent the U.S. embassy from giving emergency aid. International visitors are often crime victims. In Paramaribo and the surrounding region, burglary, robbery, and violent attacks occur frequently. Pickpockets typically target people in the capital, so travelers should leave behind their jewelry and refrain from showing cash. Visitors should remain near their lodgings after dark. Police do not patrol the Palm Garden neighborhood of the capital, so visitors should avoid the section at night. Drivers should keep windows raised and doors locked. Motorists should hide their valuables. Carjackings and thefts from vehicles occur occasionally.

Calling home

There are 81,500 land-based telephones and 320,000 cell phones in Suriname. There are 28 Internet hosts.

Diplomatic contact in the United States

Ambassador Jacques Ruben Constantijn Kross
4301 Connecticut Avenue NW, Suite 460, Washington, DC 20008
Phone: (202) 244-7488 • Fax (202) 244-5878

Diplomatic contact from the United States

Ambassador Lisa Bobbie Schreiber Hughes
Embassy: Dr. Sophie Redmondstraat 129, Paramaribo
U.S. Department of State, PO Box 1821, Paramaribo
Phone: (597) 472-900 • Fax (597) 410-025

Bibliography

"Airmail M-Bags: Airmail M-Bags Deliver a Large Amount of Mail to a Single Addressee." **www.usps.com/international/mbags.htm**. Accessed on June 9, 2008.

Backhurst, Paul. *Alternatives to the Peace Corps: A Guide to Global Volunteer Opportunities, Eleventh Edition.* Food First Books. Oakland, California (2005).

Banerjee, Dillon. *So, You Want to Join the Peace Corps: What to Know Before You Go.* Ten Speed Press. Toronto, Ontario (2000).

Banerjee, Dillon. *The Insider's Guide to the Peace Corps: What to Know Before You Go Second Edition.* Ten Speed Press. Berkeley, California (2009).

Bradley, Julie. Personal interview. May 2008.

"Burkina Faso: Destination Information." **www.lonelyplanet.com**. Accessed on June 9, 2008.

"CIA World Factbook." **www.cia.gov/library/publications/the-world-factbook/index.html**. Accessed on June 9, 2008.

A. Clark and M. Greeley *Where There Is No Restaurant.* Friends of Guinea (2004).

"Coming Out: Part One," *British Broadcasting Company.* July 2007.

"Coming Out: Part Two," *British Broadcasting Company.* August 2007.

Coyne, John. Personal interview. May 2008.

2006 Essential Guide to the Peace Corps (CD-ROM). Progressive Management (2006).

"Frequently Asked Questions." **http://ieo.okstate.edu/ieo.aspx?page=79**. Accessed on June 9, 2008.

Green, J. L., "The Nitty Gritty." April 3, 2007. **http://joyagreen.blogspot.com**. Accessed on June 9, 2008.

Hachmyer, Caitlin. *Alternatives to the Peace Corps: A Guide to Global Volunteer Opportunities, Twelfth Edition.* Food First Books. Oakland, California (2008).

Hastings, T. *The Peace Corps.* Chelsea House Publishers, Langhorne, Pa. (2005).

"International Travel" **http://travel. state.gov/travel/travel_1744.html, www.state.gov**. Accessed on June 9, 2008.

Ireland, Richard. Personal interview. April 2008.

Jenson, Lindsay. Personal interview. May 2008.

Kohn, Mark. Personal interview. May 2008.

M. Learned, "Peace Corps Equal Opportunity Policy." **www.lgbrpcv. org/articles/eeo.htm**. Accessed on June 9, 2008.

Lipez, Richard. Personal interview. May 2008.

Mc Carron, K.M. "Job Corps, AmeriCorps and Peace Corps: An Overview." July 16, 2002. **www.bls. gov/opub/ooq/2000/fall/art03.pdf**. Accessed on June 9, 2008.

Miller, Darren. Personal interview. May 2008.

"The Monarchy." **www.lesotho.gov.ls**. Accessed on June 9, 2008.

"NPCA Calendar of Events." June 9, 2008, **www.peacecorpsconnect.org**. Accessed on June 9, 2008.

"Peace Corps Manual." April 28, 2008, **www.peacecorpsjournals.com/ manual**. Accessed on June 9, 2008.

Presley, Sarah, "Teaching English (and More) in Morocco." **www.miusa.org**. Accessed on June 9, 2008.

Scheib M., "Volunteering in the Peace Corps (Paraguay)." **www.miusa.org/ ncde/stories/buckscamacho?search term=Camacho**. Accessed on June 9, 2008.

Shtogren, Zachary "Peace Corps Book," e-mail message. May 19, 2008.

"So You Wanna Join the Peace Corps." **www.soyouwanna.com/site/ syws/peacecorps/peacecorps.html**. Accessed on June 9, 2008.

Statler, Donna. Personal interview. May 2008.

"Travelers' Health: Destinations." The CDC. **wwwn.cdc.gov/travel**. Accessed on June 9, 2008.

Williams, B. *The Kingfisher Reference Atlas.* Larousse Kingfisher Chambers, New York, N.Y. (1993).

Werner D., C. Thuman, and J. Maxwell. *Where There Is No Doctor.* Hesperian Books, Berkeley, Ca. (1992).

World Factbook, The. **www. cia.gov/library/publications/ the-world-factbook/index.html**. Accessed on January 8, 2010.

Wright, David. Personal interview. June 2008.

Author Biography

Sharlee DiMenichi has taught English as a second language in Zhejiang Province, China. Her coverage of immigration and ethnic communities was recognized with a New Jersey Press Association award for excellence among young journalists.

She holds an M.S. in journalism from Columbia University and a B.A. in English and education from Juniata College, where she also studied peace and conflict studies.

DiMenichi is a past recipient of the Baker Peace Prize and Baker Peace Scholarship from Juniata College. Prior to becoming a journalist, she volunteered as a regional boycott coordinator for INFACT, was a founding member of the Lehigh Valley chapter of the Bosnian Student Project, and served as a steering committee member of the peace group Lehigh-Pocono Committee of Concern.

The *Complete Guide to Joining the Peace Corps: What You Need to Know Explained Simply* is DiMenichi's first book. She is currently researching a book of curricular materials on Holocaust rescuers.

Index

D

E

F

G

H

I